UNTIL THE LAST GUN IS SILENT

ALSO BY MATTHEW F. DELMONT

Half American

Black Quotidian

Making Roots

Why Busing Failed

The Nicest Kids in Town

UNTIL THE

LAST GUN

IS SILENT

A STORY OF PATRIOTISM,
THE VIETNAM WAR, AND THE
FIGHT TO SAVE AMERICA'S SOUL

MATTHEW F. DELMONT

VIKING

VIKING
An imprint of Penguin Random House LLC
1745 Broadway, New York, NY 10019
penguinrandomhouse.com

VIKING and VIKING ship colophon are registered trademarks of Penguin Random House LLC.

Grateful acknowledgment is made for permission to reprint the following:

Lines from "Face It Girl, It's Over." Words and music by Angelo Badalamenti,
Frank H. Stanton, and Edwin H. Morris & Co. Copyright © 1967. Used by permission.
Reprinted by permission of Hal Leonard LLC.

Lines from "Mother to Son" from *The Collected Poems of Langston Hughes* by
Langston Hughes. Copyright © the Estate of Langston Hughes. Used by permission of
Harold Ober Associates and International Literary Properties LLC.

Image credits may be found on page 327.

DESIGNED BY MEIGHAN CAVANAUGH

LIBRARY OF CONGRESS CONTROL NUMBER: 2025025120
ISBN 9780593655870 (hardcover)
ISBN 9780593655887 (ebook)

Printed in the United States of America
1st Printing

The authorized representative in the EU for product safety and compliance
is Penguin Random House Ireland, Morrison Chambers, 32 Nassau Street,
Dublin D02 YH68, Ireland, https://eu-contact.penguin.ie.

For "Small Together":
Jacque, Xavier, and Simone

And in memory of my parents,
Diane and Frank

CONTENTS

PART 2

PREFACE

This book started with a clue from my father.

We were sitting on a porch in Minneapolis, trying to make up for lost time. Prostate cancer had left him thin and tired, but his mind was still sharp. He knew I was in the early stages of researching a book about the Vietnam War, and our conversation eventually turned to his memories of the era.

He told me that after graduating from Minneapolis Central High School in 1965, he had been recruited to run track at the Air Force Academy in Colorado Springs. He seriously considered going—until something came up during the physical.

"After that," he said, "the military didn't come looking for me, and I sure as hell didn't go looking for them."

He went on to talk about friends and classmates who were drafted and served. I thought of his friend Tony, who sometimes visited when I was young. I wasn't allowed to play certain video games or make loud noises when Tony was around. I didn't understand why at the time, but looking back, it was my first lesson about the war.

After sharing these memories, my dad grew quiet. We sat there in silence, swatting mosquitoes in the warm June air, as he searched for other stories.

"Then there was this brother from Chicago or Detroit who was my same age," he said finally. "He earned the Medal of Honor, but they got him when he came back home."

He did not remember the soldier's name or many details, but the story had clearly stayed with him. The afternoon slipped into evening. It was the last time I spoke with my dad.

When I returned home, I did what historians do: I started researching.

It didn't take long to realize my dad had been remembering the story of Dwight "Skip" Johnson, a tank driver who earned the Medal of Honor for fighting his way out of an ambush in Vietnam. His life received national attention in the late 1960s and early 1970s. He was hailed as a hero by President Lyndon Johnson and attended the first inauguration of President Richard Nixon. General William Westmoreland, Michigan Governor William Milliken, and Detroit Mayor Jerome Cavanagh all spoke at dinners in his honor. There were stage plays and even a movie about his life. Poets and psychologists looked to his story to help make sense of the experiences of Vietnam veterans—both heroic and traumatic.

More than eight million Americans served in the armed forces during the Vietnam era, with about three million deployed in Southeast Asia. For a time, Skip Johnson was one of the most well-known among them. He came to symbolize the complicated legacy of a generation.

But his story, as I found it in the archives, was frustratingly incomplete. Most coverage focused on two moments: the ambush near

Dak To that earned him the Medal of Honor, and the attempted robbery in Detroit that ended his life. "Vietnam Hero Collapses Under Glory Strain," read one typical newspaper headline.

Time and again, Skip was reduced to the two worst days in his life.

He deserved better.

I set out to tell a fuller story. Friends, classmates, teachers, and his former pastor described an inquisitive and kind young man with a rich singing voice. I spoke with a dozen veterans from his unit, the Sixty-Ninth Armor, who remembered his laugh, his self-lessness, and the tight bonds formed in four-man tank crews.

With every new perspective, Skip's story came into clearer focus.

But I knew I was still missing an important piece of the puzzle. To tell Skip's story fully, I needed to speak with the person who had loved him most. So I booked a flight to Detroit to meet his widow, Katrina May.

As I drove my rental car to Starter's Bar & Grill in Southfield, Michigan, it struck me: I wasn't sure I would recognize her. We had spoken several times on the phone, but the only photos I had seen were more than fifty years old. I was relieved when she waved to me outside the restaurant.

"I recognized you from the picture on your book," she said. "And the cross-body bag gave away that you are a professor."

Katrina was a spirited septuagenarian, dressed in navy slacks and a gray cardigan. From our phone conversations, I already knew she was matter-of-fact and funny. ("I could never have been a preacher's wife—I couldn't hold my tongue long enough," she once told me.) In person, she had a warm smile and eyes that sparkled with mischief.

We found a table near the back, and I opened the recording app on my phone, unsure what the mic would pick up over the nineties R&B pulsing through the speakers. Katrina told me her son, Christopher, would join us later—and that he was the spitting image of his father.

"God must have listened when he said, 'I want a boy who looks just like me,'" she said, recalling what Skip had told her when Christopher was born.

She described how, when they were teenagers, Skip had flirted with her for months before she finally agreed to go out with him. During his deployment, they wrote letters back and forth, making each other laugh and falling in love through the mail—a kind of epistolary romance, like a Jane Austen novel set in Detroit.

Katrina stood by him when he returned home, through moments of celebration and spirals of despair. She spoke of a young man who had his whole life ahead of him—until he didn't anymore.

As Katrina filled in details from our earlier phone conversations, I found myself reflecting on how much Skip's story echoed the experiences of so many American GIs. The US Army was filled with young men like Skip—poor and working-class guys drawn from Detroit, South Boston, Watts, and thousands of small towns across the country's heartland. The more I learned about what made Skip's story unique, the more I saw how emblematic it was of a generation shaped—and forever changed—by the Vietnam War.

Like so many others, Skip began basic training just months after graduating high school. During my research, I had come across a copy of Skip's 1966 high school yearbook—the *Norwester*, from Detroit's Northwestern High School—on eBay. After lunch, I gave it to Katrina.

She ran her finger along a photo of Skip in the Glee Club, a teenager in a white shirt and black tie, smiling.

"He looks so young," she said, chuckling softly. "We were so young."

CORETTA SCOTT KING never met Skip Johnson, but she fought for him.

From her days as a student activist at Antioch College in Yellow Springs, Ohio, Coretta raised her voice against war, racism, and poverty. She envisioned a country where soldiers, veterans, their families—and all citizens—had equitable access to jobs, housing, health care, and education. She saw peace and justice as inseparable, and she worked to unite the civil rights and antiwar movements.

The Coretta Scott King you will meet in this book was a fierce and visionary leader—far more dynamic and dangerous than the demure helpmate the media so often portrayed. Though proud to be Mrs. Martin Luther King Jr., Coretta bristled at being reduced to a supporting role, often "made to sound like an attachment to a vacuum cleaner, the wife of Martin, then the widow of Martin, all of which I was proud to be," she said. "I was never just a wife, nor a widow. I was always more than a label."

Coretta spoke out against the Vietnam War earlier and more forcefully than Martin did, and he consistently praised her activism. When the television interviewer Arnold Michaelis arrived at the King family home in Atlanta on December 1, 1965, Martin was in the middle of a whirlwind year. Michaelis noted Coretta's growing visibility in the peace movement, including her speech at a major rally in Washington, DC, just days earlier.

"Did you educate your wife on activism?" Michaelis asked.

"Well, it may have been the other way around," Martin replied. "I think at many points she educated me."

Michaelis paused, caught off guard. Martin went on, recalling the early years of their relationship, Coretta's deep commitment to racial and economic justice—and to pacifism.

"I wish I could say to satisfy my masculine ego that I led her down this path," Martin said, "but I must say we went down together, because she was as actively involved when we met as she is now."

From the summer of 1965 until the end of his life, the timing and tone of Martin's public statements on Vietnam bore the imprint of Coretta's influence. She challenged him—not only privately, but publicly—to stand with her.

At a time when most politicians and civic leaders were reluctant to speak out against US military actions in Vietnam, Coretta forcefully confronted presidents, congressmen, and her fellow Americans with the moral and economic costs of the war. "What kind of country can spend billions of dollars on an unjust and immoral war in Vietnam," she asked in an August 1969 speech in Philadelphia, "but can only spend a pittance to fight a war against poverty?"

In the late 1960s, Coretta became the most visible and influential figure in the antiwar movement. She spoke at nearly every major protest rally of the era, inspiring audiences—and worrying the FBI.

In both her civil rights and antiwar activism, Coretta came to understand the quiet power of presence. "She came to help uplift our wages, to lift *us* up," recalled Annie Hall, a hospital worker who heard her speak at a labor rally in Baltimore. People drew strength from simply seeing Coretta—at a podium, in a protest march, standing beside workers or soldiers' families. Her name, her story, and her presence carried weight.

And each appearance was a chance to grow the movement—to bring more people into the coalition fighting against war, racism, and poverty.

"Sometimes we win just by showing up," she wrote.

Both Coretta and Martin helped broaden the appeal of the anti-war movement. After Martin delivered his "Beyond Vietnam" speech at Riverside Church in the spring of 1967, he began appearing more frequently as a headliner at peace rallies. One organizer told the journalist David Halberstam that King was "a good umbrella"—someone who could draw in labor unions, church groups, middle-aged Americans, and "good-hearted" citizens who might otherwise be nervous about public protests.

"Look here, we've got King, and it makes them all breathe easier," the activist said. "They think, 'Why it's King, it's all right, it's safe.'"

Coretta played a similar role before, during, and after Martin's final year as an outspoken critic of the war. She helped transform private doubt into public protest. She made it possible for millions of people to be brave together.

Coretta's critique of the Vietnam War was multifaceted. She argued that it siphoned vital resources from domestic needs, turning attention and funding away from programs that could improve the lives of American citizens. She also believed that the Cold War had narrowed the imagination of US leaders, drawing them ever deeper into a proxy battle with the Soviet Union and China. At the root of this entanglement was the domino theory—first articulated by

President Dwight Eisenhower in 1954—which warned that a Communist victory in one nation, like South Vietnam, would trigger a cascade across neighboring countries.

Coretta urged Americans to look beyond that logic. Rather than focusing on the spread of communism, she emphasized the legacy of colonialism—how Britain, France, Japan, and the United States had carved up the globe, and how, in the decades after World War II, nations in Asia and Africa were fighting for independence. When she and Martin attended Ghana's independence ceremony in 1957, she was overwhelmed with emotion as thousands of Ghanaians cheered the swearing-in of President Kwame Nkrumah. "We had never seen this happen before," she recalled, marveling at the birth of an independent Black nation.

Where the foreign policy establishment saw peril, Coretta saw possibility. On the same map that triggered fears of communism, she saw dozens of newly sovereign nations struggling to define themselves in the shadow of global superpowers. She acknowledged the complexity of the geopolitical moment—but believed it could be explained in ways that resonated with everyday Americans.

Her antiwar activism, and the wave of solidarity she inspired, had real impact. Despite their differences, both President Johnson and President Nixon paid close attention to public sentiment around Vietnam. Each weighed decisions about troop commitments, bombing campaigns, and peace negotiations against the size and visibility of organized opposition.

It was easy for the White House to dismiss fringe radicals as unrepresentative of mainstream opinion. But it was far harder to ignore a movement that spanned every demographic—and was led by someone with Coretta's gravitas.

In protesting the war, Coretta urged Americans to remember the nation's revolutionary heritage—and to side against colonialism, exploitation, and dictatorship.

"No one reading the Declaration of Independence can deny the divine inspiration of our founding fathers," she said during the many Freedom Concerts she performed in the 1960s to raise money for the civil rights movement. She saw that same dream of freedom alive in the dozens of countries in Africa, Asia, and Latin America that had "won their independence from colonial yokes."

She read widely on the history of French and American military involvement in Southeast Asia and understood the Vietnam War as part of a larger "worldwide revolution"—one that echoed America's own founding ideals.

"I don't know about you," she told her Freedom Concert audiences, "but as for me, I choose to join with that great American patriot who said, 'Is life so dear, or peace so sweet, as to be purchased by the price of chains and slavery? Forbid it, almighty God! I know not what course others may take, but as for me, give me liberty or give me death.'"

IN NOVEMBER 1968, as Coretta prepared for the family's first Thanksgiving without Martin, news broke that Skip Johnson had been awarded the Medal of Honor. The story appeared in her hometown papers—*The Atlanta Constitution*, *The Atlanta Journal*, and the *Atlanta Daily World*—as well as in newspapers across the country.

"We really had been a generation of one war after another," she told an interviewer that fall, reflecting on how World War II, the Korean War, the Cuban Missile Crisis, the Vietnam War, and the Cold

War had shaped her adult life. She worried about what that meant for returning veterans.

"Many of our young men, particularly our black men, were affected by the wars," she said. "They would go to fight the war, and they'd come back and conditions at home had not changed for them. They suffered discrimination. Many of them went to war—went into the service because they couldn't find employment in their communities, and they were drafted because they couldn't go on to college."

Coretta dedicated her life to building a better America for working-class and poor families—people who grew up in neighborhoods like Skip's in Detroit. She wanted students at schools like Northwestern High School, Skip's alma mater, to graduate to opportunity, not dead ends. She believed veterans should return to jobs and health care, not unemployment and neglect. She believed women like Katrina deserved support as they juggled work and parenthood. And she believed children like Christopher deserved more than food and shelter—they deserved to grow up in a country free from violence.

When Coretta called for a nonviolent society that prioritized peace and equality over war and racism, she wasn't speaking in abstractions. She was thinking of real people who animated her appeals.

Through the linked stories of Skip Johnson and Coretta Scott King, and those who loved them and fought at their sides, this book offers a history of the Vietnam era that is both intimate in its details and expansive in its themes. Skip and Coretta were singular, iconic figures, but their stories also reflect the lives of millions of Americans: those who fought abroad and returned to a nation unwilling to support them, and those who fought at home for peace, only to be labeled "un-American" for doing so.

This book is a story about what the Vietnam War meant for Americans. It is the story of Martin Luther King Jr.'s breaking his silence about a war he believed was devastating the country—only to be attacked by fellow civil rights leaders. It is the story of the grassroots activist and Georgia state representative Julian Bond and the Detroit congressman John Conyers Jr., who risked their political futures to oppose the war. It is the story of Dagmar Wilson, an artist and children's book illustrator, who founded Women Strike for Peace, leading thousands of mothers, grandmothers, and other women to publicly challenge US foreign policy. It is the story of the war correspondent and Howard University professor Bernard Fall, whose dispatches on the French war in Indochina offered warnings that too few American leaders were willing to hear. It is the story of the psychiatrists Robert Jay Lifton and Chaim Shatan, who used Skip's case to help develop the diagnosis for what we now know as post-traumatic stress disorder (PTSD). And it is the story of the everyday soldiers, veterans, and activists whose lives were shaped by the Vietnam War.

Both Skip and Coretta fought for America. Their stories challenge us to think more boldly about how we define patriotism. They call us to embrace a definition of patriotism that places the well-being of actual veterans and their families above symbolic tributes at sporting events. A patriotism where love for one's country is strengthened—not diminished—by dissent. A patriotism rooted in an honest reckoning with our nation's history, not in comforting myths about the past.

"We love America," Coretta told a group of Black college students in 1965. "Our job is to save the soul of America."

The title of this book comes from a speech Coretta gave three weeks after her husband was assassinated. Dressed in black and standing before eighty thousand people in New York's Central Park, she vowed to carry on the work of peace "until the last gun is silent." That call remains as urgent today as it was more than five decades ago.

PART 1

1

CORETTA

B y the end of the night, Coretta Scott King would become one of the nation's most visible—and, to some, most dangerous— critics of America's rapidly expanding war in Vietnam.

Standing before a crowd of eighteen thousand people inside New York's Madison Square Garden on a warm June night in 1965, at the "Emergency Rally on Vietnam," she had every reason to feel uneasy. She knew the FBI was watching. Civil rights activists like her were under constant surveillance, and whatever she said would end up in a government file. Outside, right-wing demonstrators picketed the rally, accusing anyone who opposed the war of being a Communist or a Communist sympathizer.

And Coretta was the only woman invited to speak that night. She would take the stage alongside US Senator Wayne Morse, the political scientist Hans Morgenthau, the pediatrician and bestselling author Benjamin Spock, the civil rights organizer Bayard Rustin, and the Pulitzer Prize–winning poet Robert Lowell, who received a standing ovation for his recent refusal to visit the White House in protest of the war.

As she waited for the actor and activist Ossie Davis, her dear friend, to introduce her, Coretta gently thumbed through her notes, making sure the pages were in order. She had spent years thinking, organizing, and marching alongside her husband. Now she was eager to use her own voice to speak for peace.

The ads for the rally billed her as "Mrs. Martin Luther King," following the custom of the era. But if anyone in the crowd expected her to be demure, she quickly set them straight.

"Have you often wondered," she began, "why it is that the same President Johnson who speaks so eloquently for civil rights and who has been so moved by the struggle for the right to vote and the anguish of the poor can be so callous about the Vietnamese, and so apparently thoughtless on foreign policy?"

She let the question hang in the air.

In the three months leading up to the rally, the number of American troops in Vietnam had more than doubled—to fifty-two thousand. On the day of the event, the State Department confirmed that President Johnson had authorized US ground forces to engage in combat if requested by the South Vietnamese Army.

Many in the arena had voted for Johnson over the Republican Barry Goldwater just the year before. Now they were openly criticizing the president's decision to commit the nation to a land war in Asia.

Coretta asked the crowd to consider the human cost of that policy.

Earlier in the evening, the father of Lt. Joe Thorne, a twenty-four-year-old from South Dakota, had taken the stage. His voice cracked as he read the telegram from the air force informing him that his son had been killed when his helicopter was shot down. He also shared one of Joe's final letters, in which the young pilot confided that he believed the war was a "hopeless operation." Thorne was one of nearly a thousand US service members to die in Vietnam in the first six months of 1965. It was painfully clear he would not be the last.

On the day of the rally, the front page of *The New York Times* detailed the US aerial bombardment campaign against North Vietnam, launched four months earlier. US Ambassador to South Vietnam Maxwell Taylor—former chair of the Joint Chiefs of Staff and one of the architects of the war—stated he was "completely opposed" to ending the air strikes.

For Coretta, the daily bombings were not distant policy—they were personal.

"Where my husband and I have lived and where we have worked, poverty and bombing are not abstractions," she told the crowd. "They are a part of the struggle of life from one day to another."

She spoke not only as a peace activist, but as a mother. How could she explain to their seven-year-old son that the federal government was on the side of civil rights marchers, she asked, "only to have him watch on the television and see the very same troops we welcomed in Alabama, throwing bombs in Vietnam?"

Casting her eyes to the second tier of Madison Square Garden, ringed with American flags and patriotic bunting, Coretta closed with a theme she would return to again and again in the years ahead.

"Ultimately, there can be no peace without justice, and no justice without peace," she said.

Calling peace and human rights the "two great moral issues of our time," she urged the audience to educate their neighbors and bring enough people "into the streets" to make the president understand that Americans favored peace over war.

"Too many men have died in Vietnam while the country grows poorer, the people starve, and democracy is stifled," she concluded. "We must begin negotiating now."

As Coretta stepped away from the podium to thunderous applause, Bayard Rustin embraced her. A committed pacifist and conscientious objector during World War II, Rustin had organized the rally on behalf of the National Committee for a Sane Nuclear Policy (SANE). Coretta had first met him when he spoke to her ninth-grade class in Alabama about India's independence movement, and later when he visited her college in Ohio. He introduced her to pacifism in her teens, and she watched as he helped bring Gandhi's nonviolent resistance strategies into the heart of the civil rights movement. Rustin knew as well as anyone how much it meant for Coretta to step into the spotlight as an activist.

He picked up on one of the themes from her speech to close the rally.

"The time is so late, the danger so great," he bellowed, "that I call upon all of the forces that believe in peace to take a lesson from the labor movement, and the women, and the civil rights movement, and stop meeting indoors, but go into these streets until we get peace!"

The crowd rose to its feet, clapping and shouting in approval.

With that rousing call to action, more than two thousand people followed Rustin, Coretta, and the other speakers out of the Garden for a midnight march to United Nations Plaza. The line of demonstrators stretched for eight blocks, lining Broadway as curious theatergoers looked on. Freedom songs and chants of "End the war in Vietnam" and "Bring the troops home" echoed off buildings, then slowly faded into the summer night.

THE SEEDS OF Coretta Scott King's antiwar activism were planted in the fertile soil of Alabama. Her parents, Bernice McMurry and Obie Scott, were born and raised in Perry County, where their families had lived since the end of slavery. McMurry was the first Black woman in the area to drive a car and taught herself to cut hair so she could work alongside her husband in the barbershop they ran out of their home. Scott was the only Black man in town with a truck, which he used to move logs. The work put him in direct competition with local white men, who threatened him whenever he delivered lumber to the train station. He was routinely stopped on the road, cursed at, and threatened at gunpoint—but he never backed down. He began carrying a revolver, kept in plain sight in his truck, a warning to anyone who might think he was an easy target.

"If you look a white man straight in the eyes, he can't harm you," he told Coretta.

The Scotts were third-generation landowners, but even landownership did not shield them from racism and violence. On Thanksgiving night in 1942, when Coretta was fifteen, white vigilantes burned their house to the ground. The family survived, but nearly everything they owned was destroyed—Coretta's favorite dresses, books, photographs, and record albums all gone.

"The postcard from hell was my first taste of evil," she remembered, "the kind that shows up at your door in such a way that you can never forget its smell, its taste, its sting."

A few years later, Scott saved enough money to buy a sawmill. Two weeks after the purchase, when he refused to sell to a white logger, the mill was burned to the ground. The arsonists were never identified.

Throughout it all, Obie Scott never showed fear, even though Coretta and her siblings spent many nights worrying if he would make it home alive.

"He had the ability to deny people with ugly agendas the power to chase him from his mission," she recalled. "Fortunately, I learned early how to live with fear for the people I loved. . . . When fear rushed in, I learned how to hear my heart racing, but refused to allow my feelings to sway me."

She was also not afraid to play rough. A self-described tomboy, she climbed trees and wrestled with siblings, cousins, and friends.

"If another child angered me, I would fight, real hard," she remembered. "I used to fight my sister and brother when they did anything that I didn't like, so they used to call me mean."

When Coretta graduated as valedictorian of her high school in 1945, she knew she wanted to leave the South. That fall, she enrolled at Antioch College, where her older sister, Edythe, had matriculated two years earlier. She majored in music and education—the first was her passion, the second practical.

At Antioch, she felt most at home among student activists.

"Hearing young people . . . give their firm convictions and conceptions concerning certain public issues was astonishing," she wrote. She joined the campus NAACP, race relations committee, and a newly formed peace group. They organized rallies in support of students who were conscientious objectors.

"Pacifism felt right to me," she said, "it accorded with what I had been taught as a Christian: to love thy neighbor as thyself."

But even at a progressive institution like Antioch, Coretta encountered the quiet betrayal of liberal hypocrisy. When she was barred from completing a required student teaching rotation at the all-white Yellow Springs public school, no professor, administrator, or classmate spoke up on her behalf. She fumed at the contradiction between the school's values and its silence. The same "glib advocates of Democracy," she wrote, tolerated racism in their own backyard.

"Do you then wonder why America as a leader among nations in the world today cannot command more respect among the common people who make up the majority of the citizens of the world?" she asked in her senior essay. From then on, she vowed to seek out people whose actions aligned with their ideals.

Coretta's pacifism and support for civil rights led her to join the local chapter of the Progressive Party and attend its national convention in July 1948 as a student delegate. When she arrived in Philadelphia that summer, she was electrified by the atmosphere. More than twenty-five thousand people crowded into Shibe Park, including throngs of young people who made the gathering feel more like a festival than a political convention. At twenty-one, Coretta was one of thousands of students *The Pittsburgh Courier* described as "free souls who were unfettered by customs or accepted routines."

While the Progressive Party nominated Henry Wallace—President Franklin D. Roosevelt's former vice president, who had been replaced on the 1944 ticket by Senator Harry Truman—Coretta was especially struck by the prominent role played by Black delegates and speakers. She heard fiery speeches from Edgar Brown, a founder of the National Negro Council, the Philadelphia teacher Goldie Watson, and John E. T. Camper, a Baltimore physician and World War I veteran.

"What do we want?" asked the playwright, composer, and activist Shirley Graham in her keynote. "That our children may dwell in peace. PEACE without battleships, atomic bombs and lynch ropes; PEACE without murderers masked as statesmen; PEACE without military conscriptions and mangled, torn bodies lingering on in veterans' hospitals; PEACE in which to work and build."

Peace, she emphasized, was not simply the absence of war—it was a question of national priorities. Why, she asked, was the United States backing the French war in Indochina? Why pour resources into the "hell of war," when that same money could be used for health care, housing, food, and education?

As Graham concluded to a standing ovation, Coretta joined the crowd chanting, "Jim Crow must go."

Building on Graham's speech, the Iowa attorney and newspaper publisher Charles P. Howard delivered a sharp critique of US foreign policy. Howard, who had served as a second lieutenant with the Ninety-Second Division, 366th Infantry in France during World War I, accused President Truman of using the Cold War to justify a sweeping peacetime expansion of America's global military footprint.

"We are told that warships in the Mediterranean are necessary; that bomber bases in Africa are necessary," Howard said. "We are told that there is a dire threat to our security, and that we must arm to the teeth to protect ourselves from the Soviet Union."

Coretta was struck by how Howard, who at one point waved a stalk of Iowa corn to rally the crowd, used homespun pragmatism to challenge the basic assumptions of national security.

But within the Progressive Party, the person who most influenced her was Paul Robeson. That summer, she had the chance to perform on the same program as the pioneering singer, actor, and activist at a meeting of the party's Ohio chapter. After the concert, Robeson praised her singing and urged her to continue her training. Coretta was deeply moved—by his encouragement, but also by the figure he cut onstage, combining song with searing political commentary.

"After watching Robeson's performance, I tucked it away in my memory," she later wrote. "When I began my freedom concerts to raise funds for the movement, I patterned my concerts after his performances."

For many years, Coretta avoided discussing her affiliation with the Progressive Party.

"The party was often accused of having links to communism," she later explained, "and I did not want to besmirch my reputation."

But in the summer of 1948, she was alive to new political visions for America—and inspired by the possibility that art, activism, and global justice could be part of the same fight.

AFTER SHE GRADUATED FROM ANTIOCH, Coretta's dream of a singing career led her to Boston, where she enrolled at the New England Conservatory of Music in 1951. She arrived in the city with just fifteen dollars in her pocket, living on peanut butter, graham crackers, and the occasional piece of fruit until she found work as a domestic helper in the home of an Antioch alum.

In her second semester, a classmate asked if she would be interested in going on a date with a promising young minister from Atlanta who was studying for his PhD at Boston University's School of Theology. At first, Coretta was not interested. She could not imagine herself as a minister's wife. But her friend, eager to play matchmaker, gave her phone number to the young man anyway. He introduced himself as M. L. King Jr.

"He doesn't look like much," Coretta recalled thinking when they first met. "But when he talked, he just radiated so much charm he became much better looking as he talked."

She laughed at his typical male smoothness—what she later called his "intellectual jive." She recalled him saying, "You know, every Napoleon had his Waterloo. And you know, I'm like Napoleon. I'm at my Waterloo and I'm on my knees."

On their first date, they talked about peace, war, and racial and economic justice. Coretta had the distinct sense he was testing her, probing her thinking. She admired his intellect and maturity but was caught off guard when, as he was driving her home, he declared, "You have everything I ever wanted in a wife."

"Martin showed every sign of someone falling in love at first sight," she remembered. "But for me, it was an overload, too much to handle at one time."

Still, with each date, she found more to like. He was a good dancer, compassionate, and shared her love of concert music. They spoke deeply about religion, philosophy, and politics.

"I saw that my views were more global and pacifist, while his were more focused on direct action to change the oppressive structures of black America," she said.

During their courtship, Coretta fell deeply in love but still wrestled with the idea of giving up her concert career to become a minister's wife.

Coretta and Martin were married on June 18, 1953, on the lawn of the Scott family home in Marion, Alabama, in a ceremony officiated by Martin's father, Daddy King. She wore a pastel-blue dress and, asserting her independence, told her imposing father-in-law that she would not recite the traditional marriage vow to "obey" and "submit" to her husband.

"The language made me feel too much like an indentured servant," she said.

After the wedding, they returned to Boston to complete their coursework. In August 1954, they moved to Montgomery, Alabama, where Martin became the pastor of Dexter Avenue Baptist Church. Montgomery was home to a vibrant network of Black organizers and activists, including Jo Ann Robinson, president of the Women's Political Council, and E. D. Nixon, head of the local NAACP chapter. These groups were working to register Black voters and to challenge the daily humiliations of Jim Crow segregation. One of their most urgent targets was the city's bus system, where Black riders were routinely threatened and harassed by white drivers.

"The system was operated so as to make blacks feel less than human," Coretta recalled. "Imagine what it was like to get on a Montgomery bus with your children."

The dam burst on December 1, 1955, when Rosa Parks—a lifelong activist and secretary of the local NAACP—was arrested for refusing to give up her seat to a white passenger. In the days that followed, E. D. Nixon and other leaders recruited Martin to head a newly formed organization, the Montgomery Improvement Association, which launched a citywide boycott of the bus system. Over the next thirteen months, more than forty thousand Black residents took part. They walked miles to work, organized massive carpool networks, and held the line.

The Montgomery bus boycott propelled Martin into the national spotlight, where he would remain for the rest of his life.

Life was changing quickly for Coretta too. During their first year in Montgomery, she sang in the church choir, taught Sunday school, and helped Martin with his sermons—listening, offering critiques, typing drafts. It was a practice they would continue in the years to come.

Coretta Scott King concert program, 1956

Martin doted on her during her first pregnancy. Their daughter Yolanda—nicknamed Yoki—was born on November 17, 1955, just before the bus boycott started.

What had started as Coretta's effort to be a "good minister's wife" had become a collaborative partnership.

"I felt very much involved in what he was doing," she remembered.

As the civil rights movement gained momentum, Coretta's national profile grew as well.

In 1957, she helped launch SANE to raise awareness about the dangers of nuclear testing. She performed in fundraising concerts and often stood in for Martin at public events. By 1962, the couple had three young children—Martin Luther King III was born in 1957, Dexter in 1961—and Martin had mixed feelings about Coretta's growing national presence. He was uneasy with her traveling the country for singing and speaking engagements, and hesitant about her taking on a larger role in the movement.

During one tense exchange, he told her, "You see, I am called by God, and you aren't."

"I have always felt that I have a call on my life, too," Coretta replied. "I've been called by God, too, to do something. You may not understand it, but I have a sense of a calling too."

Martin seemed unconvinced. He countered, "Well, somebody has to take care of the kids."

"No problem, I will do that," Coretta retorted.

She saw that he looked crestfallen. "You aren't totally happy being my wife and the mother of my children, are you?" he asked.

"I love being your wife and the mother of your children," she said. "But if that's all I am to do, I'll go crazy."

Coretta knew she was an activist and a leader in her own right. Soon, others would recognize her stature as well.

CORETTA WAS HEARTENED when Martin encouraged her to accept an invitation from Women Strike for Peace (WSP) to travel to Geneva, Switzerland, in March 1962, as part of an international effort to ban atomic testing.

Founded in 1961 by the children's book illustrator Dagmar Wilson and the lawyer Bella Abzug, WSP was a loose network of mostly middle-class women who rallied against nuclear weapons and war.

"We decided it was up to the women because the men are trapped in the course of daily events," Wilson said, after an estimated fifty thousand women joined marches in sixty cities on November 1, 1961, calling for an "End to the Arms Race—Not the Human Race." She led fifteen hundred demonstrators to the base of the Washington Monument, while President Kennedy watched from a White House window.

Most of the protesters were housewives and mothers. Some were new to activism; others had long been involved with peace groups such as SANE and the International League for Peace and Freedom. Wilson, who planned the protest with friends in the backyard of her Washington, DC, home, was stunned by the turnout.

"The girls are only beginning to feel their power," she said. "Let's face it, wars can no longer be won; wars are antediluvian. We simply have to abolish them."

Coretta welcomed the opportunity to travel with women who shared her passion for peace. On April 1, 1962, she was one of fifty women who boarded a Swissair flight from New York's Idlewild airport to attend the United Nations disarmament conference in Geneva. Among them was a woman who had survived Nazi repression in Poland, and another who had lived through the atomic bombing of Hiroshima. Two other Black women joined Coretta on the trip: the newspaper columnist Valena Williams and Dr. Uvee Mdodana, an activist deeply involved in women's groups and religious organizations.

The New York Times featured a photo of Coretta with other protesters at the airport, describing her as one of the "women known through their husbands' reputations." Still, she was the only woman quoted in that article—and in several others—marking her as the group's highest-profile participant.

"I go to Geneva because I am concerned that disarmament and suspension of nuclear tests may well be mankind's last chance for survival," she told *The Pittsburgh Courier* before the trip. "No sober minded person can ignore the possible ominous effects of a continuation of the arms race and atmospheric tests. Not only will this increase the possibilities of an accidental war, but it will lead to a poisoning of the atmosphere that will be ruinous to generations yet unborn."

For a generation that had already lived through World War II and the Korean War—and was now living through the Cold War— the fear of nuclear holocaust was palpable.

In the years leading up to her trip to Switzerland, Coretta had accompanied Martin on journeys to Ghana, Nigeria, London, Paris, Rome, Greece, Lebanon, and Egypt. She was better traveled and more worldly than President Johnson and many members of Congress. Foreign dignitaries and press often treated Martin as the de facto ambassador of Black America—and Coretta as its First

Coretta Scott King, Richard Nixon, and
Martin Luther King Jr. in Ghana, 1957

Lady. In India, they dined with Prime Minister Jawaharlal Nehru, and Coretta sang spirituals at several stops during their tour.

But this trip felt different.

Though no stranger to international travel, Coretta arrived in Geneva with a sense that she was beginning to establish an identity—and an agenda—distinct from her husband's. She and the US delegation joined women from Scandinavia, England, Australia, and the Soviet Union in a march to the Palace of Nations, home of the United Nations office in Geneva. Together, they delivered a petition with fifty thousand signatures to the US negotiator Arthur Dean and Soviet Deputy Foreign Minister Valerian Zorin, the cochairs of the seventeen-nation disarmament conference.

Dean received the women icily. He insisted that there were complex foreign policy considerations and technical details about fissionable materials that they could not possibly understand.

"It's all rather reminiscent of some of the games our 6-year-olds play," Wilson said of the Geneva talks. "They make the rules as they go along and when they are not winning they change them. . . . The men in Geneva are not 6-year-olds. They are grown men and are entrusted with the greatest responsibility—the destiny of the human race."

When the women returned to New York after their weeklong trip, Coretta spoke on their behalf: "The women are disappointed that we did not achieve our purposes in Geneva, but we will not give up our fight for peace."

Always a voracious reader, Coretta followed reports about America's growing military presence in Vietnam with mounting concern. In *The New York Times* that November, the journalist David Halberstam described how nearly eight thousand US troops were engaged in a "private war, with its endless debate over the rules as to when to shoot the enemy, when not to shoot the enemy, and what constitutes the enemy." The accompanying photographs—showing US Special Forces advising Vietnamese soldiers—made it hard to believe the United States was not already at war.

Coretta's role with Women Strike for Peace quickly drew the attention of the FBI, which believed the group's leaders were influenced by the Communist Party. Similar suspicions had long fueled the bureau's surveillance of Martin. The FBI had been monitoring him since the Montgomery bus boycott in 1955. By the end of 1963, Attorney General Robert Kennedy had authorized wiretaps on the Kings' home phone, the Southern Christian Leadership Conference (SCLC) offices in Atlanta, and the office of Stanley Levison, one of Martin's closest advisers.

J. Edgar Hoover provided Robert Kennedy with regular reports on Martin and other civil rights leaders. Just weeks after Coretta returned from Switzerland, Hoover received a field report titled "Coretta Scott King, aka Mrs. Martin Luther King, Jr. INFORMATION CONCERNING (SUBVERSIVE CONTROL)." The memo stated that the House Un-American Activities Committee (HUAC) had requested passport files on all fifty women who had traveled to Geneva. Coretta's photograph and her parents' names were forwarded to the FBI field offices in Atlanta and New York, along with the physical description from her passport application:

Height: 5'4½"

Hair: Black

Eyes: Brown

Marks: None

Occupation: Housewife

The report is a chilling reminder of the official surveillance Coretta, like Martin, endured.

Although Coretta didn't see the classified FBI memo at the time, the suspicions some government officials held about WSP were no secret. In December 1962, HUAC subpoenaed a dozen WSP members to testify in an investigation into Communist infiltration of the peace movement. More than a hundred women packed the hearing room, cheering Dagmar Wilson as she declared that the group welcomed anyone who opposed nuclear war, regardless of their political affiliation. Outside, dozens more women marched in freezing temperatures, carrying signs that read "Peace is American."

Congressman Clyde Doyle, a Democrat from California, accused the women of offering "strong encouragement to the Communists in this country to continue their infiltration of 'Women Strike for Peace.'"

With HUAC attacking her fellow activists and the FBI hounding her husband, Coretta doubled down on her commitment to the peace movement. In May 1963, she published a half-page ad in *The California Eagle* calling on other Black women to join the cause.

"Peace Among Nations and Peace in Birmingham Ala. Cannot Be Separated!" she wrote.

CORETTA WAS UNABLE to attend the Women Strike for Peace rally in Washington, DC, that May. She had given birth in March to the couple's fourth child, Bernice Albertine King, named after her grandmothers.

It had been a difficult pregnancy. Hip pain made it nearly impossible for Coretta to walk down the stairs, and her doctor ordered bed rest during the final weeks. The postpartum period brought new challenges as well: Just one day after Bernice's birth, Martin left to lead a massive civil rights campaign in Birmingham.

On April 12, he was arrested and taken to jail. Coretta, caring for the children at home, had no way of contacting him. She feared for his safety.

Alone for a week in a Birmingham cell, Martin penned what would become one of the most important statements of the civil rights era—a letter defending nonviolent protest as a patriotic call to conscience. The movement, he wrote, was "bringing our nation back to these great wells of democracy which were dug deep by the founding fathers in their formulation of the Constitution and Declaration of Independence."

He returned to that same patriotic theme on June 23, 1963, in Detroit, where more than 125,000 people marched down Woodward Avenue to protest racism and inequality. Speaking at Cobo Hall, he declared: "I have a dream. It is a dream deeply rooted in the American dream."

He repeated the phrase again and again—condemning the murders of Emmett Till and Medgar Evers, invoking the words of Abraham Lincoln and Thomas Jefferson, and offering a vision of justice that resonated deeply with the crowd. He tapped the aspirations of many of those in the audience: "I have a dream this afternoon that one day right here in Detroit, Negroes will be able to buy a house or rent a house anywhere that their money will carry them and they will be able to get a job."

Applause thundered through the arena. Coretta, who had stayed home with the children, listened to a recording of the speech later, as she often did, and offered Martin feedback on which parts struck her as most powerful.

Two months later, Coretta and Martin traveled together to Washington, DC, for the March on Washington for Jobs and Freedom. She was up into the early morning hours of August 28, watching and listening as Martin worked on the final draft of his speech. When she awoke near sunrise, she found him gazing out the hotel window, anxious about how many people would show up. Organizers had hoped for a hundred thousand. Commentators expected far fewer.

As the couple made the short walk from the Willard Hotel to

the National Mall, the growing crowd buoyed their spirits. Chartered buses and trains had delivered waves of people into the capital. By the afternoon, as many as 250,000 stood along the reflecting pool stretching before the Lincoln Memorial. Millions more watched on television.

Coretta was awed by the grandeur of the moment—but also deeply disappointed. Despite the vital roles women had played in building the movement and organizing the march, they were dismissed and disrespected by its leadership. When she asked to join the main procession down Constitution Avenue, Martin replied curtly, "The wives are not going to march."

There was no seat reserved for her on the platform. No women were permitted to deliver a major address.

"This was very upsetting to me," she later recalled, "especially when there were so many battle-weary female veterans who deserved the opportunity to speak."

She thought of Ella Baker, Daisy Bates, Fannie Lou Hamer, Diane Nash Bevel, Rosa Parks—women who had helped give life to the movement.

"The list was endless," she said. "But that's how chauvinistic the leadership was at that time."

Still, when Martin rose to speak, Coretta recognized the phrases she had heard him worrying over the night before. As a trained singer, she noticed how the crowd lifted him, how his voice took on a "strong and beautifully resonant tone."

When he said, "I still have a dream," she knew he had left the prepared speech behind. He was returning to the theme he had first sounded that summer in Detroit. The words were not written on the page, she said. They were "tucked inside him."

It was the most iconic speech Martin would ever give—and one of the most famous speeches in American history.

After the march, Coretta joined Martin in a limousine to the White House. Top civil rights leaders—including NAACP Executive Secretary Roy Wilkins, Student Nonviolent Coordinating Committee (SNCC) Chairman John Lewis, and A. Philip Randolph, who had first envisioned the March on Washington two decades earlier—were scheduled to meet with President Kennedy and Vice President Lyndon B. Johnson.

"I'd like to go," Coretta told Martin.

She had spoken with President Kennedy by phone several times and thought she might never have another opportunity to meet a sitting president. She wanted to thank him for his support when Martin had been jailed, and to commend him for a recent step toward peace: The United States had joined Great Britain and the Soviet Union in signing the Limited Test Ban Treaty just weeks earlier.

"You can't go," Martin told her, "because you are not invited."

He explained that she was not on the official list of visitors and attending would violate protocol.

When the limousine arrived at the White House gate, Martin and the men went inside. Coretta and Aminda Badeau Wilkins, the wife of Roy Wilkins, hailed a cab and returned to the hotel.

Although Coretta was not welcomed at the White House, the president's schedule that day closely mirrored the very issues she was fighting to bring together—civil rights and peace—though from a different perspective.

That morning, Kennedy had met with leaders from the Defense Department, State Department, and CIA to discuss the growing instability in South Vietnam. The self-immolation of a Buddhist monk, Thich Quang Duc, had drawn international attention to the persecution of Buddhists under South Vietnamese President Ngo Dinh Diem.

After the civil rights leaders departed, Kennedy reconvened the meeting—this time joined by Vice President Johnson—to discuss the consequences of a military overthrow of the Diem regime.

Less than three months later, a group of Vietnamese army officers staged a coup, assassinating Diem and his brother Ngo Dinh Nhu.

IN OCTOBER 1962, Americans looked on anxiously as a dispute over the deployment of nuclear missiles in Europe and the Caribbean led the United States and the Soviet Union to the brink of war. Coretta was watching news coverage of the Cuban Missile Crisis while getting seven-year-old Yolanda ready for school.

"If they don't stop talking about Cuba, I'm not going to live to get to be seventeen," Yolanda said. "We are all going to be blown up and I don't want to be blown up."

Coretta tried to reassure her, telling her that both she and Martin were working every day to bring about peace. She explained that this was why she had traveled to Geneva—and why she would soon be going to the United Nations.

"Yes, Mommy," Yolanda replied, "but you better be glad that you lived to be grown." It was heartbreaking for Coretta to hear her daughter worry that her young life might be cut short.

Coretta woke early on November 1, 1963, to catch a flight from Atlanta to New York. She joined 350 members of Women Strike for Peace to celebrate the group's second anniversary with a march on United Nations Plaza.

Coretta Scott King with Women Strike for Peace founder
Dagmar Wilson at a march on United Nations Plaza,
New York City, November 1963

Carrying a sign that read "Let's Make Our Earth a Nuclear-Free Zone," Coretta led the march alongside Dagmar Wilson and the New York civil rights activist Marie Witherspoon.

Other women held signs calling for "A Peace Economy with Jobs for All."

The group presented a scroll to UN Secretary-General U Thant, pledging to support the UN's ongoing work for disarmament, human rights, and equality.

"You who have the truest motives have worked in complete unity with the United Nations," Thant told them.

After the march, the women gathered at the Church Center for the United Nations, where they met with several women delegates from newly independent nations in Africa and Asia, as well as representatives from Communist bloc countries. Their conversations hummed with possibilities, mapping potential alliances beyond the Cold War binary of the United States versus the Soviet Union.

Coretta was the featured speaker. She emphasized that the peace and civil rights movements were intertwined. At the close of the gathering, Wilson presented her with an award from WSP in recognition of her leadership.

After leaving New York that afternoon, Coretta arrived in Washington, DC, just minutes before the start of another WSP event at National Baptist Memorial Church. She joined Wilson and former Congressman Byron Johnson for a panel titled "From Armaments to Abundance." After Johnson described how the United States was spending billions of dollars on military weapons and equipment, Coretta told the audience that such money could be better spent meeting urgent needs at home. She asked them to think back to the issues that had brought tens of thousands of people to the capital that summer—jobs, housing, education, health care.

"There cannot be peace outside our nation without peace within our nation," she said. "No peace without racial justice and no racial justice without peace."

Before returning to Atlanta the next morning, Coretta met for breakfast with Sue Cronk, a reporter for *The Washington Post*'s For and About Women section. Over scrambled eggs and toast, Cronk asked Coretta about how she managed the demands of being an activist, wife, and mother.

Coretta said she felt a deep emotional connection to the movement—and admitted she sometimes felt "ashamed" that she had never been jailed. It was not practical for her to protest in that way, she explained. "Martin's absent from home so much that the children need me all the more."

Cronk noted that Coretta's "hurried trip to Washington . . . was an exception to her stay-at-home rule." As they finished breakfast, Cronk asked what it was like to be married to a symbol of the civil rights movement.

Coretta said living with Martin was not hard, but the constant demands on his time were. Then she paused for a moment, before confessing that since their home was bombed in 1956, she never stopped worrying about his safety—or the safety of her family. Being married to a symbol was, she said, a life of "constant fear."

Three weeks later, back home in Atlanta, Coretta heard Martin call to her from the living room. President Kennedy had been shot. They held hands and prayed that the president would survive. When the news of his death arrived, Martin fell silent.

"This is exactly what's going to happen to me," he told her. "I keep telling you, this is a sick society."

Coretta felt a chill course through her body and struggled to speak.

"I had no words to comfort him, to assure him that it wouldn't happen," she recalled. "I felt he was right."

THE NATIONAL MOURNING that followed President Kennedy's assassination did little to stop political attacks on Coretta. In their newly launched syndicated column, Rowland Evans and Robert Novak warned of a "dangerous alliance" between the civil rights and peace movements—an alliance they blamed, in part, on Coretta's leadership. Citing her recent role in the Women Strike for Peace rally at the United Nations, they wrote: "Placards at some rallies these days are combining the civil rights movement's demand for 'Freedom' and the disarmament movement's demand for 'Peace' into the slogan of 'Peace and Freedom Now.'"

They feared Coretta was inspiring thousands of young people to follow her lead.

"Many of the white youths currently demonstrating against segregation in the South cut their eye-teeth against United States possession of nuclear weapons," they argued.

But if her critics hoped to silence her, they were disappointed. In May 1964, Coretta traveled to Norfolk, Virginia, to receive an award from the Links, a civic organization of upper-class Black women. She accepted the honor, she said, on behalf of the millions of women engaged in the same struggle.

"I can never really be free until every black man from Johannesburg, South Africa, to Jackson, Mississippi, is free," she said. "I cannot rest until freedom and justice become realities for all people."

By October 1964, Martin was exhausted from his relentless travel and speaking schedule. Coretta encouraged him to check into Saint Joseph's Hospital in Atlanta for a checkup—and some much-needed rest.

The next morning, Coretta received a call from a reporter: Martin had been awarded the Nobel Peace Prize. At thirty-five, he was the youngest person ever to receive the honor, and only the second Black American to do so. The first, Ralph Bunche, had won in 1950 for brokering a peace accord between Israel and Egypt as a United Nations emissary.

"It was a great tribute," Coretta recalled, "but an even more awesome burden. I realized, as well as he did, the tremendous responsibility this placed on him, and I felt it too."

She sensed that the prize carried a deeper meaning they could not fully grasp at the time.

"It felt like he had been given a commission to really go out and do something. The prize was recognition for something that had not been achieved. It was almost a frightening kind of feeling."

Not long after the award ceremony, Coretta said to Martin that she hoped he would soon take on a more active and public role in the peace movement. She believed that was what they were both called upon to do.

Later, she told the Associated Press reporter Kathryn Johnson that after more than a decade living with the "threat of death always present," the Nobel moment felt like standing on a "mountaintop." She wished they could stay there forever.

FBI Director J. Edgar Hoover had other desires.

He already harbored a vendetta against Martin, convinced that the civil rights movement was infiltrated by Communists and posed a threat to national security. Hoover also resented Martin's public criticism of the FBI for failing to protect civil rights activists in the South. The Nobel announcement only deepened his fury, and he escalated his efforts to discredit Martin.

On November 18, at a press conference in Washington, DC, Hoover called Martin "the most notorious liar in the country." This remark was reported in newspapers nationwide.

Days later, one of Hoover's assistant directors mailed a blackmail package to the King home. It contained a typed letter filled with explicit allegations about Martin's extramarital sex life, along with an audiotape allegedly meant to corroborate them. The letter warned that the material would be made public in a month's time, and said, ominously, that "there is only one thing left for you to do."

Coretta opened the package, assuming it was a recording of one of Martin's speeches. It is impossible to know exactly what she felt in that moment. She had heard rumors of his infidelity before but had always refused to believe them.

"I don't have any evidence, and I never had a gut feel that told me he had strayed," she later wrote.

She shared the letter and recording with Martin. Both of them believed it was a coordinated effort to destroy their marriage—and push him toward suicide.

Regardless of the personal content, the package offered unmistakable proof of the FBI's surveillance campaign and its intent to undermine Martin and the movement. The scope of the effort and the vitriol that motivated it were terrifying.

"Each of us had been discounting as 'paranoid' our suspicions that our home phones as well as our office phones had been tapped," Coretta later recalled. "Now we put two and two together."

Martin's closest adviser, Ralph Abernathy, put it even more bluntly: "The FBI had become our enemy just as surely as the Ku Klux Klan."

FROM THE HIGH of the Nobel Prize ceremony in Oslo to the low of Hoover's smear campaign, Coretta kept pushing for peace. News from Vietnam only deepened her sense of urgency.

In early February 1965, the Vietcong attacked a US Army base near Pleiku, in the Central Highlands of Vietnam. In response,

President Johnson authorized Operation Rolling Thunder, an aerial bombing campaign targeting military and industrial sites in North Vietnam. Privately, Johnson expressed grave doubts about the war's direction.

"It looks to me that we're getting into another Korea," he had told National Security Adviser McGeorge Bundy the year before. "It just worries the hell out of me. I don't see what we can ever hope to get out of this."

He recognized how easy it was for a nation to get into war—and how hard it was to get out.

"What the hell is Vietnam worth to me?" he asked Bundy. "What is it worth to this country?"

While Martin strategized in Selma, Alabama, with his SCLC colleagues James Bevel and Hosea Williams, SNCC's John Lewis, and others to advance a voting rights campaign, Coretta embarked on a multicity speaking and singing tour of the West Coast.

In March, she served as the keynote speaker at a Women Strike for Peace luncheon at the Beverly Hills Hotel. Before a predominately white audience of 550 women, she praised Black women as the "backbone" of the civil rights movement—and urged the women present to join the fight.

"If women would march and demonstrate all across the land protesting situations such as that which exists in Selma, Alabama, it would help immeasurably," she said to applause.

From Los Angeles, Coretta traveled to San Francisco and then to Seattle to perform a series of Freedom Concerts. Her mix of music and narration captivated standing-room-only audiences. In several cities, crowds gathered outside venues to listen on loudspeakers.

Politically attuned concertgoers recognized her performance style as a tribute to Paul Robeson, the legendary singer and activist who had been blacklisted for his political views. Those unfamiliar with that context were moved by her stories of the freedom struggle, from the Montgomery bus boycott to the present.

As she traveled, Coretta followed the news from Alabama closely. Earlier in the year, she had joined Martin for marches in Selma and for mass meetings and protests in her hometown of Marion, thirty miles northwest of Selma. When twenty-six-year-old deacon Jimmie Lee Jackson was shot and killed by an Alabama state trooper during a peaceful voting rights demonstration in Marion, the news hit Coretta hard. Jimmie Lee's aunt had been one of her best friends in high school. His death made her feel, she later said, that the Constitution's promises to Black Americans were "penned in invisible ink."

In response to Jackson's death, more than five hundred activists staged a march through Selma on Sunday, March 7. Led by Lewis and Williams, they crossed the Edmund Pettus Bridge—only to be met by a wall of state troopers and local police.

Television cameras and photographers captured what happened next: Police beat marchers with nightsticks. Deputies on horseback trampled protesters. Tear gas choked the crowd. The nation watched in horror.

News from Selma ran alongside another flashpoint: On March 8, the first regular US combat units arrived in Vietnam.

Civil rights leaders began making increasingly explicit references to the war. At Howard University in Washington, DC, Martin called war "obsolete" and one of the three "howling evils" of modern society.

"The war in Vietnam is accomplishing nothing," he said. "I feel we are following the wrong course of action in Vietnam."

In Alabama, he eulogized Jimmie Lee Jackson with a sharp indictment of federal priorities: Jackson was murdered "by the timidity of a federal government that spends millions of dollars for troops in Vietnam and can't protect its citizens in this country."

SNCC Chairman John Lewis—who suffered a skull fracture in Selma and was among dozens hospitalized—made the point even more bluntly: "I don't see how President Johnson can send troops to Vietnam—I don't see how he can send troops to the Congo . . . and can't send troops to Selma, Ala."

Two days after what would come to be known as Bloody Sunday, Coretta performed in Seattle at Garfield High School. FBI agents filed reports on her West Coast travels, noting that members of the Communist Party allegedly attended a reception at Mount Zion Baptist Church following her speech.

While Coretta was in Seattle, Martin led a second march in Selma. Reporters asked her if she was concerned about his safety.

"You realize that what you are doing is pretty dangerous, but we go with the faith that what we are doing is right," she said at a news conference. "If something happens to my husband, the cause will continue. It may even be helped."

The movement, she insisted, was much bigger than Martin. People would continue to follow the path of nonviolence.

Coretta finished her Freedom Concert tour with stops in Portland and Denver, raising more than twenty thousand dollars for the movement. She returned to Atlanta eager to see her children and settle into the family's new home. After years of renting and staying with friends and family, the Kings had finally purchased a house: a four-bedroom home at 234 Sunset Avenue, in a working-class, predominately Black neighborhood in southwest Atlanta called Vine

City. Coretta hoped that the house would be a refuge from the "death and bloodshed" engulfing the country.

Martin was still in Selma when Coretta joined seventy million Americans watching President Johnson address a joint session of Congress. The president described Selma as a "turning point in man's unending search for freedom," invoking Lexington, Concord, and Appomattox as historical parallels. Civil rights, he said, was an issue that "[laid] bare the heart of America itself."

"The real hero of this struggle is the American Negro," Johnson said. "His actions and protests, his courage to risk safety and even to risk his life, have awakened the conscience of this Nation. . . . He has called upon us to make good the promise of America. And who among us can say that we would have made the same progress if not for his persistent bravery, and his faith in American democracy."

Coretta was moved by the sincerity and urgency in Johnson's voice. When he declared, "We shall overcome," it felt—for the first time in a long while—as if the tide might be turning in favor of the movement.

On March 21, she traveled to Greensboro, North Carolina, to speak at North Carolina A&T College. Addressing an audience of more than a thousand Black students from A&T and Bennett College, she urged them to join a global nonviolent revolution for peace and freedom.

"It is in South Africa, it is in Selma, Alabama," she said. "We want to be free, and we want to be free now—everywhere."

Confronting the red-baiting attacks that had been used to discredit civil rights and peace activists, Coretta affirmed the students' right to be both critical and patriotic.

"We love America," she said. "Our job is to save the soul of

America. We cannot have a united America until we are all treated equally. This is our greatest bulwark against communism."

Black Americans, she argued, weren't asking for special treatment. They were simply demanding what had always been promised: full citizenship, equal treatment, and a real share in the American dream.

After her speech, Coretta left campus and rushed to the Greensboro airport to catch a flight to Montgomery. There, she rejoined Martin and five thousand others determined to complete the march from Selma to the state capital.

That night, at the "Stars for Freedom" concert organized by Harry Belafonte, Coretta took the stage alongside performers including Sammy Davis Jr., Odetta, Nina Simone, and Tony Bennett. She spoke of how meaningful it was to return to Montgomery ten years after the bus boycott—and then read Langston Hughes's "Mother to Son," a poem about perseverance in the face of hardship. It was a piece both she and Martin returned to often in difficult times.

Unlike the earlier Selma marches, this time the demonstrators had federal protection. Outraged by the violence unleashed on peaceful protesters—and by Alabama Governor George Wallace's intransigence—President Johnson federalized the Alabama National Guard and sent more than two thousand army soldiers and federal marshals to ensure the march could proceed safely.

"We were no longer treated like enemies of the state," Coretta wrote, recalling the show of force.

Federal troops flanked the highways. Sharpshooters stood watch from rooftops. Helicopters hovered overhead.

"Finally our lives had some value, were deemed worthy of protection," she reflected.

At the Pentagon, army command and communications officers monitored live reports from both Montgomery and Vietnam.

WHEN CORETTA ARRIVED at Madison Square Garden on June 8, 1965, for the "Emergency Rally on Vietnam," she had already delivered dozens of lectures and concerts across the country. At each stop, she made the case that the movements for peace and civil rights were inseparable—and that America's escalating involvement in Vietnam threatened both racial justice and the nation's global credibility.

Although she had been active in every major civil rights campaign from Montgomery to Selma, Coretta—like many women in the movement—was often made to feel that her role was peripheral. That she was not a leader. That her voice did not matter.

But on that stage in New York, with eighteen thousand people hanging on her every word, she claimed her place as one of the movement's most forceful critics of the Vietnam War.

Her bold position provoked the ire of President Johnson. While Johnson liked to publicly dismiss antiwar activists as "sob sisters and peace societies," he and his advisers quietly worried that large-scale protests could constrain his military options.

In April, after committing an additional twenty thousand ground troops, National Security Adviser McGeorge Bundy issued National Security Action Memorandum No. 328, warning, "The President desires that . . . premature publicity be avoided by all possible precautions."

Johnson did not publicly discuss the military actions he had authorized until late July 1965—and even then, he offered the American people no clear explanation of how the war would be won or how long it might last. Inside Washington, few political or military leaders dared to express more than private doubts. The cost of dissent was too high.

"Both the President and the congressional leaders were afraid of an open national debate," General William Westmoreland later reflected.

Coretta's headlining of a mass rally at Madison Square Garden helped drag the war issue into the public consciousness—exactly what President Johnson hoped to avoid. It took courage to speak out on such a controversial issue. A Gallup poll from that year found that only 10 percent of Americans "felt the urge to organize or join a public demonstration" about any issue—and of that group, only 10 percent cited Vietnam as the cause that might move them to protest.

Coretta saw every protest, every speech, every appearance as a chance to persuade more of her fellow citizens to raise their voices.

By the summer of 1965, demand for Coretta as a speaker had surged. She traveled to Chicago to keynote the Women's International League for Peace and Freedom luncheon, and then to Columbus, Ohio, where she appeared alongside the baseball legend Jackie Robinson, Office of Economic Opportunity Director Sargent Shriver, and the Mississippi civil rights leader Aaron Henry at the national assembly of the United Presbyterian Church.

Women Strike for Peace continued their media campaign. In June 1965, they ran a large advertisement in *The New York Times* that showed a white teenager in a cap and gown. The headline read: "He graduates in June '65, will he die in Vietnam in June '66?"

The subhead added: "American mothers will not remain silent while their sons are sent to Vietnam to kill and be killed."

At the time, there were nearly seventy-five thousand US troops in Vietnam—a number expected to rise to two hundred thousand by early 1966. Public opinion on the war was divided. Polls showed 26 percent of Americans favored ending US military involvement, 21 percent supported escalation, 20 percent backed current policy, and the rest were undecided.

Later that month, Coretta traveled to Detroit to speak at the annual Women's Day at Greater Macedonia Baptist Church. Her themes—peace and freedom—remained constant.

"Each of us must take part," she told the congregation, "if we are ever to live in a world free of hatred and free of fear of being bombed and free from war."

The parishioners in the Detroit church, like communities across the country, were beginning to follow the war more closely. Young men from the city—boys barely out of high school—were already among the thousands of American troops in Vietnam. Locals tried to make sense of a distant war through the stories of these young men: their letters, their homecomings, and, for too many, their funerals. When Coretta spoke of peace and freedom, she was thinking of these lives—the lives most vulnerable to the violence of war and racism.

2

SKIP

The first time Dwight "Skip" Johnson visited Washington, DC, it was to receive the Medal of Honor. On November 19, 1968, Skip—a twenty-one-year-old from Detroit—stood in the East Room of the White House before an audience that included General William Westmoreland, who commanded US forces in Vietnam, Secretary of Defense Clark Clifford, and members of Congress, his mother, his younger brother, and his fiancée. President Lyndon Johnson, whose party had lost the election just weeks earlier, stepped to the podium for what would be his final medal ceremony.

"Five heroic sons of America come to us today from the tortured fields of Vietnam," President Johnson began. "They come to remind us that so long as that conflict continues, our purpose and our hopes rest on the steadfast bravery of young men in battle."

While Johnson often used such ceremonies to scold antiwar protesters, this time he focused squarely on the veterans being honored.

"These five soldiers in their separate moments of supreme testing

Dwight "Skip" Johnson receives the Medal of Honor from
President Lyndon B. Johnson on November 19, 1968.

summoned a degree of courage that stirs wonder and respect and
an overpowering pride in all of us," he continued. "Through their
spectacular courage, they set themselves apart in a very select company. They represent the contribution of more than half a million
young Americans to a world of order and of peace."

When Skip approached President Johnson to receive his medal,
his hands trembled.

His muscles, he later said, "jumped like frogs." He offered a
quiet "Thank you" as the president hung the nation's highest military honor around his neck: a five-pointed star suspended by a light-
blue ribbon embroidered with thirteen white stars.

"It came as a shock to me," Skip said of the award. "Something
like this never crosses your mind."

At the reception that followed, Skip confided to the president,
"The ceremony was the only time I was really scared."

His twelve-year-old brother, who had to stand on a chair to see the stage, proudly told reporters and politicians, "That's my big brother."

Reading the Medal of Honor citation, President Johnson praised Skip's "conspicuous gallantry" as a tank driver in the Sixty-Ninth Armor. But unlike the other four recipients honored that day, Skip was also conspicuous as a Black soldier and veteran.

By 1968, the US military depended on the service and sacrifice of Black Americans to a degree that was unimaginable just two decades earlier. Black troops like Skip were more visible in Vietnam than in any previous American war—a shift that military leaders, politicians, and even some civil rights advocates pointed to as a sign of progress.

In many ways, the presence of Black soldiers on the front lines seemed to represent the fulfillment of long-fought civil rights demands: equal opportunity, equal duty, equal honor. When newspapers across the country published photographs of Skip, standing tall in his US Army uniform with the Medal of Honor around his neck—an award no Black soldier had received during World War II—he appeared to be the embodiment of the American hero.

HEROES HAVE HISTORIES. The White House seemed an unlikely destination when Skip was growing up in Detroit.

Born in 1947, he was raised in the Jeffries Housing Projects, where he lived with his mother, Joyce Johnson Alves, and his young brother, David. Joyce worked as a psychiatric nursing attendant at the local Veterans Administration hospital. She did not talk much about her work, but occasionally she shared stories of the patients she cared for—veterans of World War I, World War II, and Korea, some of whom still relived their battlefield traumas decades later. These fleeting glimpses painted a far more harrowing portrait of war than the heroic combat scenes Skip's friends watched in movie theaters.

Skip never met his biological father but loved his stepfather, Brenton Alves. A Jamaican immigrant, in the early 1950s Alves had come as a migrant farmworker to the United States, where he met and married Joyce. When Skip was nine, immigration officials deported Alves, claiming he had entered the country under an assumed name. Suddenly, not yet a teenager, Skip became the man of the house. Joyce gave him long lists of chores and depended on him to keep David out of trouble while she was at work.

In the 1950s and early 1960s, the Jeffries Homes were like a small town of twelve thousand residents tucked into a massive city of 1.6 million. The fifty-acre complex—thirteen high-rise towers surrounded by low-rise buildings—could seem intimidating to outsiders. But for those who lived there, it was a tight-knit community of low-income families, seniors, and a few Wayne State University students and staff.

The modest park and playground were always crowded. Children made up nearly three quarters of the population. Bright, curious, kind, and funny, Skip got along with just about everybody—even if his gentle streak sometimes meant he was left out of tackle football games.

"We did not want to pick Skip because everybody knew Skip wouldn't hit anybody hard enough," recalled his classmate Ron Scott.

Growing up at Jeffries, Skip learned to stay aware of his surroundings. Walking home from school, he kept an eye out for the older boys who lingered on street corners—sometimes flashing switchblades to intimidate the younger kids. Just as carefully, he avoided the police who patrolled the neighborhood. When Skip was almost ten, he saw two officers beat a teenager they suspected of stealing a car. More than fifty adults and children gathered to protest the assault, but one of the officers barked, "He's not related to you—go mind your business!"

After that, Skip crossed the street whenever he saw a squad car. It felt like the police were always looking for a reason to stop and harass kids who looked like him.

The same distrust followed him into Jefferson Junior High. Each morning, Skip and hundreds of other kids from Jeffries crossed an overpass spanning the Lodge Freeway. They joked with each other, radios buzzing with the latest Motown hits. They were ordinary kids, but many teachers didn't see them that way. They saw problems instead of potential: Black, poor, and too often dismissed.

"Most of these kids are just plain dumb," one teacher told a reporter from the *Detroit Free Press*. "You'll never teach them anything."

Another referred to the students as "welfare leeches" when some forgot to bring pencils to school. While nearby white schools had open seats, Jefferson was overcrowded and under-resourced, making it harder for both students and teachers to succeed.

Conditions were not much better during Skip's first year at Northwestern High School. In October 1962, more than twenty-five hundred students and three hundred parents boycotted the school to protest the neglect. They carried signs that read "D-Day at N'Western: Disappointment, Distrust, and Disgust"; "Education is cheaper in 1962 than welfare in 1972"; and "We are not sardines, give us more room."

The protest was led by Reverend Albert Cleage, a fiery activist minister with deep ties to Northwestern. He had graduated from the school, as had several of his siblings and cousins. His two daughters, Kristin and Pearl, were students who joined the boycott.

A Black teacher and activist, Ernest Smith, saw the conditions at Northwestern as a microcosm of racism in Detroit—and across the nation. "White racism infests the North as well as the South," he wrote in *Illustrated News*, a civil rights newspaper published by the Cleage family. "It is not merely a matter of 'emotions' or 'education,' as the do-gooders think. White racism is structured. It is made of organizations, institutions, and social interests. It cannot be shaken by words."

Students and parents were protesting not just poor facilities but a school system built on decades of intentional inequality. Administrators racially gerrymandered attendance boundaries, segregated Black teachers into overcrowded Black schools, and operated union apprenticeship programs that routinely excluded Black students—cutting them off from future employment opportunities.

"Segregated Northwestern's chief defect is, in fact, this: it is the bastard child of white-racism, No'th'n style!" Smith argued. "It is as much a segregated school as one in the middle of the Black Belt of Mississippi or Alabama."

The boycott at Northwestern was part of a national wave. In the 1960s, majority-Black high schools in cities like New York, Chicago, Philadelphia, Boston, and Los Angeles erupted in similar protests. As the military draft expanded, the stakes of educational inequality grew more urgent. Students in well-resourced schools were being prepared for college, while working-class students like Skip were being prepared for Vietnam.

Conditions began to improve in 1964, when Jessie Kennedy became the first Black high school principal in Detroit. She brought new energy and vision to Northwestern, inviting the South African singer Miriam Makeba, the civil rights activist James Meredith, and the Detroit Urban League's executive director, Francis A. Kornegay, to speak with students. The local educator Catherine Carter Blackwell shared stories from her travels in Africa, while Congressman— and Northwestern alum—John Conyers spoke about voting rights and foreign policy.

Kennedy wanted students to imagine possibilities that existed beyond the school's walls. "See what has been done," she told them.

Working with her teachers, Kennedy launched new initiatives like the Current Topics Study Club and the Negro History Club. She asked her friend the Northwestern alumna Mary P. Motley to donate her personal library—hundreds of books on African and African American history—and persuaded Ivan Ludington, the owner of a Detroit book and magazine distribution company, to contribute two thousand books and monthly issues of major magazines to create a new reading room in the school library.

Motown Records' founder, Berry Gordy Jr., also stepped in. He donated copies of the label's spoken-word recordings, including their first such album: Martin Luther King Jr.'s 1963 speech in Detroit. Gordy called it "required listening for every American child, white or Black."

Skip and his classmates listened as King described segregation in Detroit as "a cancer in the body politic," no less destructive than segregation in the South.

"This social revolution taking place," King declared, "can be summarized in three little words. They are the words 'all,' 'here,' and 'now.' We want *all* of our rights, we want them *here*, and we want them *now*."

Where the school's hallways had once been bare and the library shelves sparse, students now passed portraits of famous Black Americans. They could read about current-day newsmakers and explore ideas that stretched beyond Detroit's borders. Under Kennedy's leadership, Northwestern's teachers believed in their students—and challenged them to believe in themselves.

For Skip, the difference was night and day. It opened his eyes to where life might take him after high school.

WHILE HE WAS not particularly interested in politics, it was impossible to ignore the war in Vietnam. In social studies, students debated US air strikes and President Johnson's decision to commit ground troops. Every Wednesday afternoon, the school's Current Topics Study Club met in the library, where students pored over the *Michigan Chronicle*, the *Detroit Free Press*, *Ebony*, *Life*, and other newspapers and periodicals—eager to understand both the war unfolding more than eight thousand miles away and the protests it had sparked across the country. Even in Latin class, the war was unavoidable. Reading *The Iliad*, Mrs. Eula Cutt asked her students to draw connections between the experiences of Achilles and modern-day combat veterans.

Outside the school walls, one event in particular shook the students: the story of Alice Herz. In March 1965, Herz—an eighty-two-year-old German Jewish refugee—poured a flammable fluid over her body and set herself ablaze outside Detroit's Federal Department Store.

Herz had joined the Women's International League for Peace and Freedom in 1916. She fled Nazi Germany with her daughter in the early 1930s, was imprisoned in a French internment camp during World War II, and eventually settled in Detroit. There, she became a fixture of the city's antiwar and civil rights movements. Herz cofounded Detroit Women for Peace, supported Coretta Scott King and Women Strike for Peace, and never missed a protest.

She had seen Martin speak at Cobo Hall and marched in solidarity with Selma protesters just a week before she took her own life.

"I've seen her around for years," said a sergeant in the Detroit Police Department's "Subversive Squad." "She was just a pacifist. You know, always on the march whenever someone—anyone—was demonstrating against war. . . . I don't think she ever missed a meeting of any of those peace organizations."

In a note tucked into her pocketbook, Herz explained her deep concern about the war in Vietnam. She charged a string of US presidents—Truman, Eisenhower, Kennedy, and now Johnson—with misleading the American people, allowing Congress "to appropriate endless billions of dollars for an Arsenal of Destruction—unlimited." To make her voice heard, she wrote, she had chosen "the flaming death of the Buddhists."

Rosa Parks and Congressman John Conyers attended a remembrance ceremony for Herz at the First Unitarian Universalist Church.

The Federal Department Store where she died was only a couple of miles up Grand River Avenue from Northwestern High. Several students heard about the incident before it even appeared in the newspaper. It added to the growing sense of unease and urgency Skip and his classmates felt when they discussed the war.

It was a scene playing out in high schools across the country—especially in working-class communities where college deferments were out of reach. Only a few months in age separated them from the tens of thousands of young Americans already deployed to Vietnam.

In July, President Johnson announced that draft calls would double to thirty-five thousand per month. Military service was no longer a distant possibility—it was fast becoming a certainty. At Northwestern, few students had the resources to avoid it. There were no strings to pull. Skip and his classmates paid close attention to how other young people—students, athletes, musicians, protesters—were responding to the draft.

At Northwestern, students read about a group of young civil rights activists in McComb, Mississippi, who, in July 1965, began urging Black Americans to resist the draft. The Mississippi youth were devastated to learn that one of their former high school classmates and fellow activists—twenty-three-year-old Private John D. Shaw—had been killed during a search-and-destroy mission in Vietnam. They responded by circulating a flyer that challenged the legitimacy of the war and the draft.

Affiliated with the Mississippi Freedom Democratic Party (MFDP), which had been founded the previous year to challenge the state's all-white Democratic Party, the activists argued that until Black people had freedom in Mississippi and across the country, young Black men should not honor the draft—and Black mothers should discourage their sons from going to war.

"Negroes have caught hell here under this <u>American Democ-</u>

racy," the flyer read. "No one has a right to ask us to risk our lives and kill other Colored People in Santo Domingo and Viet Nam, so that the White Americans can get richer."

They also encouraged Black soldiers already serving to protest from within the military. They pointed to Pvt. David Ovall, a young white soldier who staged a seventeen-day hunger strike at Fort Monmouth in New Jersey. The army eventually discharged him, ruling him "unsuitable for military service due to defective attitude."

Though the flyer was intended for local circulation, it drew national attention, with newspapers, television, and radio stations all covering the protest. *The New York Times* ran a headline: "Mississippi Negroes Being Urged to Dodge Draft."

The backlash was swift. Mainstream civil rights organizations had largely avoided taking a strong public stance against the war, wary of alienating President Johnson and being branded unpatriotic. The firestorm around the McComb flyer showed those fears were well founded.

Hodding Carter III, a liberal white journalist in Mississippi, called the leaflet "close to treason." Even Charles Diggs, a Black US congressman representing parts of Detroit and its suburbs, called the notion of young Black men resisting the draft "ridiculous and completely irresponsible."

Amid this criticism, Lawrence Guyot, executive director of the Mississippi Freedom Democratic Party, tried to clarify the organization's position. He issued a press release explaining that the anti-draft flyer was produced by local activists in McComb, not officially sanctioned by the MFDP. Still, he expressed sympathy with their frustrations.

"It is very easy to understand why Negro citizens of McComb, themselves the victims of bombings, Klan-inspired terrorism, and harassment arrests, should resent the death of a citizen of McComb while fighting in Vietnam for 'freedom' not enjoyed by the Negro community of McComb," he wrote.

Just days later, on August 9, 1965, more than eight hundred people marched from the Washington Monument to the Capitol in an effort to link the civil rights and antiwar movements.

"In Mississippi and Washington the few make decisions for the many," organizers declared. "Mississippi Negroes are denied the vote; the voice of thirty per cent of Americans now opposed to the undeclared war in Vietnam is not heeded and all Americans are denied access to facts concerning the true military and political situation."

Bob Moses, who had organized voter registration drives as a leader in both SNCC and the Mississippi Freedom Democratic Party, co-led the march. He saw a deep connection between the domestic fight for civil rights and the international fight over US foreign policy.

"Negroes better than anyone else are in a position to question the war," he said. "Not because they understand the war better, but because they understand the United States."

Police arrested more than 350 demonstrators. Dozens had been splattered with red paint hurled by neo-Nazi counterprotesters. *Life* magazine ran a full-page color photo of two march leaders—the pacifist historian Staughton Lynd and the World War II conscientious objector David Dellinger, who cofounded the pacifist journal *Liberation*—drenched in red. Their faces, hair, and clothes looked soaked in blood. On the opposite page, *Life* published a picture of white students in New York burning their draft cards.

"For many young Americans," the article read, "dodging the draft has become a game."

Paul Glover, Skip's social studies teacher at Northwestern, used current events to help students connect the news to their own lives.

"What will you do if you are drafted?" he asked one afternoon. "Or if your brothers or boyfriends are drafted?"

Skip hesitated. He didn't know what he'd do if his name came up. When he thought about military service, he thought of the veteran he knew best: Rev. Carl Hort, the pastor at his family's church. Faith Lutheran Memorial was a small congregation, fewer than sixty members, and Reverend Hort knew everyone by name. He worked closely with Skip, encouraging him to serve as an altar boy and to join the church's Explorer Scout group.

Hort, who grew up in a white rural community in Oklahoma, had served as an army rifleman during the Battle of the Bulge. He often spoke to Skip about the 761st Tank Battalion—known as "The Black Panthers"—an all-Black unit that distinguished itself in major European campaigns. Their heroism, he said, had inspired him to become a pastor in a predominately Black congregation in Detroit. Hort was proud of his service and shared those memories freely with the young men of the church.

Some of Skip's classmates were eager to enlist. Northwestern's Junior Reserve Officer Training Corps (JROTC) program had about two dozen members, including David Clark Riley and Robert Thornton. Riley's father had served in the army, and his uncle had fought as a marine in Korea. Wearing the JROTC uniform, Riley felt seen and respected—he liked the discipline of leading underclassmen in drill and practicing on the rifle range.

Thornton, a champion miler on the school's track team, also

came from a military family. His uncle had served in the Eighty-Second Airborne. He dropped out of school after eleventh grade to enlist in the marines. At his induction ceremony in the Detroit federal building, a marine corporal with a buzz cut shouted at the recruits, "Are you prepared to give your life to your country? That's either a yes, sir, or no, sir."

The words echoed off the limestone walls.

"To be honest with you," Thornton recalled, "I later peed in my pants."

Other students were both inspired and unsettled by the stories they heard from Lt. Christopher Sturkey, a Detroiter and draftee who had served in the 614th Tank Destroyer Battalion during World War II. Sturkey earned a battlefield commission and the Silver Star for his bravery during the battalion's push through Germany's Siegfried Line. When he visited Northwestern in 1965, he spoke about arriving in France and receiving a rousing pep talk from General Patton. He told students how the all-Black 614th earned the respect of white GIs through their courage and effectiveness in combat. But he did not sugarcoat the violence. He described how they had to kill Nazi troops who refused to surrender.

"They wanted it the hard way and that's just the way they got it," he said.

Even so, Sturkey's pride in his service was tempered by anger over the way Black veterans were treated when they came home. After the war, he returned to Detroit to surprise his wife at the defense plant where she worked. He arrived about half an hour before her shift ended and decided to grab a hamburger at nearby White Tower restaurant. Dressed in full uniform, with campaign ribbons and battle stars, he took a seat at the counter.

The waitress looked him up and down. Then she said flatly: "We don't serve niggers in here."

"Here I was," Sturkey recalled, "supposed to be some kind of a hero returned from war and this is the first thing I hear from some poor white hash-slinging bitch I've been fighting for."

The students at Northwestern knew this kind of story well. Many had grandfathers, fathers, and uncles who had served in World War I and World War II in the segregated military—only to return to a country that refused to honor their sacrifice.

The disrespect did not fade over time. It festered. And for a generation staring down the draft, it shaped how they saw the war in Vietnam.

Draft resistance came directly to Northwestern High in the fall of 1965, Skip's senior year. One afternoon, a few dozen students were milling around after school when a barrel-chested man stood on the sidewalk and shouted: "Destroy the draft!"

It was General Gordon Baker Jr.—the first Black American to openly refuse military induction. He handed out anti-draft leaflets to students at Northwestern and other majority-Black high schools across Detroit, as well as to college students and autoworkers around the city.

Baker, a twenty-four-year-old Detroiter, worked in the foundry at Ford Motor Company and took classes at Wayne State University. There, he cofounded Uhuru (Swahili for "freedom"), a student group that fought against police brutality, housing discrimination, and educational inequality.

His politics were shaped by local activists like James and Grace Lee Boggs and by the words of the Black nationalist Robert Williams, whose *Radio Free Dixie* broadcasts challenged white supremacy across the South. He saw Malcolm X speak in Detroit several times. In 1964, Baker spent two months in Cuba, building solidarity with radical student activists from Asia, Africa, and Latin America.

So when a letter from the local draft board arrived, asking about his fitness for military service, Baker responded with force. He published an open letter to the draft board rejecting the war and condemning American hypocrisy. In it, he connected the war in Vietnam with apartheid in South Africa, the assassination of the Congolese leader Patrice Lumumba, the murder of Medgar Evers, and the bombing of the Sixteenth Street Baptist Church in Birmingham.

"With all of this blood of my non-white brothers dripping from your fangs," he wrote, "you have the AUDACITY to ask me if I am 'qualified.'"

Baker's letter was published in *Soulbook*, an underground newspaper distributed by Bobby Seale, who would cofound the Black Panther Party the following year. In both tone and substance, Baker's words anticipated the Panthers' fierce opposition to the Vietnam War.

"My fight is for Freedom," Baker wrote.

> Therefore, when the call is made to free South Africa; when the call is made to liberate Latin America from the United Fruit Co., Kaiser and Alcoa Aluminum Co., and from Standard Oil; when the call is made to jail the exploiting Brahmins in India in order to destroy the Caste System; when the call is made to free the black delta areas of Mississippi, Alabama, South Carolina; when the call is made to free Harlem, New York, to FREE 12TH STREET

HERE IN DETROIT!: when these calls are made, send
for me [and] it shall be an honor to serve!

Skip did not necessarily share Baker's radical politics. But the
reference to Twelfth Street hit home. He crossed it every day on his
way between Jeffries and Northwestern High.

AS A TEENAGER, Skip often visited his cousin Tom Tillman, whose
family lived on the West Side in a racially mixed neighborhood of
modest single-family homes. Kids played in the streets and left their
bicycles beside their houses, unlocked. Day-to-day life felt less tense
than at Jeffries, and Skip could finally let his guard down.

It did not take long before a girl in his cousin's neighborhood
caught his eye. He started finding excuses to swing around the
block and flirt with her.

The problem was, Katrina Lyn May wasn't interested—at least
not at first. She was about to turn fifteen, and Skip had just turned
sixteen.

"I was not interested in being bothered. I was too busy playing
baseball in the street," Katrina recalled. "And besides, my mother
would not let me date yet anyway. It got to the point where when I
would see him coming, I would just go in the house. I wouldn't
care if it was a hundred degrees—I would go in the house and close
the door. That's how I met Skip."

Smart, athletic, and pretty, Katrina lived with her parents and
grandfather in a single-story brick house at the corner of Central and
Garden Streets. When they left the Black Bottom neighborhood in

the mid-1950s, they were the first Black family to move onto the street. While Black homeowners faced violence in other parts of Detroit, the Mays got along well with the Polish and Jewish families in their neighborhood.

Katrina's grandfather would sit outside for hours, talking with the older Polish man next door—two elders passing the time in a community of mostly young families.

Her father had served in the army during World War II; her uncle had fought as a marine in the Korean War, where he lost his left arm in combat. These family stories, combined with Katrina's precocious appetite for the news, shaped her early views on Vietnam.

"I had been reading the newspaper since I was about ten, and I would read it from cover to cover," she said.

By 1965, she had consumed hundreds of articles on the war and seen hours of footage on her family's new RCA color television.

"You couldn't turn on the news without seeing film footage from Vietnam," Katrina remembered. "That war was played out on the television. And we'd be sitting there, and we'd actually be looking to see if we knew anybody in all that mayhem."

Katrina was not an antiwar activist, but the news from Vietnam made her angry.

"This is not a new war," she told her uncle one evening. "Korea poured over into Vietnam. One war just pours into the other."

The domestic news was just as unsettling. Over the summer of 1965, Katrina read about civil rights protesters being beaten in Selma, Alabama—and about a weeklong uprising in Watts, a Black neighborhood in Los Angeles, that left thirty-four people dead and more than a thousand injured. The *Detroit Free Press* ran images of National Guardsmen with rifles aimed at crowds.

Katrina's parents had lived through the 1943 Detroit race riot, and she knew that the same conditions that sparked Watts—concentrated poverty, racial discrimination, police brutality—existed in her city. She couldn't help but wonder: Would one riot pour into another?

And yet, she was also a teenager looking forward to her sixteenth birthday in August.

Her aunt, a supervisor for Detroit Parks and Recreation, reserved the neighborhood recreation center for the birthday celebration. The *Michigan Chronicle*'s Women's Section later reported that two dozen friends and family attended—including an eighteen-year-old high school senior named Dwight "Skip" Johnson.

Katrina and Skip went on their first date later that fall.

"I always had a thing for tall, dark, and handsome," she later joked.

Katrina May, 1967   Skip Johnson, 1966

That birthday party was the first time Skip's name appeared in a newspaper. It would not be the last.

THE YOUNG SOLDIER'S EYES stopped Skip in his tracks.

It was a typical afternoon in the fall of 1965, and Skip was on his way to choir practice. He passed the familiar portraits that lined the hallways at Northwestern: Harriet Tubman, Frederick Douglass, Ida B. Wells-Barnett—Black luminaries meant to inspire.

But then he noticed something new. In the window of the library, just beyond the framed pictures of iconic historical figures, there was a small, taped black-and-white photograph. It had been clipped from a newspaper article and showed the face of one of the first Black soldiers killed in Vietnam: Private First Class Milton Lee Olive III.

Milton Lee Olive, 1965

Olive was eighteen, from Chicago. He had enlisted in the army, completed jump school, and deployed to Vietnam as a paratrooper with the 173rd Airborne—the "Sky Soldiers." He had only been in-country for four months when his platoon moved through thick jungle in the "Iron Triangle," north of Saigon, pursuing Vietcong fighters.

An enemy soldier lobbed a hand grenade into the middle of the platoon.

Before anyone had time to react, Olive shouted, "I've got it!" He grabbed the grenade and fell on it, absorbing the blast. He saved the lives of his fellow soldiers.

"It was the most incredible display of selfless bravery I ever witnessed," said his platoon leader, 1st Lt. James Sanford.

Olive would become the first Black American awarded the Medal of Honor for service in Vietnam.

When Skip saw the picture, Olive—helmet on, parachute pack strapped tight—seemed to stare back at him. Skip did not think of heroism, sacrifice, or medals. All he could think was how *young* he looked. Skip was just a few months younger than this fallen hero.

Milton Olive III's father traveled to Detroit for an Armed Forces Day celebration and spoke with a *Michigan Chronicle* reporter. The grief was still raw.

"I thought of taking sleeping pills and laying down and not waking up," he confessed.

He described how Milton was born breech—how doctors doubted the underweight baby would survive, and how Milton's mother died hours later from birth complications. Milton spent much of his childhood with his paternal grandparents in Mississippi.

In Chicago, he learned photography from his father, who had

once run a studio, Olive & Olive, with his late wife on the South Side.

Milton later returned to Mississippi for high school and became involved in the civil rights movement. Fearing for his safety, his grandparents sent him back to Chicago. His father urged him to finish school, find work—or join the military.

With few real opportunities available to Black teenagers, Milton volunteered for the army.

"We all do a man's job and wear a man's clothes and call ourselves men," he wrote to his father from Vietnam, "but some of us are still little boys."

In Detroit, Milton's father showed the *Chronicle* reporter half a dozen photos of Milton at different stages of life. He remembered that the family called him "Skipper," while his army buddies called him "Preacher" because he often read the Bible and did not cuss. As he gently turned the photos over in his hands, "the sadness closed in."

He had been saving money to help his son start a life when he returned from the war.

"My first wife died giving birth to this boy," he said, his voice low, "and he was the only child I had and now he is gone."

Skip was still thinking about Milton Olive when he went to church that Sunday.

Reverend Hort asked the congregation to pray for the servicemen in Vietnam. Heads bowed. When Skip closed his eyes to pray, he could see Milton's face.

"SHE EDUCATED ME"

Vietnam dominated dinner table conversations across the country, and the Kings were no exception. On Thanksgiving in 1965, Martin and Coretta hosted a holiday meal at their Atlanta home with their four children, SCLC board member Marian Logan and her husband Dr. Arthur Logan, and three young SCLC staffers. Coretta served turkey and stuffing, followed by cakes and pies for dessert. But the talk at the table quickly turned to the war.

When Martin brought up Vietnam, the Logans cautioned him against speaking out publicly—it could cost the movement critical political and financial support. Martin turned to the younger guests, eager to hear what they were hearing from their peers.

"My friends are concerned," said Stoney Cooks, a project director with SCLC. "People are angry, confused, and scared about the war and the draft."

Throughout the conversation, Cooks noticed how uneasy Martin seemed. "It was like it was a burden on him," he later recalled.

The day after Thanksgiving, Coretta traveled to Washington, DC, to speak out against the war in a massive protest rally. That weekend, she joined a delegation of march leaders for a meeting in the Executive Office Building next to the White House. The group included Sanford Gottlieb, political director of the National Committee for a Sane Nuclear Policy (SANE); Dr. Benjamin Spock, who had appeared with Coretta at the Madison Square Garden rally in June; Norman Thomas, a minister and frequent presidential nominee of the Socialist Party; and Congressman George Brown Jr. of California, a World War II veteran who would later cast the lone dissenting votes against Department of Defense appropriations in 1966 and 1968.

As she arrived for the meeting, Coretta thought back to two years earlier, when she was left waiting at the White House gate while Martin and other male civil rights leaders met with President Kennedy after the March on Washington. Now, she was walking into a grand federal building, just steps from the West Wing. She hoped to make the case for peace directly to one of President Johnson's top advisers.

Instead, the delegation was ushered into a conference room with Chester Cooper, a Vietnam specialist and aide to National Security Adviser McGeorge Bundy. Also present were Joseph Laitin, the associate White House press secretary, and Clifford Alexander, the president's associate special counsel on civil rights. Alexander—the highest-ranking Black official in the White House—had met the Kings several times before. He greeted Coretta warmly.

The meeting was courteous but disappointing. Coretta and her colleagues urged the administration to declare a ceasefire, halt the bombing campaign in North Vietnam, and begin good-faith negotiations. Cooper listened politely but responded with a line they had heard before: The United States was ready to talk, but only if North Vietnam agreed to negotiate without preconditions. Until then, he said, "the war has to go on—bombings as well."

"Very frankly, we got very little satisfaction," Thomas told reporters after the meeting.

The organizers' spirits were buoyed by the more than twenty-five thousand marchers who arrived by bus, train, car, and plane from across the country. Some hitchhiked from California. In New York and New Jersey, hundreds scrambled to organize carpools after bus drivers refused to transport passengers to an antiwar rally.

"Our members are veterans of two or three wars," a union leader explained. "They belong to the American Legion and the Veterans of Foreign Wars. . . . They feel that what these people are doing is giving aid and comfort to the enemy."

Among the marchers were hundreds of members of Women Strike for Peace. The group placed advertisements for the march in *The Washington Post* and dozens of local papers. Addressed as "A message to our sons in Vietnam," the ad commended the "bravery" of young soldiers, then listed the reasons why the women were marching to end the war:

We do not want you to die for a corrupt Saigon regime
whose own people do not support it.

We do not want you to kill women and children whose
only crime is to live in country ripped by civil war.

We do not want you to destroy a small defenseless country
which in no way threatens American security.

What made the United States special, the group argued, was that "women like us" could voice disagreement with the military, the State Department, and even the president.

Coretta took up that theme in her speech, identifying herself as a mother concerned about the well-being of *all* children, regardless of where they lived.

"Freedom and destiny in America are bound together with freedom and justice in Vietnam," she said. Speaking in the shadow of the Washington Monument, she praised democracy as the foundation of American greatness—"in spite of the bombings in Alabama as well as in Vietnam." But she warned that the nation was in danger of losing its way.

"Unless America learns to respect the right to freedom and justice for all, then the very things which we hold dear in this country will wither away in the hypocritical ritual of the preservation of national self-interest."

For two hours, demonstrators marched in front of the White House carrying signs that read "Honor Peace, Stop the Bombings" and "War Erodes the 'Great Society.'" *The New York Times* noted that the crowd was largely middle class and white—people who, as the reporter put it, "would not have been out of place at the Army-Navy game."

"I expected to see a bunch of crazy-looking beatniks," a police officer told *The Washington Post*, "but this is really a respectable-looking group." A four-year-old, hustling to keep pace with her parents, held a lollipop-shaped placard that read "Peace in Vietnam, Please."

Across the street, in Lafayette Square, counterprotesters heckled the marchers. They waved banners that read "Bomb Hanoi" and

"Burn Teach-in Profs." One member of the American Nazi Party, dressed in army fatigues and combat boots, clutched a bright red gas can and a sign offering "Free Gasoline and Matches for Peace Creeps." The American Legion distributed flag buttons that read "Americans are serving the cause of freedom in Vietnam" and "I wear my country's flag to show that I support their efforts." Overhead, a skywriting plane—hired by an American Legion post in Brooklyn—etched a message: "Shame on You."

Watching it all, Coretta shook her head. She thought of the thousands of Black veterans of World War II and Korea—men like Medgar Evers, Amzie Moore, and Hosea Williams—who had served their country with distinction, only to be barred from joining segregated American Legion posts. And now, their patriotism was being questioned.

March organizer Sanford Gottlieb had been working toward this day for more than a decade. Unfazed by the hecklers and critiques, he focused on the bigger picture. A lithe thirty-nine-year-old with a forthright manner, Gottlieb had graduated from Dartmouth on a navy scholarship in 1946. While pursuing graduate studies in political science at the Sorbonne, he met Vietnamese students who described the guerrilla tactics being used to repel French troops in their homeland. In 1949, he joined a crowd of a thousand marching down the Champs-Élysées, wearing a suit and tie and chanting, "La paix au Vietnam!" ("Peace in Vietnam!").

"I wouldn't call myself a pacifist," he said on the eve of the Washington rally. "But I do believe in peace as the only rational sort of existence." He put this belief into action as political director of SANE, crisscrossing the country to encourage voters to pressure lawmakers on disarmament.

Gottlieb envisioned the march as a broad display of mainstream opposition to the war. He carefully avoided radical slogans or demands that could be used to discredit the movement. Monitors were instructed to ask marchers to carry only signs with authorized phrases, and to surround anyone carrying a Vietcong flag with demonstrators holding American flags.

The march followed a four-day summit of the National Coordinating Committee to End the War in Vietnam, which brought together more than a hundred civil rights, labor, peace, and radical organizations. When leaders from Students for a Democratic Society and other leftist groups challenged his strategy, Gottlieb shot back.

"If you want to be a little in-group and talk to each other the rest of your lives, all right," he said. "But another approach would be to strain your minds and think."

Despite tensions, the groups reached a precarious unity. Most agreed to join the rally and abide by the guidelines, helping make it the largest US protest of the Vietnam War up to that point.

Although the march was more disciplined than defiant, it was still deemed too controversial for most civil rights leaders to attend. Martin had originally been scheduled to speak but withdrew weeks earlier after Senator Thomas Dodd, a Democrat from Connecticut, publicly rebuked him for urging the Johnson administration to pause its bombing campaign and pursue a negotiated settlement in Vietnam.

Dodd insisted that King had "absolutely no competence to speak out about complex matters of foreign policy," adding that his comments "will make it impossible for me hereafter to regard Dr. Martin Luther King with quite the same respect." Other politicians and newspaper editors piled on. Some invoked the Logan Act, which prohibits unauthorized American citizens from negotiating with foreign governments, to suggest that King's remarks were borderline criminal.

"If a Negro minister can defy the United States Government, then *anything* goes," a Los Angeles woman wrote in an angry letter to King.

Under mounting pressure, Martin decided to temporarily limit his public statements on the war. "I really don't have the strength to fight this issue and keep my civil rights fight going," he confided to his advisers.

Several other leading Black civil rights leaders—John Lewis of SNCC, James Farmer of the Congress of Racial Equality (CORE), and Bayard Rustin—were listed as march sponsors but did not attend. Behind their various excuses was a clear message: They had heeded President Johnson's warning not to cross him on Vietnam. "The sparsity of civil rights leaders indicated they were having second thoughts about involving their organizations in a foreign policy protest," the *New York Times* reporter John Herbers noted dryly.

This left Coretta as the lone Black speaker at the rally. Looking out over the vast crowd, she felt both inspired by the chorus of voices joining her call for peace and sharply aware of how much work remained to bridge the civil rights and antiwar movements. As the marchers made their way past the White House lawn, she overheard a group of young SNCC members trying to start a freedom song. After several attempts, they gave up. "There's too many white folks here," one of them muttered.

President Johnson, watching the protests from his ranch in

Texas, where he was spending Thanksgiving with his family, tried to project calm. He said that dissent was part of democracy and that Americans had every right to criticize foreign policy. At the same time, he argued that "the great majority" of Americans supported his administration's actions in Vietnam.

In his holiday message to the troops, Johnson declared that true support did not come in the form of marches, placards, or petitions, but in "raising our voices in a single prayer of thanks for your courage and your dedication." Still, the mounting casualties—more than thirteen hundred American soldiers had been killed in combat in 1965—weighed heavily on him. He was haunted by the growing pile of condolence letters to grieving parents.

One of his aides, trying to offer solace, read to him a passage from Aeschylus:

> Women know who they sent forth
> But instead of the living
> Back there comes to every house
> Armor and dust from the burning.

Johnson asked for a copy of the lines and returned to them frequently in the months that followed.

FOR CORETTA, Martin, and many of their allies in the civil rights movement, one of the deepest tragedies of America's military escalation in Vietnam was the way it drained resources from President Johnson's Great Society programs—especially the War on Poverty. "Our aim is not only to relieve the symptom of poverty, but to cure it and, above all, to prevent it," Johnson declared in his January 1964 State of the Union address. Now, money that might have gone toward housing, education, and nutrition for the poor was instead funding fighter jets, tanks, bombs, and bullets.

In 1965, CORE Chairman James Farmer warned that it was impossible for the federal government "to mount a decisive war against poverty and bigotry while it is pouring billions down the war against people in Vietnam." Even *The Christian Science Monitor*, known for its restraint, observed that "Vietnam has distorted the budget. . . . If war takes more money there will presumably be less for the Great Society."

President Johnson's State of the Union address on January 12, 1966, deepened the growing concerns among civil rights and antiwar activists. "I believe that we can continue the Great Society while we fight in Vietnam," Johnson declared. But the numbers told a different story. In the coming year, Vietnam-related spending would rise by $5.8 billion—nearly ten times the increase proposed for all other federal programs combined.

"The cup of peril is full in Vietnam," the president told the nation. "It just must be the center of our concerns."

At times, Johnson insisted that the war and domestic reform were not in conflict but part of the same global vision. "My foreign policy is the Great Society," he told India's ambassador. In another speech, he declared, "We mean to show that our dream of a great society does not stop at the water's edge. . . . All are welcome to share in it and all are invited to contribute to it." But the fiscal realities suggested otherwise, both at home and abroad.

"The 'War on Poverty' may find out in 1966 how it feels to be poor," one United Press International story quipped, a line reprinted in *The Chicago Defender* and the *Los Angeles Sentinel*. Martin believed that the nation's priorities had gone astray: "If our country can spend $800 a second, $2 billion a month, $24 billion a year to fight a war in Vietnam . . . it can spend billions of dollars to put God's children on their own two feet."

He sensed, correctly, that critics of Johnson's domestic reform agenda were all too eager to see the war siphon money from anti-poverty programs. "In a real sense," he later lamented, "the Great Society has been shot down on the battlefield of Vietnam."

The historian Arthur Schlesinger reached the same conclusion. In his 1967 book on the Vietnam War, *The Bitter Heritage*, he wrote, "The Great Society is now, except for token gestures, dead."

It was just before midnight on January 3, 1966, when the twenty-one-year-old college student and navy veteran Sammy Younge Jr. pulled his beige Volkswagen Beetle into the parking lot of a Standard Oil gas station in Tuskegee, Alabama. Over the past year, Younge had crisscrossed the South as an organizer with SNCC. He helped Fannie Lou Hamer register voters in Ruleville, Mississippi, and visited Stokely Carmichael in Lowndes County, Alabama, during the early days of what would become the Black Panther Party.

Raised in a middle-class family, Younge had traded his suit jacket for a denim coat and dungarees, which he paired with his navy boots. He spoke with the cadence of a preacher—repeating phrases for emphasis, his voice humming and cracking. The "only thing that could keep him still was the Movement," recalled his childhood friend and fellow activist Wendy Paris.

That night, when Younge entered the gas station, he asked to use the restroom. The attendant, sixty-eight-year-old Marvin Segrest, told him the indoor restroom was for white customers and employees only. If he needed to go, Segrest said, he could use the toilet out back.

"You haven't heard of the Civil Rights Act?" Younge replied.

Segrest pulled a silver pistol from behind the counter and ordered Younge to leave. As the two men exchanged profanities, Younge backed away toward a nearby bus station. Segrest fired two shots. The second bullet struck him in the head.

Segrest was arrested the next day and charged with second-degree murder. Later that year, an all-white jury found him not guilty.

Gwen Patton, a Tuskegee classmate of Younge's, was outraged by his murder—and by the injustice that followed. "I wanted some action," she recalled after Segrest's acquittal. "I wanted a riot right there in the courthouse."

That afternoon, hundreds of Tuskegee students marched from campus into town. The crowd bristled with anger and raw energy—a different kind of protest than the carefully orchestrated marches led by Martin's SCLC.

"People were just filling the streets, and they weren't singing no freedom songs," Patton said. "They were mad. . . . All of a sudden you heard this 'Black Power, Black Power.' People felt what was going on. They were tired of doing this whole nonviolent bit."

The students swarmed the town square, where a twenty-foot-tall statue of a Confederate soldier had loomed over the county seat of majority-Black Macon County for six decades. Some came armed. Others carried makeshift Molotov cocktails made from Listerine bottles and Tampax. "They were using things they learned from

ROTC," said SNCC organizer Scott Smith, but "they were using these things for offensive measures."

The students painted a yellow stripe down the statue's back and scrawled "Black Power" and "Sam Younge" in thick black letters. "Every time the paintbrush hit," Smith recalled, "a roar came up from those students."

At Younge's funeral, John Lewis was struck by the irony of an American flag draped across the casket. "Here was a man who had served his country," he said, "and what had it gotten him?"

Cleveland Sellers, another SNCC leader, saw a movement expanding in real time. "We didn't need to look just at America and Alabama," he said. "We needed to be looking at Cape Town and Sharpeville, South Africa. We needed to be looking at other kinds of progressive movements and countries around. That our struggle was a much larger struggle than we had all anticipated in the beginning."

SNCC staff had debated making a public statement on Vietnam before but held off, worried that doing so might alienate donors. After Younge's murder, their hesitation evaporated.

On January 6, 1966, John Lewis faced a room of reporters and declared that SNCC was unequivocally opposed to US involvement in Vietnam. "We believe the United States government has been deceptive in its claims of concern for freedom of the Vietnamese people," he began, "just as the government has been deceptive in claiming concern for the freedom of colored people in such other countries as the Dominican Republic, the Congo, South Africa, Rhodesia, and in the United States itself."

Then came the heart of the message:

The murder of Samuel Younge in Tuskegee, Alabama, is not different than the murder of people in Vietnam, for both Younge and the Vietnamese sought, and are seeking, to secure the rights guaranteed them by law. In each case, the United States government bears a great part of the responsibility for these deaths. Samuel Younge was murdered because United States law is not being enforced. Vietnamese are murdered because the United States is pursuing an aggressive policy in violation of international law. The United States is no respecter of persons or laws when such persons or laws run counter to its needs and desires.

Lewis ended by expressing SNCC's support for draft resisters and suggesting that national service through civil rights work should be a legitimate alternative to military duty.

The statement drew national headlines—just as twenty-five-year-old Julian Bond, SNCC's communications director, was about to be sworn in to the Georgia House of Representatives. A charismatic and cerebral son of a prominent Black family, Bond had won his seat with 82 percent of the vote, campaigning under the slogan "A vote for Bond is a vote out of bondage."

He was one of seven Black politicians elected that year to a statehouse that had been all-white since Reconstruction, nearly a century earlier.

Bond quickly became the center of national controversy. Reporters flooded him with calls, asking if he endorsed SNCC's antiwar statement.

Yes, he told them. He was a pacifist. He believed most of his constituents in Atlanta—a majority-Black district, where the Kings lived—opposed the war too. He recalled watching young draftees board a bus for Fort Benning. One Black recruit had turned to the sergeant and said, "You didn't want us to go to school with you, you didn't want us to sit at lunch counters with you and now you want us to go overseas and fight and die with you."

Bond added wryly, "Each draft notice begins: 'Friends and neighbors,' but none of my friends are on my local draft board."

Though Bond had been declared 1-Y—mentally, physically, or morally unfit for service—due to a civil rights arrest, he knew dozens of young activists who had been drafted. "Sammy getting killed heightened our awareness of the essential wrongness of asking these young men to defend the country overseas," he said. He told reporters he admired "the courage of draft-card burners" and affirmed his support for SNCC's statement.

The condemnation was immediate and ferocious.

Georgia's lieutenant governor, Peter Zack Geer, called Bond a "glaring, sad and tragic example of a total lack of patriotism to the United States of America." Newspaper editorials denounced him as disloyal, reckless, even treasonous. White House officials sprang into action, contacting Black civic leaders and newspaper editors to shore up support for the president's Vietnam policy—and to isolate Bond and SNCC.

The fissures widened quickly. The national leadership of the NAACP and the Urban League condemned SNCC's statement. Privately, NAACP head Roy Wilkins sent President Johnson a telegram praising his Vietnam stance as the "right call."

On January 10, 1966, instead of taking the oath of office, Bond stood in a hallway of the Georgia statehouse as legislators accused him of treason. The vote to expel him passed 184 to 12. When the final tally was read aloud, Bond broke down in tears.

He vowed to fight back. His attorneys filed for an injunction in federal court, arguing that the state had violated his First Amendment rights.

Two days later, Martin met privately with Bond. Though Martin had often clashed with SNCC over tactics, he announced he would lead a march calling for Bond's reinstatement. Asked by reporters if he supported SNCC's antiwar statement, he hedged: "I have never encouraged evading the draft, and I am not prepared at this point to encourage evading the draft." But he left no ambiguity about Bond's right to speak freely.

Addressing a crowd of more than a thousand outside the Georgia statehouse, Martin reminded them that Abraham Lincoln had

In January 1966, the Georgia state legislature refused to swear in Julian Bond because of his opposition to the Vietnam War.

opposed the Mexican-American War as a congressman, and quoted John F. Kennedy's wartime reflection: "War will never cease until that distant day when the conscientious objector enjoys as much respectability and prestige as the warrior enjoys today."

That Sunday, Martin took up the theme again from the pulpit of Ebenezer Baptist Church. "We aren't doing enough to end the war in Vietnam," he said. "America must hear the truth, if we are going to survive as a nation, somebody has got to have vision, somebody must be willing to stand up and be criticized and called every bad name, out of love for this country. Nobody should be considered disloyal because they dissent."

Martin was speaking about Bond, but he was also speaking about Coretta and himself.

In the coming weeks, Martin continued to champion Bond's right to protest. Alongside Harry Belafonte, John Conyers, Ossie Davis, Ruby Dee, A. Philip Randolph, Dagmar Wilson, and dozens of other artists, activists, and politicians, he signed a full-page advertisement in *The New York Times* urging Americans to defend "Bond's Right to Dissent."

At a United Nations luncheon in Bond's honor—organized by Belafonte and cohosted by delegates from fifteen African nations—Martin called for solidarity between African Americans and Africans and declared "absolute support for our brother Julian Bond." In his regular My Dream column for *The Chicago Defender*, Martin noted the hypocrisy of Georgia legislators who questioned Bond's loyalty to the Constitution even as they fought to keep Black citizens from voting. "I support Bond in his right as a citizen to disagree with our foreign policy," King wrote.

Bond's SNCC colleagues responded by launching the Atlanta

Project, an ambitious campaign to return him to the statehouse and organize grassroots action around local issues—from tenant abuses by slumlords to the wider injustices of war.

Twenty-two-year-old Gwen Patton, who had led demonstrations in Tuskegee after Sammy Younge's murder, was among its leaders. So was Michael Simmons, a twenty-one-year-old from Philadelphia who had left Temple University to join SNCC full-time. When Simmons received his draft paperwork, he answered the questions on "native country" and "date and port of entry" with two lines that said everything: "Africa, 1619."

When he appeared before the draft board, Simmons turned it into a performance of protest.

Beginning on August 16, 1966, members of the Atlanta Project staged daily protests outside the Twelfth Army Corps and Induction Center in Atlanta. Arriving before dawn, they carried hand-made signs with phrases like THE VIETCONG NEVER CALLED ME "NIGGER." Army personnel responded with hostility—spitting, jeering, and even flicking lit cigarettes from the second-floor windows at the protesters below.

On the day he was called for induction, Simmons knocked on the center's front door again and again, insisting on speaking with the officer in charge. He figured if he was turned away, he could not be guilty of avoiding the draft. But the Atlanta police had a different idea. After several tense days of confrontation, officers stormed the scene, dragging Simmons and eleven other protesters away. They were beaten, clubbed, and choked into submission.

The following day in court, Judge T. C. Little convicted them of disturbing the peace, resisting arrest, and disobeying an officer. The protesters received jail terms of two to three months. Little made no attempt to disguise his personal bias. "I'm not giving them stiff sentences based on their color but because I have a son in Vietnam who is fighting to defend the principles of freedom and democracy," he told SNCC's attorney.

But SNCC had prepared for this. Patton had been tasked with avoiding arrest in order to coordinate a media response and sustain momentum. The next morning, she returned to the induction center leading a small group of women dressed in black. In stark contrast to the previous week's chants and confrontations, they stood in solemn silence. Their signs read: WE MOURN THE DRAFTING OF BLACK MEN and WE MOURN THE 400 YEARS OF LYNCHING AND CASTRATION OF THE BLACK MEN IN THIS COUNTRY.

The soldiers watched them from behind the gates with a mixture of scorn and confusion.

Through the fall of 1966, Patton, Simmons, and the other members of the Atlanta Project traveled across the Midwest and Northeast, building ties with emerging antiwar and Black liberation groups. In New York, they met with Black Women Enraged; in Detroit, with the Inner City Organizing Committee; and in Boston, with Afro-Americans Against the War in Vietnam. These groups viewed opposition to the Vietnam War as part of a broader rethinking of how Black people related to both the United States and the world.

Earlier that year, the Atlanta Project articulated this vision in an influential and controversial "Black Consciousness Paper." It argued that Black communities must control their own political and cultural direction, and that white allies should organize against racism within white institutions. It was a call not just for protest but for power.

They called it Black Power.

Mainstream media soon fixated on Stokely Carmichael, who succeeded John Lewis as SNCC chairman in May 1966 and coauthored *Black Power: The Politics of Liberation* the following year. Carmichael's rise symbolized SNCC's shift from a multiracial coalition to a sharper emphasis on Black militancy. But the call for self-determination was always larger than any one leader—it emerged from the lived experiences of organizers and residents in Black communities across the country.

As internal debates deepened, Bond found himself increasingly out of step with SNCC's new direction. He believed in interracial coalitions and in working to change the system from within, even as the organization moved in the opposite direction. "I felt uncomfortable with it," he later said of SNCC's evolution under Carmichael. That fall, Bond resigned to focus on his legal battle with the Georgia legislature. After a federal court upheld his expulsion, Bond took his case to the US Supreme Court.

On December 5, 1966, the court ruled unanimously in *Bond v. Floyd* that the Georgia legislature had violated Bond's First Amendment rights. Elected officials, the justices held, could not be punished for expressing dissenting views on controversial public issues—even on something as contentious as the country's war effort in Vietnam. The decision affirmed broad free-speech protections for legislators and delivered a stinging rebuke to those seeking to silence a new generation of Black political leaders.

Bond finally took his seat on January 9, 1967—one year after being expelled. Several white legislators refused to speak to him. James "Sloppy" Floyd, a World War II veteran who had led the campaign to keep Bond out of office, walked out of the chamber when the young representative rose to take the oath.

As JULIAN BOND fought for his political life, Martin faced growing doubts about the direction of the civil rights movement. In 1966, he turned his attention to Chicago, launching a campaign against segregation in housing, employment, and education. That January, Martin and Coretta moved into an apartment on the city's West Side to establish a community base for their fight against poverty. What they found stunned them. "The level of poverty called to mind our travels through Bombay a few years before," Coretta said. That winter and spring, she shuttled between Chicago and the family's home in Atlanta.

Martin hoped Chicago would be a proving ground for expanding the movement beyond the South. But resistance was fierce. During an open-housing march, white residents—some waving Confederate flags and signs painted with swastikas and "White Power"—hurled bottles, bricks, and cherry bombs at the demonstrators. A rock struck Martin in the back, knocking him to his knees. "I've never seen anything like it in my life," he said. "I think the people of Mississippi ought to come to Chicago to learn how to hate."

Chicago's powerful mayor, Richard J. Daley, blamed King for the unrest and made sure the White House knew it. In a phone call with President Johnson, Daley fumed: "He's not your friend. He's against you in Vietnam. He's a goddamn faker. . . . I don't know how the hell we approach it. It's the most dangerous thing we have facing our country."

Daley wasn't alone. As protests mounted and King's message broadened to include antiwar activism, Johnson's advisers warned that white support for "big and bold" programs benefiting Black communities was evaporating. When a proposed Civil Rights Act failed in the Senate that September, it confirmed what Johnson already feared: The political will that had powered the early victories of the movement was beginning to crumble.

"This is not an easy time for me," Martin told a conference of radio and television news directors in Chicago that fall. "It is not a pleasant or noble time for the civil rights movement. We stand in one of those valley moments now, not on the peak of achievement of a more democratic society."

That sense of gloom deepened on December 14, when *The New York Times* reported that the FBI had been engaged in widespread wiretapping—including surveillance of the Kings' personal phone calls. "We've assumed all along that our phones are tapped," Martin told reporters, "but we haven't known whether it's the local government, the federal, or what." The public confirmation of his worst suspicions strained his already faltering relationship with President Johnson, who was well aware of J. Edgar Hoover's campaign, and with Robert Kennedy, who had approved the wiretaps during his time as attorney general.

Coretta was outraged that dissent continued to be treated as disloyalty. "If the FBI wants to find the wellspring of radicalism," she later said, "tell them not to look on the campus . . . or in the haunts of so-called revolutionaries. Tell them to look to the White House and in the marbled halls of Congress. The policies there radicalized more young people than a million books by revolutionaries."

Martin was in Washington, DC, the day after the wiretap story broke, to testify before a US Senate subcommittee on the "Federal Role in Urban Affairs." Describing himself as both an "American citizen" and an "American Negro," he warned that the nation's priorities were dangerously out of balance. While patriotic fervor fueled massive spending on the military and space programs, the War on Poverty faced impatience, indifference, and hostility.

"At present the war on poverty is not even a battle, it is scarcely a skirmish," he said. He urged the senators to understand that "the waste of war" had grave domestic consequences. "The security we profess to seek in foreign adventures, we will lose in our decaying cities. The bombs in Vietnam explode at home; they destroy the hopes and possibilities for a decent America. . . . The chaos of the cities, the persistence of poverty, the degenerating of our national prestige throughout the world are compelling arguments for achieving peace agreements."

The New York Times, The Washington Post, The Chicago Defender, and dozens of other newspapers covered the speech, marking it as Martin's most forceful public condemnation of the war since Senator Dodd's rebuke more than a year earlier.

Coretta was proud. "Until 1967, Martin had been content to leave it to me to march, protest, and mount public challenges to the war in Vietnam," she recalled. She believed that her vocal activism made it "easier to assuage his conscience about not being more strongly involved himself," she wrote. Still, she consistently challenged him to embrace his role in advocating for world peace.

Coretta also understood the historical weight of her work. In 1966, she asked her sister, Edythe, to begin documenting their family's story. Edythe set to work interviewing Coretta, relatives, and close friends, while gathering family records, newspaper clippings, and school materials. Coretta knew that she and Martin were not only living through history but helping to shape it—and she was determined to preserve that legacy as it unfolded.

Coretta's sense of urgency in the fight for peace deepened as the war escalated. By the end of 1966, the United States had deployed 385,000 military personnel in Vietnam—more than double the previous year. More than 5,000 Americans were killed that year, and more than 30,000 were wounded. The toll among North Vietnamese and Vietcong fighters was even greater, though the United States exaggerated the numbers and Hanoi minimized them, each side eager to shape the narrative of who was winning. Tens of thousands of Vietnamese civilians had already been killed or maimed—only a fraction of the devastation still to come.

Where Coretta and other peace activists saw a human tragedy produced by reckless foreign policy, American officials saw a problem of manpower. In Washington, military leaders devised a plan they believed could meet the growing demand for troops while also appearing to support the War on Poverty. Under the guidance of Secretary of Defense Robert McNamara, the US military launched a program to recruit at least one hundred thousand men from poor neighborhoods into combat service.

They went looking for men like Skip Johnson.

4

BASIC TRAINING

S kip Johnson was inspired. Congressman John Conyers Jr. had that effect on people. Sitting in the Northwestern High School auditorium with 175 graduating seniors clad in red caps and gowns, Skip listened as Conyers described his journey from Detroit to Capitol Hill.

"When I graduated from Northwestern in 1947, I sat right there," Conyers said, pointing to a seat in the third row. "I bet it's still squeaky," he joked, drawing laughter from the students.

He told them how he had studied music in high school, but his father would not let him pursue it professionally. Instead, he joined the Michigan National Guard for two years before enlisting in the US Army and attending officer candidate school in 1950. He earned a commission as a second lieutenant in the Army Corps of Engineers and served in the Korean War. His unit was stationed behind the front lines, managing aircraft repairs and watching for enemy planes.

Conyers had not traveled far beyond Detroit until the army sent him overseas. "I like to think that my worldview was broadened by my military experience," he said. Still, he admitted that he and other soldiers often asked themselves, "What are we doing here? Why are we fighting?" He told the students that young troops in Vietnam were asking those same questions now.

After the war, Conyers used GI Bill benefits to attend Wayne State University, where he earned a BA and a law degree. He said he entered politics to improve life for working people in Detroit. "I was drawn to the struggle because my dad was a labor organizer for the UAW [United Auto Workers]," he said.

Running on the slogan "Jobs, Justice, and Peace," Conyers was elected to Congress in 1964. The following year, he hired Rosa Parks to his staff and praised her to the students as the "mother of the civil rights movement."

When Conyers arrived in Washington, DC, he was one of only six Black members of Congress. He argued for voting rights, pushed for civil rights legislation, and spoke out against US military involvement overseas.

"Don't be afraid to stand up to people in power," he told the students.

To prove his point, Conyers described how, in May 1965, he voted against President Johnson's request for seven hundred million dollars in supplemental appropriations to fund the war in Vietnam. The final vote was 408–7. Conyers was one of only two freshman congressmen to defy the president.

"I do not support the present policy in Viet Nam," he said on the House floor. He told the students he would continue voting against war funding, arguing that the money could be better spent ensuring that the War on Poverty was more than "just a skirmish."

Skip and his classmates were used to seeing Conyers around Detroit. He marched with teenagers protesting police brutality and school segregation. He visited Northwestern regularly—guest-lecturing in classes and walking the halls with newspaper reporters to call attention to the school's crumbling infrastructure. Conyers demanded overdue upgrades to the science labs, the cafeteria, and even the JROTC rifle range.

At a time when young Black people—especially students like Skip—were often blamed for the country's problems, it meant everything that a congressman would fight for them, their school, and their city.

"He made people in this town believe in their own strength," a Conyers campaign aide told *Ebony*.

While Skip was inspired by what Conyers had accomplished, his own prospects felt more modest. His grades were solid, though not strong enough to earn a college scholarship. He was grateful when a family friend helped him land an entry-level job at a General Motors plant where Cadillacs were manufactured. The work was grueling, but the pay was good. At a time when Detroit's industrial economy was beginning to falter—and blue-collar jobs were becoming harder to come by, especially for Black teenagers—Skip was proud to have steady work and to help his mother with rent and bills.

Outside of work, the summer of 1966 started off quietly. He played basketball at the park with neighborhood kids and listened to Detroit Tigers games on the radio, rooting for left fielder Willie Horton, a fellow Jeffries alum who had led Northwestern to a city baseball championship several years earlier.

On Fridays, Skip would ride the bus over to visit his cousin Tom

Tillman, always hoping to run into Tillman's neighbor, Katrina Lyn May. "I think he was tired of the Jeffries Projects girls," Katrina recalled. She gradually warmed to him. "He was smarter than I expected." That summer, Skip persuaded Katrina to go to the movies, a double date with his cousin and one of her friends. She appreciated his silliness. "We stopped at a traffic light, and while the light was red, he and his cousin both got out and they swapped places," she remembered. "Next red light, they did the same thing. That was the kind of fun we had."

Skip remained smitten, but Katrina, with her senior year of high school ahead of her, was not ready to go steady with anyone—at least not yet.

Coming home from his shift on a humid June evening, Skip checked the mail and found the same letter that awaited thousands of young men across the country each month. It began:

> *Greetings:*
>
> *You are hereby ordered for induction into the Armed Forces of the United States.*

The Selective Service letter directed him to report at the Greyhound bus terminal at 130 East Congress Street in Detroit the following month. "Willful failure to report at the place and hour of the day named in this Order subjects the violator to fine and imprisonment," it warned.

Skip had been anticipating the draft for months, unsure how he would feel when the notice finally arrived. Now, staring at a letter that would change the trajectory of his life, he thought of his mother and younger brother. When his stepfather was deported a decade earlier, he'd taken on adult responsibilities. His family relied on him, and he liked being relied on. If he were sent to Vietnam, who would take care of the people he loved?

He was also scared. Reports of US casualties were everywhere—on the evening news, in magazines, splashed across the front pages of newspapers. What worried him most was how many of the fallen soldiers looked like him. The number of Black servicemen killed in the early stages of the Vietnam War was a particular source of dread.

Early in 1966, the Pentagon released data showing that Black troops made up 14.8 percent of the army in Vietnam but accounted for 18.3 percent of the US military deaths there between 1961 and 1965—even though Black people comprised just over 11 percent of the total US population.

"Negroes Dying Faster Than Whites in Vietnam," read the headline in the *New York Amsterdam News*, a leading Black newspaper. "It is not likely to give comfort to Negroes battling to gain equality on the home front to learn that they are being given more than an equal opportunity to die for their country on the battlefield of Vietnam," its editors declared.

The disparity in casualties gave critics of the war new ammunition. They noted that fewer than 2 percent of local draft board members were Black, and twenty-three states had no Black board members at all. In Louisiana, the Grand Dragon of the Ku Klux Klan had led the state's all-white draft board for a decade, until NAACP protests forced his removal. In Georgia, the chairman of the Atlanta draft board publicly referred to Julian Bond as "that nigger," lamenting, "We sure let him slip through our fingers."

These draft boards wielded enormous power, including the ability to determine who qualified for draft deferments, with student deferments often based on scores from the Selective Service Qualification Test.

"The draft deferment test brings the circle of racial discrimination full cycle," argued Congressman Adam Clayton Powell Jr., who represented Harlem. Powell charged that standardized testing favored white, middle-class students. "First, we provide inferior education for black students. Next, we give them a series of tests which many will flunk because of an inferior education. Then we pack these academic failures off to war."

Rev. Albert Cleage made a similar argument in his fight to improve Detroit's public schools, including his alma mater Northwestern, where his daughter Pearl graduated the same year as Skip. "If you can't learn anything in high school, it's off to Vietnam to get killed off," Cleage contended.

In Harlem, an activist group called Black Women Enraged urged defiance of draft notices, printing flyers that read, "Black Men! Whitey's plan for you is death in Vietnam. Choose jail. Stay here and fight for your manhood."

Even among Black troops already serving in Vietnam, there was growing unease that they were being used as cannon fodder. "I think we're being killed off," said a Black marine private stationed in Dong Ha. "I think we're being used."

At the same time, some Black leaders offered more optimistic interpretations of the outsize role Black troops were playing in the war. "I feel good about it," said Lt. Col. George Shoffer, one of the highest-ranking Black officers. "Not that I like the bloodshed, but the performance of the Negro in Vietnam tends to offset the fact that the Negro wasn't considered worthy of being a front-line soldier in other wars." Whitney Young, executive director of the National Urban League, echoed that sentiment after visiting Vietnam at President Johnson's request. A World War II army veteran, Young argued in his newspaper column that "race is irrelevant" in Vietnam and that in "the muck and mire of a war-torn land, colored soldiers fight and die courageously as representatives of all America."

There was data to support his view. In 1966, 66 percent of Black soldiers in the army reenlisted, compared to just 20 percent of white soldiers. A Harris poll that same year found that two thirds of Black respondents believed Black Americans had better chances to advance in the military than in civilian life.

On June 30, 1966, just days before Skip was scheduled to report, three soldiers from Fort Hood, Texas, made national headlines by refusing to deploy to Vietnam. The "Fort Hood Three"—James Johnson, a Black private first class from Harlem; Private Dennis Mora, a Puerto Rican from Spanish Harlem; and Private David Samas, the son of Lithuanian and Italian immigrants from California—stood before a bank of reporters and television cameras to read a joint statement.

"We represent in our backgrounds a cross section of the Army and of America," they began. "We speak as American soldiers. We have been in the army long enough to know that we are not the only GIs who feel as we do. Large numbers of men in the service either do not understand this war or are against it."

They condemned the conflict as "unjust, immoral, and illegal," and urged other soldiers to follow their lead. "Contrary to what the Pentagon believes, cannon fodder can talk," they declared.

Their public defiance—the first time enlisted men openly refused orders to Vietnam—shocked the military and inspired antiwar activists. Folk singer Pete Seeger wrote a protest song, "Ballad of the Fort Hood Three," in their honor. The three soldiers were court-martialed, dishonorably discharged, and sentenced to three years of hard labor.

WHILE DEBATES OVER THE DRAFT raged in newspapers and city halls, thousands of young men like Skip simply reported for induction.

The night before he left, Skip pulled his little brother aside. He told him to steer clear of neighborhood bullies, stay away from the police, and be good to their mother. She was up early the next morning, already dressed for work, and made him breakfast. She gave him a long hug and teared up when the door closed behind him.

Skip arrived at the Greyhound terminal just after sunrise and took his place in line with dozens of other Detroit recruits. He had not spent much time outside the city, and as the bus rolled through rural Ohio, the stretches of farmland felt oddly soothing—like they belonged to another world entirely.

A scruffy blond kid a few rows up joked loudly about how many Vietcong he planned to take out and how many medals he would bring home. Skip rolled his eyes, figuring the loudmouth had watched too many John Wayne movies.

By midafternoon, the bus pulled into Fort Knox, forty miles south of Louisville. As he stepped off, Skip caught sight of a large yellow sign with black block letters: WELCOME TO THE UNITED STATES ARMY.

A sergeant barked at them to fall in line and shut up. The sun beat down and heat from the asphalt rose through Skip's shoes. The men stood in their civilian clothes, sweating and silent, until they were called into the reception station. One man locked his knees and fainted, dropping to the pavement.

Processing at Fort Knox reminded Skip of the Cadillac plant back in Detroit. Men moved from station to station like cars on an assembly line. A tailor measured him for a uniform. A barber took clippers to his already short hair, buzzing it down to the scalp. He stood in line for a series of shots to his right arm, then sat stiffly for a photo—an unsmiling mug shot that became his army ID.

At the next station, a clerk asked him a series of questions:

Are you married?

Do you have any dependents?

Do you wear glasses?

Colorblind?

Are you a conscientious objector?

Do you have a twin brother?

Do you have a police record?

"No," Skip said, again and again.

After the last stop, the men were herded into an auditorium, where the deputy commander of the training center stood waiting onstage. He told the recruits to expect the training to be rigorous and demanding.

"We are going to give you the military training which is going to turn you into a soldier," he said. "So that your reactions in times of stress are going to be a combination of instinct, native ability and intelligence, reinforced by training that will give you the skills to react effectively."

The times of stress came quickly. Skip practiced hand-to-hand combat, learned to lob grenades, and stabbed a rubber tire with the bayonet on his rifle until his arms ached.

"What is the spirit of the bayonet?" a drill sergeant bellowed.

"To kill without mercy!" the recruits shouted in reply.

They marched the three steep hills of Fort Knox—Agony, Misery, and Heartbreak—each climb made worse by the eighty-pound packs strapped to their backs. On the confidence course, they scrambled over wooden obstacles and crawled through mud while a sergeant hollered, "Get off those elbows! Chest to the ground! Pull with your hands!"

Skip was shouted at so often by so many voices that when he lay in his bunk at night, commands still ricocheted through his head.

In the barracks, the men complained about the food, argued over which sergeant was the meanest, and swapped stories about girlfriends at home—some real, others wishful. A few held out hope they would be stationed in Germany after training, but they all knew the truth: Most of them were going to Vietnam.

The war was never far away. One training area on base was designed to simulate combat in Vietnam, complete with thatched huts, thick vegetation, and underground tunnels. The sergeants called it, using the racist slang of the era, "Gook Village."

No detail was left to chance. The men watched training films on everything from brushing their teeth to avoiding sexually transmitted diseases. Then came the propaganda reels. In *Why Vietnam?*, a Department of Defense film from 1965, a narrator explained America's noble mission to save a small country from Communist aggression.

"This is a different kind of war," the narrator intoned. "There are no marching armies or solemn declarations. But this is really war. It is guided by North Vietnam and it is spurred by Communist China."

In clips, President Johnson, Secretary of Defense Robert McNamara, and Secretary of State Dean Rusk explained that the United States had first sent advisers to train South Vietnamese forces, only to be drawn deeper into combat after hostile actions in the Gulf of Tonkin.

"We want no wider war," McNamara assured viewers.

A few recruits hissed in the back of the room; others laughed uncomfortably. Skip did not react. Compared to the newspaper articles and editorials his high school teachers had passed around, the film felt heavy-handed—more sales pitch than truth.

Meanwhile, the sergeants were frank about the dangers of combat. Training was designed to show the recruits that any failure could lead to death.

"I don't believe I have any right to discuss whether you should kill a man," one platoon sergeant said. "I do know one thing, gentlemen: If a man attempts to shoot me or kill me, I definitely will attempt to stop him in the fastest way possible."

The men sat holding their weapons, listening with rapt attention.

"When you get out in the jungle in Vietnam, I don't believe the thought of killing a man will enter your mind if you get hit from three sides," he continued. "Automatically, the only thing that's going to go into your mind is self-preservation. You probably won't have anything in your mind except survive, survive, survive."

His voice rose.

"The man is out to kill you, gentlemen."

If they did not accept that fact, he warned, they would go home in a body bag. The men sat with that lesson for months. It scared them to believe the sergeant. It scared them more not to.

IN THE FALL, Skip received a letter with a newspaper clipping from home—proof of the sergeant's warning made real. Marine Private First Class David Clark Riley, his former classmate at Northwestern, had been killed in action in Quang Tri Province.

Skip remembered David well, carrying the American flag as part of the JROTC color guard. The clipping included an interview with David's father, James Riley, whose eyes were red with grief as he clutched a photo of his son in uniform.

"He was proud of being a Marine," the father said. "His uncle had been in the Marine corps and I have been in the service, and he felt that being a Marine was the best that could happen to him."

When a marine sergeant came to inform him of his son's death, Mr. Riley could not bring himself to believe it. He called Congressman Conyers in Washington, DC, who confirmed the tragic news.

Marine Sergeant Robert Thornton, another Northwestern alum, had seen David in Vietnam just days before he was killed. "I died on my feet," Thornton said after hearing the news from his lieutenant. Thornton considered David a half brother; the Rileys had taken Thornton in as a teenager when his mother could not make ends meet.

At Mrs. Riley's request, Thornton escorted the body back home. After seeing the head wound David had suffered, he quietly decided the funeral would be closed casket.

David was the first person Skip knew personally who was killed in Vietnam.

At Detroit's New Bethel Baptist Church, JROTC cadets from Northwestern stood alongside a Marine Corps honor guard at the memorial service. Skip, unable to attend, spent that Sunday in the Fort Knox chapel. He bowed his head and prayed for David—and for the family that had once cared for David like their own.

After the funeral, Thornton spent his thirty-day leave in Detroit with his girlfriend, who later became his wife. She noticed something in him had shifted. He was quieter, distant.

"You don't leave that kind of violence," he told her.

Eight weeks after arriving at Fort Knox, Skip graduated from basic training and was assigned to an armor unit there. He stayed for Advanced Individual Training (AIT), learning how to drive, maintain, load, and fire the M48A3 Patton tank.

The power of the machine was undeniable. Firing its 90 mm cannon caused full-body reverberations. A visiting reporter, after watching nearly a thousand rounds fired over two hours, described the experience as physically painful—despite wearing earplugs—"like someone poking hard at your eardrum with a blunt stick." Days later, his ears still rang.

Operating a tank required close teamwork among the four-man crew. Barry Davis, a nineteen-year-old white draftee from Ventura, California, served in Skip's platoon. "Dwight was very nice, very athletic, and quiet," Davis recalled. "He got along with everybody."

Like most military units, their platoon brought together young men from across the country. One day, Davis thought a fight was about to break out: A wiry white soldier from the South—who looked, someone joked, like Alfred E. Neuman from *Mad* magazine—made a racist comment in front of a broad-shouldered Black tanker from Tampa. Words were exchanged. But before punches could fly, others stepped in. Somehow, the two ended up as friends. By the end of training, they were staging comedy skits to entertain the platoon.

Skip also liked to make people laugh. After lights out in the barracks, he would let out a high-pitched, nasally wail that sounded like a crying baby.

"Everybody would say, 'What *is* that?'" Davis recalled. "Well, it was Dwight. It was the darnedest thing you ever heard."

He completed tank training at Fort Knox in late 1966, just as nights turned bitterly cold. Temperatures dropped below freezing, and the drafty barracks offered little relief. A bout of tonsilitis left Skip exhausted. Sleep was hard to come by, but he was relieved to have completed both basic and AIT.

That December, his deployment orders came through. He would ship out to Vietnam with B Company, First Battalion, Sixty-Ninth Armor.

He studied the unit's insignia—a black panther crouched on a green-and-white shield, with the words VITTESSE ET PUISSANCE ("Speed and Power") emblazoned beneath. He hoped the months of training would be enough to prepare him for whatever lay ahead.

SECRETARY OF DEFENSE Robert McNamara felt like he knew Skip Johnson—even though he had never heard of him. To McNamara, "Skip Johnson" was a type: one of thousands of young men from poor and working-class backgrounds for whom military service could serve as a lifeline. At a Veterans of Foreign Wars convention in New York in August 1966, McNamara announced Project 100,000, a sweeping initiative to induct one hundred thousand men into the military each year—most of whom had previously failed the Armed Forces Qualification Test.

McNamara cast the project as a fusion of military necessity and social uplift. Framing it as an extension of President Johnson's War on Poverty, he declared that tens of thousands of men, "most of them with 'poverty-encrusted' backgrounds, would be 'salvaged' for military duty." The program, he claimed, would "rehabilitate the nation's subterranean poor" and "cure them of the idleness, ignorance, and apathy" that defined their lives.

"The poor of America . . . can be given an opportunity to serve in their country's defense," McNamara said, "and they can be given an opportunity to return to civilian life with skills and aptitudes which for them and their families will reverse the downward spiral of human decay."

The logic behind Project 100,000 drew heavily on the thinking of the scholar and White House adviser Daniel Patrick Moynihan. In 1963, Moynihan authored *One Third of a Nation: A Report on Young Men Found Unqualified for Military Service*, which argued that mass disqualification from the draft reflected a deeper national crisis. Two years later, his controversial report *The Negro Family: The Case for National Action* advanced the theory that entrenched family behavior patterns and family instability—not structural inequality—had created a "culture of poverty" in Black communities.

Moynihan saw the military—"a world run by strong men and unquestioned authority"—as the antidote. "The biggest opportunity to do something about Negro youth has been right under our noses all the time," Moynihan argued in an internal White House memo. "Very possibly our best hope is seriously to use the armed forces as a socializing experience for the poor, until somehow their environment begins turning out equal citizens."

Moynihan believed that expanding military service could directly reduce racial disparities in unemployment. "If 100,000 nonwhite men were added to the Armed Forces, and resulted in a decrease of 100,000 in the unemployed, that unemployment rate would drop from 11.5 percent to 6.4 percent," he calculated. At a time when Coretta Scott King, Martin Luther King Jr., and other activists charged that the war was draining resources from domestic programs, Moynihan and McNamara urged President Johnson to see the military as an anti-poverty tool.

Over five years, McNamara's initiative brought more than three hundred thousand men into the military who otherwise would have been deemed unfit for service. Nearly 40 percent of these "New Standards Men" were Black. "The plain fact is that our PROJECT 100,000 is succeeding beyond even our most hopeful expectations," McNamara told the National Association of Education Broadcasters in November 1967.

The program appealed to the White House in part because it expanded the draft pool without politically risky steps like activating reservists or drafting large numbers of college students—measures that could have ignited even more antiwar protests.

Instead, military recruiters scoured the country for other Skip Johnsons: poor and working-class men of all races. Project 100,000 deepened the inequalities of a draft system that already favored those with more money, education, and connections. In the wealthy

Detroit suburbs, parents set up businesses in Canada and put their kids in charge to qualify them for deferments. Just across the Detroit River lay safety, but for Skip, fleeing to Canada was unthinkable.

"We're setting up a kind of class warfare," Lt. Col. Jim Williams later said. "I wonder about the morality of a nation that lets the disadvantaged do the fighting." Even General Westmoreland came to describe the draft policy as "discriminatory and undemocratic," resulting, he admitted, "in the war being fought mainly by the poor man's son."

Some young soldiers rationalized the danger of combat in monetary terms. Roger Harris, who went from Roxbury—the heart of Boston's Black community—to the marines, remembered thinking, "If I die, at least my mother would get $10,000 life insurance benefit and be able to buy a house. She'd be rich."

Across the country, casualty data reflected stories of opportunity—or the lack of it. In Illinois, men from working-class neighborhoods where the median family income was under five thousand dollars were four times more likely to be killed in Vietnam than those from areas where family incomes exceeded fifteen thousand. More people from South Boston, a predominately Irish American section of the city, died in Vietnam (twenty-five) than Harvard graduates (twenty-two). Latino neighborhoods in Los Angeles also saw a disproportionate number of casualties. In Beallsville, Ohio—a rural town of just 450 residents—fifteen young men went to Vietnam. Several did not return. "They got our boys because this is a poor town and the boys can't afford to go to college," Mayor Ben Gramlich said, after the town's sixth military funeral.

Thomas Edison High School in North Philadelphia—a working-class neighborhood not unlike Skip's own—lost more than sixty young men in Vietnam, the highest known death toll of any high school in the country. At Northwestern High, each month seemed to bring news that another former classmate had been wounded or killed in Vietnam: Wayne V. Glenn, hit by shrapnel in March 1966; Charles H. Shelton, died of gunshot wounds in June 1966; George H. Dorsey Jr., killed in Tay Ninh in February 1967.

Project 100,000 quickened the pace of these losses. "When Mc-Namara says he is going to draft 30 percent of the black people out of the ghettos," Stokely Carmichael told an audience at Morgan State University, "baby, that is nothing but urban removal."

Skip was one of 382,000 men drafted in 1966—more than in any other year of the Vietnam War. As the Department of Defense increasingly turned to poor and working-class teenagers to fill its ranks, the average draftee looked more like a Black kid from the projects in Detroit than not.

Skip was not yet twenty when he left Fort Knox for Vietnam. He had not asked to become a symbol—but in many ways, he was. He stood for a generation whose lives would be forever shaped by a war they did not choose.

BREAKING SILENCE

Coretta sat in her living room, chatting with a friend from church, when she heard footsteps outside. It was half past nine—too dark to see beyond the walkway leading up to the house.

Suddenly, a brick slammed against the concrete porch. Moments later, a thunderous explosion rocked the house. Smoke filled the living room. Broken glass and splinters covered the floor.

Shaken by the impact and her friend's screams, Coretta raced to the back bedroom, where her infant daughter, Yoki, lay crying in a bassinet. Just as she scooped up the baby, the doorbell rang. For a moment, she feared the bombers had returned to finish the job.

This time, thankfully, the ominous visitor turned out to be a neighbor offering to help.

The house bombing—during the early weeks of the Montgomery bus boycott in January 1956—served as a wake-up call about her family's safety. "I was shocked into a new reality," Coretta said.

"The perpetrators would do anything, even commit murder, to stop us."

In the days that followed, Coretta felt something stir in her chest—a deep, anxious uncertainty about how to protect her family and respond to this terror. She thought back to the fire that destroyed her childhood home, and the lessons her parents taught her about survival. "I don't think any black person growing up in the Deep South escaped the reality that a black person's life could be taken by whites without any consequences," she later wrote.

She called on faith to temper the fear. It would not be the last time tragedy crystallized her calling. "That's really when I made the commitment to go all the way," she said.

Coretta told this story often, to audiences all over the country. It explained how she came to dedicate her life to the fight for peace and civil rights. By recalling the visceral emotions she felt after the bombing, she also hoped to express a universal truth: that as a parent she felt a fierce responsibility to protect her children.

When Coretta spoke out against the war in Vietnam, she often did so as a mother—concerned not only for her own children but for children around the world. This framing was common among women activists, but for Coretta, it was more than rhetoric. It reflected her core values and shaped the alliances she sought.

In December 1966, she became a founding supporter of the Committee of Responsibility, a group of doctors, clergy, and concerned citizens who worked to bring Vietnamese children—some burned and disfigured by napalm, others who had lost limbs in the fighting—to US hospitals for plastic surgery and prosthetics treatment.

The following month, the Committee of Responsibility sponsored articles in *Ramparts* and *Ladies' Home Journal*, pairing their advocacy with more than a dozen searing images: a toddler whose arm had been amputated below the elbow; a young boy with a badly burned hip; a baby swaddled in newspaper for lack of a blanket. "For countless thousands of children in Vietnam, breathing is quickened by terror and pain, and tiny bodies learn more about death every day," the *Ramparts* article read.

The FBI took notice. In its file on Coretta, the bureau flagged her involvement with the Committee of Responsibility, which it viewed with suspicion as a group attempting to "dramatize and propagandize US 'atrocities' in Vietnam."

Martin picked up a copy of *Ramparts* magazine during a layover at the Miami airport in January 1967. He was traveling with Bernard Lee, an activist and his personal assistant, en route to Jamaica, where Martin hoped to make progress on a new book—*Where Do We Go from Here: Chaos or Community?*—before enjoying a much-needed vacation with Coretta.

Sitting down for lunch, Martin opened the magazine and stared at the photographs. He was sickened. "He froze as he looked at the pictures from Vietnam," Lee remembered. "He saw a picture of a Vietnamese mother holding her dead baby, a baby killed by our military." When Martin pushed his plate away, Lee asked what was wrong.

"Nothing will ever taste any good for me until I do everything I can to end that war," he said.

Martin was so engrossed by the images that he may not have noticed the article named Coretta—"Mrs. Martin Luther King, wife of the civil rights leader"—as a supporter of the Committee of Responsibility. Her affiliation gave the group added credibility. She understood that images of suffering children could move people—including her husband—to speak out more forcefully. The pictures,

Martin later said, led him to an unavoidable truth: "There is an existential moment when you must decide to speak for yourself; nobody else can speak for you."

When Coretta and Martin returned to Atlanta in early February 1967, they shared a renewed commitment to ending the war in Vietnam. Martin told his advisers he planned to accept several invitations to speak at antiwar events that spring, even if it permanently fractured his relationship with President Johnson or jeopardized financial support for SCLC. Coretta soon traveled to Montreal, where she addressed local religious groups and previewed the Christian Pavilion at the upcoming Expo 67 International and Universal Exposition.

"Unless we have a peaceful world outside, we will never have security inside," she said. "There are many people working together for peace but, unfortunately, we lack a symbol or personality." She believed Martin could become that symbol.

Two days later, on February 25, Martin made his first public appearance in two months at a conference on Vietnam in Beverly Hills, California, sponsored by *The Nation*. He spoke alongside four prominent critics of President Johnson's foreign policy: Senators Ernest Gruening (D-Alaska), Mark Hatfield (R-Oregon), Eugene McCarthy (D-Minnesota), and George McGovern (D-South Dakota). Martin delivered his first major speech devoted entirely to Vietnam, entitled "The Casualties of the War in Vietnam." "A war in which children are incinerated, in which American soldiers die in mounting numbers is a war that mutilates the conscience," he declared.

He gave the audience of more than fifteen hundred a sobering history lesson: In the decade following World War II, the United

States funded France's effort to recolonize Vietnam. After Vietnamese nationalists defeated the French, the United States propped up a corrupt and repressive regime in South Vietnam. Rather than supporting the Vietnamese people's right to self-determination, he argued, "we are engaged in a war that seeks to turn the clock of history back and perpetuate white colonialism."

To make matters worse, King argued, the war had become a direct threat to vital domestic programs. Great Society initiatives—designed to tackle poverty and racial inequality—were becoming casualties of foreign policy. King shared a startling estimate: The war budget amounted to $322,000 for every enemy killed in war, while the War on Poverty allocated just $53 per person in need. "It challenges the imagination to contemplate what lives we could transform if we were to cease killing," he said.

He closed with an anguished but patriotic message: "Let me say finally that I oppose the war in Vietnam because I love America. I speak out against it not in anger but with anxiety and sorrow in my heart, and above all with a passionate desire to see our beloved country stand as the moral example of the world. I speak out against this war because I am disappointed with America. There can be no great disappointment where there is no great love. I am disappointed with our failure to deal positively and forthrightly with the triple evils of racism, extreme materialism and militarism. We are presently moving down a dead-end road that can lead to national disaster."

The following month, Coretta echoed and expanded these critiques in an interview with *The Atlanta Constitution*. "We entered this war in support of colonialism," she argued. "We insinuated our military might into a civil conflict, we equated our interests with those of corrupt and dictatorial regimes, we ignored the principle of self-determination, we shunned efforts by the United Nations to stop the war to the point of bombing, burning and annihilating civilians, including innocent women and children."

The newspaper profiled Coretta as a member of "Atlantans for Peace." Founded a year earlier, the group met regularly—among themselves and with other local organizations—to study the history of US foreign policy and discuss recent news coverage of the war. The group had, the paper noted, "scores of arguments at their command and books and sources to back them up."

Coretta told the reporter she hoped to persuade more religious people to embrace nonviolence and oppose "the evils which breed war—poverty, racism, greed, and arrogance." She was outraged that while the government poured billions into fighting abroad, "we ignore and even jeer at the plight of my people at home." She admitted it often felt like she was swimming against a strong tide. She and other antiwar activists, she said, faced "constant denunciation" and warned that these efforts to "stifle dissent would smother democracy."

On March 25, Martin led his first antiwar march in Chicago, walking alongside Dr. Benjamin Spock. He urged the crowd of five thousand people to "combine the fervor of the civil rights movement with the peace movement."

The backlash was swift. Days later, *Saturday Review* editor Norman Cousins announced that the magazine would no longer publish King's writing, accusing him of fueling a "Hate America" movement.

It was a stinging rebuke—but tame compared to what lay ahead. For two months, Martin had weighed whether to accept an invitation to speak at a major antiwar rally scheduled for April 15 in New York. The event, organized by the SCLC veteran James Bevel and a coalition of activists calling themselves the Spring Mobilization Committee to End the War in Vietnam, promised to be a significant public demonstration against the war. But Martin's advisers were uneasy. They feared he would be perceived as aligning too closely with more radical speakers on the program, including the SNCC leader and Black Power advocate Stokely Carmichael.

In the end, Martin agreed to participate—but on his own terms. Instead of appearing at the rally, he would deliver an earlier address at New York's Riverside Church, sponsored by a more moderate group called Clergy and Laymen Concerned About Vietnam. Martin had preached regularly at Riverside over the previous decade, but this speech, entitled "Beyond Vietnam: A Time to Break Silence," would be different.

On April 4, more than three thousand people filled the pews at Riverside to hear him speak. The crowd greeted him with a standing ovation. When the applause subsided, Martin thanked John Bennett, president of the Union Theological Seminary, Rabbi Abraham Heschel of the Jewish Theological Seminary, and the historian Henry Steele Commager, who would join him for a panel discussion after the speech.

Martin called on the crowd to join the ranks of those who had moved "beyond the prophesying of smooth patriotism to the high ground of firm dissent based upon the mandates of conscience and the reading of history." From the opening lines, it was clear that Martin was speaking not only as a civil rights leader but as a moral witness.

He admitted that his own journey to campaigning for peace had not come easily. But the War on Poverty, he charged, had been "broken and eviscerated, as if it were some idle political plaything of a society gone mad on war."

The crowd was hushed now, save for the occasional cough or the rustle of a program. Martin spoke with a steady cadence and measured tone, eschewing the dramatic flourishes for which he was known. Over the course of nearly an hour, reading from a draft written by the historian Vincent Harding, a trusted adviser and professor at Spelman College, he delivered a sweeping, unflinching indictment of US foreign policy.

He described how American intervention had thwarted Vietnamese independence movements and praised the courage of conscientious objectors at his alma mater, Morehouse College. He urged the audience to look beyond Vietnam—to Guatemala, Cambodia, Mozambique, and South Africa—and to examine the global consequences of US militarism. On this night, Martin spoke more like a professor than a preacher, offering a moral education on the costs of empire.

He mourned what the war was doing to poor and working-class Americans—the Skip Johnsons of the country and their communities. "It was sending their sons and their brothers and their husbands to fight and to die in extraordinarily high proportions relative to the rest of the population," he said. "We were taking the black young men who had been crippled by our society and sending them eight thousand miles away to guarantee liberties in Southeast Asia which they had not found in southwest Georgia and East Harlem."

Black and white soldiers could fight side by side in "brutal solidarity," he continued, yet were forbidden from living on the same city block in places like Detroit. "I knew that I could never again raise my voice against the violence of the oppressed in the ghettos," he said, "without having first spoken clearly to the greatest purveyor of violence in the world today—my own government."

Though less well known than his "I Have a Dream" speech, Martin's "Beyond Vietnam" address was just as much a turning point—and one he would not have reached without Coretta's influence. For years, she had been the family's public voice on the war, challenging politicians, military leaders, and ordinary citizens to bring it to an end. Privately, she urged Martin to follow his conscience, reminding him that he was called to be more than a civil rights leader. It was her sense of moral urgency that made him break his silence.

THE RESPONSE TO KING'S SPEECH was immediate—and overwhelmingly hostile. Within days, the nation's most influential magazines and newspapers—*Life, Newsweek, The Washington Post, The New York Times*—cast Martin as reckless, naïve, even disloyal. He had, in their view, overstepped his bounds. By drawing a connection between "two public problems that are distinct and separate," *The New York Times* editorialized, "Dr. King has done a disservice to both. The moral issues in Vietnam are less clear-cut than he suggests; the political strategy of uniting the peace movement and the civil rights movement could well be disastrous for both causes."

Many of Martin's longtime allies in Black leadership circles also disagreed with his stance. The baseball legend Jackie Robinson, whose eldest son was serving in Vietnam, said King was "utterly on the wrong track." Ralph Bunche, the Nobel Peace Prize laureate, called the speech a "serious tactical mistake" and urged Martin to choose between civil rights and antiwar activism. Whitney Young, head of the Urban League, also warned that the goals of the two movements were not easily reconciled. Senator Edward Brooke of Massachusetts—the lone Black member of the Senate—also voiced disapproval. Recently returned from a fact-finding mission in Vietnam, Brooke advocated for continued bombing until North Vietnam agreed to peace talks. He said that by linking civil rights to Vietnam, Martin had done "irreparable harm" to the cause.

The sixty-member board of the NAACP, the nation's largest civil rights organization, voted unanimously to condemn the speech. "By involving himself in the peace movement, King indicates that Vietnam is number one on his agenda and civil rights is either number three, four or five," NAACP Director Roy Wilkins told an audience at Yale University. Wilkins insisted he was not a hawk or a dove, but a civil rights leader first. "If I'm going to cry about something, I'm going to cry about the murder of Wharlest Jackson in Natchez, Miss., rather than about civilians in Vietnam," he said, referencing the recent car bombing of a civil rights activist and Korean War veteran. "Is it wrong for people to be patriotic?" Wilkins asked. "Is it wrong for us to back up our boys in the field?"

The Pittsburgh Courier, one of the nation's most influential Black newspapers, said King was "preaching the wrong doctrine." Quoting reporting from Vietnam by the war correspondent Ethel Payne, the editors described Black soldiers as "dismayed at much of the draft card burnings and other anti-war actions in this country." While many longed to be home, "to a man they are equally as determined to see this job through," the editorial concluded. The paper's cartoonist, Sam Milai, echoed the sentiment with a series of illustrations that criticized King's stance on the war.

The military brass weighed in as well. Addressing hundreds of newspaper executives at the Associated Press annual luncheon, General Westmoreland said American troops were "dismayed, and so am I, by the recent unpatriotic acts here at home." Days later, in a televised address to Congress, Westmoreland drew cheers when he insisted that domestic dissent would not weaken America's resolve, promising to apply "unrelenting military, political and psychological pressure" to the enemy.

President Johnson viewed Martin's public condemnation of the war not only as political dissent but as a profound betrayal. Within the White House, aides called him a traitor and a Communist. Long distrustful of King, FBI Director J. Edgar Hoover saw an opportunity to deepen the rift. "Based on King's recent activities and public utterances, it is clear that he is an instrument in the hands of subversive forces seeking to undermine our nation," Hoover wrote in a memo to the president. Convinced, Johnson urged Carl Rowan, a prominent Black syndicated columnist, to publish an article in *Reader's Digest* alleging that King was under Communist influence. Johnson and King never spoke again.

Even Martin's father, Daddy King, initially disapproved of his son's stand against the war.

Coretta found the media backlash predictable, but she was deeply hurt by the chorus of criticism from longtime civil rights allies. Still, she believed the speech marked the next step in a larger, divine journey. Ever since Martin received the Nobel Prize in 1964, she had told him that there was a vital role for both of them to play in achieving world peace. Now, she imagined a scroll unfurling—

revealing a shared story that they would continue writing together over the months and years ahead.

When friends suggested that Martin had turned his back on civil rights, Coretta did not hesitate to correct them. "Those persons who do not agree with my husband now do not understand the meaning of his whole life," she said. "You cannot believe in peace at home and not believe in international peace. He could not be a true follower of a non-violent philosophy and condone war. You think of him as a politician, but he feels that as a minister he has a prophetic role and must speak out against the evils of society. He sees war as an evil, and therefore he must condemn war."

Why is it surprising, she asked, to see a religious leader oppose war? "When the Pope spoke against the war, everyone applauded; but when a black man named Martin Luther King speaks, they criticize him."

Out of the media glare, Martin returned to the themes of his Riverside speech in Sunday sermons at Ebenezer. "This helped a lot of the congregation to understand perhaps for the first time what the war was all about," Coretta recalled, "because he really reviewed the history of the conflict in his sermon as well as giving his positions against it." She believed that the controversy had, in its own way, expanded his audience. More people were listening now. More people were beginning to connect the fight for civil rights with the call for peace.

Despite the barrage of criticism, the Kings felt emboldened in the spring of 1967. Martin, unburdened, was finally saying what he believed. Coretta, long unwavering in her opposition to the war, stood beside him—buoyed by his courage and renewed in her own.

WITH A NEW SENSE of purpose, Coretta and Martin set out for opposite coasts to headline major antiwar rallies on April 15, 1967. Coretta traveled to San Francisco, where more than twenty thousand people marched a four-mile route through Market Street, Golden Gate Avenue, and the Haight-Ashbury neighborhood to Kezar Stadium. They came from Oregon, Southern California, the Bay Area, and beyond for the largest antiwar protest the West Coast had seen.

Union members marched wearing buttons, hats, and jackets displaying their local affiliations. "Stanford Physicians for Peace" wore long white lab coats. A group from Denver paid forty-two dollars each to charter a bus; their leader, Mary Walter, a partially paralyzed woman in her fifties, completed the march in her wheelchair. Cold winds, bursts of rain, and even hail swept across the route, but spirits remained high.

Most of the marchers were under thirty, and "the hippie character of the march-rally was never in doubt," one newspaper reported. Spontaneous street dances broke out in Golden Gate Park—a prelude to the coming "Summer of Love." The hopeful energy reminded Coretta of her days as a student delegate at the Progressive Party convention in Philadelphia two decades earlier.

Marchers plucked lilies, irises, and daffodils from sidewalk gardens. Residents opened their apartment windows and turned up their radios so the crowd could follow live coverage of the rally.

A few hundred counterprotesters lined the route. Frank Kastl Sr., whose son was fighting in Vietnam, held a sign reading "Support Our Men in Vietnam." "I believe in their right to march," he said, "but not to disagree with the system that gives them the right to march." San Francisco Mayor John Shelley responded to the march by proclaiming "U.S. Serviceman Appreciation Week," drawing praise from California's new governor, Ronald Reagan. Surveying the tepid response at the USO on Market Street, one mayoral aide admitted, "You can't undo the work of 24,000 marchers."

As the crowd poured into Kezar Stadium, the rally quickly exceeded its sixty-thousand-person capacity—more than the hometown 49ers had drawn for any game that year. Marchers packed the stands, shaking off the day's cold rain to hear an eclectic mix of a dozen speakers. The Black Panther Party leader Eldridge Cleaver spoke. So did the actor Robert Vaughn, best known for *The Man from U.N.C.L.E.*, and Grace Mora Newman, sister of Dennis Mora—one of the Fort Hood Three soldiers who refused orders to serve in Vietnam.

A large banner draped across the stage read: "Vietcong Never Called Us Nigger" and "Stop the War in Vietnam." Julian Bond called American militarism a "cancer" and warned that unless the Johnson administration changed course, the country would see more riots in the summer of 1967.

The march had begun at 10:00 a.m., and the crowd shivered through the long afternoon. When Coretta finally took the stage at the fifty-yard line, she was undeterred.

"Fellow peacemakers," she began, "I tell you this from the Sermon on the Mount: *Blessed are the peacemakers, for they shall become the children of God.*" She warned that the war in Vietnam was corroding the nation's moral core. "I know what bombing does to an oppressed people," she said. "Let me tell the experts who are planning our military strategy that bombing only makes an oppressed people more determined to throw off the yoke of oppression."

Coretta called President Johnson an "uncertain President," too easily swayed by poor advice from his military and foreign policy advisers. Her voice rose as she reached her conclusion: "For God's sake, let us stop the bombing."

Twenty-five hundred miles away, in New York City, Martin made the same urgent plea: "Stop the bombing." He repeated the phrase seven times in his thirty-minute speech outside the United Nations, drawing thunderous cheers from the crowd of more than 125,000 protesters. He argued that the war was deepening inequality at home and making life worse for poor Americans—especially Black Americans. "We are willing to make the Negro 100 percent of a citizen in warfare," he said, "but reduce him to 50 percent of a citizen on American soil."

Earlier that day, the protesters had gathered in Central Park's Sheep Meadow, chanting, "Hey, hey, L.B.J., how many kids did you kill today?" Several young men set their draft cards on fire, including Gary Rader, a clean-cut Special Forces reservist and Northwestern University graduate. Rader wore his Green Beret uniform as he struck the match—an image that was published in newspapers across the country. "I had learned how to maim or kill a person with my hands and feet in a few seconds, and I was damned proud of it," he wrote later. "Suddenly, one day I realized what had happened to me, and was disgusted. I am not as of this moment a pacifist; but the Army, having given me a full appreciation of violence, had turned me toward non-violence better than any other experience in my life."

While Martin did not endorse draft card burning, he urged

Black Americans—and "white persons of good will"—to resist the war by becoming conscientious objectors.

In addition to Coretta and Martin anchoring the Spring Mobilization Committee rallies in San Francisco and New York City, antiwar protests erupted across the country and around the world on April 15, 1967. In Northfield, Minnesota, five hundred students and teachers from St. Olaf College and Carleton College marched through the center of the small town. In Birmingham, Alabama, eighty demonstrators—mostly housewives—marched past crowds of weekend shoppers. In Spokane, Washington, one hundred protesters rallied under signs that read "We weren't born to burn." Across the Pacific, five hundred members of Japan's Peace-for-Vietnam Committee marched through downtown Tokyo. Thousands more filled the streets of London, Mexico City, Paris, Vancouver, and other cities.

At his ranch in Texas, President Johnson followed the protests through updates from FBI Director Hoover. Speaking on television, Secretary of State Dean Rusk dismissed the demonstrations as unhelpful. "The worldwide Communist apparatus is working very hard," he warned, adding that the protests could prolong the war rather than hasten peace.

Days later, at a Medal of Honor ceremony honoring Marine Sergeant Peter Connor, Johnson doubled down, warning that the country would pay a price for actions of antiwar activists. Fallen warriors like Connor, he argued, were facing "bullets and mortar shells," not "placards and debating points."

In private, he was even more blunt: "Stop the bombing, just means kill more American Marines."

Speaking at Christ Church near Harvard University a week later, Martin called for volunteers to launch a nationwide "Vietnam summer." Estimating that 35 to 50 percent of Americans were deeply concerned about the war, he argued it was time to engage those still undecided. "It is time to move from demonstrations and university teach-ins to a nationwide community teach-out," he said.

The initiative called for grassroots organizing around anti-draft activities, backing peace candidates in state and local elections, and passing citywide referendums demanding an end to the war. "We aim at more than changing a vote or two in Congress," read a pamphlet distributed at the news conference. "We seek to defeat Lyndon Johnson and his war."

Rumors swirled that Martin would run for president on a third-party peace ticket, with Dr. Benjamin Spock as his running mate.

In the weeks that followed, Martin barnstormed the country delivering speeches, organizing rallies, and urging action. David Halberstam, profiling Martin for *Harper's Magazine*, spent ten days on the road with him and compared the pace to that of a presidential campaign. The audiences, speeches, and cities started to run together, Halberstam wrote. "Only the terrible constancy of the pressures remained."

Coretta's travel schedule was nearly as intense as Martin's. On May 17, she was in Washington, DC, where she joined Spock and James Bevel to lead a group of two hundred protesters from Lincoln Congregational Church, in the historically Black Shaw neighborhood, to the White House. Steady rain fell as they reached the northwest gate and waited to deliver a petition demanding an end to the war. "Can we see the President?" Coretta asked Nathaniel

Davis, the National Security Council staffer who received the petition through the iron grillwork. "No, he's tied up, but I'll transmit it to him," Davis replied.

As the group turned to leave, someone in Lafayette Park hurled an egg that narrowly missed Coretta and hit Spock, splattering yolk across his chest. A counterprotester, who identified himself as a member of a White Power Committee, shouted, "Dirty lousy traitors who are stabbing our boys in Vietnam in the back."

Spock was unfazed. "They don't realize that what we're doing is far more patriotic when you're reasonably convinced this war can't be won," he told a reporter.

From DC, Coretta traveled to Pittsburgh, where she performed at the American Baptist Convention, singing spirituals including "I Ain't Got Time to Die," among other songs. After the concert, she sat for an interview with Willa Mae Rice, the *Courier*'s religion columnist.

Coretta described the ongoing challenge of balancing her roles as a wife and mother of four, her concert schedule, and her commitment to the civil rights and peace movements. Asked how Martin's stance on Vietnam had impacted his work, Coretta acknowledged some supporters had fallen away—but insisted that many more had come forward.

"God called him to be more than a race leader," she said. "He is appealing to the conscience of this nation to find anew the great moral and spiritual values, which are inherent in the Declaration of Independence and the Bill of Rights in the Constitution."

She returned to this theme at a Freedom Concert at First Baptist Church in suburban Beverly, Massachusetts, in late August. After singing "The House I Live In," she repeated the lyric "What is America to me?" and let the question hang in the air.

That summer, more than 150 rebellions and riots erupted in cities across the country. In nearby Boston, a sit-in protest against the city Welfare Department escalated in the Roxbury neighborhood. Two hundred police officers, armed with riot guns, shotguns, and bayonets, converged on the area. Thirty people were arrested and dozens hospitalized.

Conditions were far worse in other cities, including Skip Johnson's hometown of Detroit, where dozens were killed and more than a thousand injured in the July uprising.

America had a choice to make, Coretta told her audience. The forces of nonviolence, peace, and love had to act before it was too late.

She invoked the proud legacy of abolitionists in Massachusetts—but reminded parishioners that the church had not always stood on the right side of history. "Slavery could not have lasted so long without the sanction of the Christian church," she said. That history demanded vigilance, and the urgency of that earlier fight must now be applied to the struggles against racism, poverty, and war.

Coretta continued supporting Women Strike for Peace, which ran a half-page ad in *The New York Times* on September 18 denouncing President Johnson and the war. "We women gave you our sons," the ad read, "you use them to kill and you returned 12,269 caskets and 74,818 casualties to heartbroken mothers."

Two days later, WSP cofounder Dagmar Wilson led five hundred protesters in a march from Lafayette Park down Pennsylvania Avenue to the Selective Service headquarters. They carried a black coffin marked "Not My Sons—Not Your Sons—Not Their Sons—Support Those Who Say No."

Among the marchers was Vivian Williams, mother of Pvt. Ronald Lockman, a twenty-three-year-old Black soldier arrested and court-martialed the week before for refusing to board a troop plane to Vietnam. "My war is being fought in the ghettos of Philadelphia, not Vietnam," Lockman told a reporter.

After the April marches in San Francisco and New York, Coretta had told Martin, "It's time for the women of this nation to take a very strong position against the war. If enough women dedicated themselves to the task of ending the war, that would make a tremendous impact on the government." She shared the idea with fellow members of Women Strike for Peace.

Several months later, an ad appeared in *The New York Times* featuring a picture of Coretta with the message: "Mrs. Martin Luther King Jr. Says Join Me in Washington January 15." The ad was placed by the "Jeannette Rankin Brigade," a coalition of peace groups and women's liberation organizations named after the eighty-seven-year-old former congresswoman and lifelong pacifist. In a coauthored letter published in *The Atlanta Constitution*, Coretta encouraged women across the country to attend the peace rally in the nation's capital. She would miss Martin's thirty-ninth birthday to lead the rally.

"History shows us that no political ideology has ever been destroyed by military might, nor any political problem solved by the killing of young men," she argued. "We are seared to the soul by the constant television chamber of horrors, which has recently brought into our homes the spectacle of American bulldozers in Vietnam pushing large piles of dead Viet Cong into unmarked bunkers and trench graves."

More than five thousand women answered the call to join the Jeannette Rankin Peace Parade. Marching six abreast through slush and snow from Union Station to Capitol Hill, many wore black and walked in silence. "We've had 10,000 women sit back and let their sons be killed in Vietnam," Rankin had said earlier. "If we had 10,000 women willing to go to prison, that would end it. You cannot have wars without women."

After years of being one of the few Black women at Women Strike for Peace events, Coretta was encouraged by the broader turn-out. When a reporter asked Bobbie Hodges, a member of the Los Angeles chapter of the Black Panther Party, why she had traveled across the country to attend, Hodges answered plainly, "I don't think Black people should be in this war."

Hodges joined Coretta, Rankin, and Dagmar Wilson in a small delegation allowed inside the Capitol to present a petition to House Speaker John McCormack (D-Massachusetts). Coretta recalled that he received them politely but refused to discuss the war. When Hodges noted that Black servicemen were dying at disproportionate rates, McCormack replied, "I don't think in terms of black and white—I think in terms of Americans."

Several marchers recognized Marie Tuck, a Black mother from Cleveland, from news stories about her sons' opposition to the war. Her twenty-six-year-old son David had served a year in Vietnam as a radio-telephone operator in the Twenty-Fifth Infantry, calling in artillery rounds. "After my son returned from Vietnam he was very moody," Marie said. "He changed a lot and something seemed to be worrying him."

Before long, David began speaking about what he had seen, first in lectures at Cleveland-area colleges, and later at the Bertrand Russell International War Crimes Tribunal in Copenhagen in December 1967.

Marie's younger son, twenty-year-old Thomas, arrived at Fort

Knox for basic training a year after Skip Johnson left. When Thomas refused to pick up a rifle, he was court-martialed and sentenced to thirty days of hard labor in the stockade. After his release, he vowed to persuade other soldiers to oppose the war. "I'm with them one hundred percent," Marie Tuck said of her sons. "I take my stand with my sons for peace and an end to the war, not only for my sons but for the lives of all black and white soldiers."

While Marie marched with the Rankin Brigade, not everyone shared its tone or tactics. Some more militant activists felt constrained by the emphasis on mourning mothers and peaceful respectability. "Mrs. King and Mrs. Wilson had to promise to do nothing illegal so that church women would join the Brigade," said twenty-four-year-old Carol McEldowney.

As Coretta and the other march leaders delivered speeches at the Omni Shoreham Hotel, several hundred protesters broke away and staged a funeral march at Arlington National Cemetery. Their leaflets advertised "The Burial of Traditional Womanhood" and urged women to resist the "roles of supportive girl friends and tearful widows, receivers of regretful telegrams and worthless medals of honor."

Where Coretta saw motherhood as a way to connect with a broader coalition of women from different backgrounds, some younger feminists argued that appealing to power through maternal grief only reaffirmed a political system that kept women on the sidelines.

Both Coretta and Martin continued to grapple with the challenge of building and sustaining coalitions in volatile and unpredictable political terrain. Their efforts to bridge the peace and civil rights movements often left them feeling drained or discouraged.

For Martin, the long, hot summer of 1967 had been especially painful. "He got . . . in a state of depression that was greater than I had ever seen it before the riots," Coretta recalled. "He said people expect me to have answers and I don't have any answers. He said I don't feel like talking to people. I don't have anything to tell them."

Friends noticed his downward turn as well. "He talked about death all the time," SCLC Executive Director Andrew Young remembered. "Martin was keeping a hell of a pace."

Yet even amid that despair, in the early months of 1968, Martin announced the Poor People's Campaign and reorganized SCLC to support it. Setting out on a "person-to-person" tour, he sought to recruit a nonviolent army of poor Americans of all races to travel to Washington, DC, and occupy the National Mall. If lawmakers were forced to confront poverty in the shadow of the White House and Capitol, he reasoned, they might finally take action.

The campaign demanded bold, systemic reforms: a guaranteed annual income, affordable housing, and full employment. The goal was to sustain a peaceful but disruptive presence, one that would "plague Congress and the President until they do something," Martin warned.

In March 1968, Martin announced that thousands of people—traveling by foot, bus, and mule train—would converge on the nation's capital on April 22 and remain as long as necessary. "We believe the highest patriotism demands the end of that war in Vietnam and the opening of a bloodless war to final victory over racism and poverty," he said. "Flame throwers in Vietnam fan the flames in our cities. I don't think the two matters can be separated, as some people continue to feel."

He also made it clear that he would not support President Johnson's bid for reelection. After praising the president's early work on civil rights, Martin lamented that Johnson's obsession with Vietnam had undercut his domestic agenda. "I must say I'm very disappointed, and I think a change is absolutely necessary," he said in a press conference before addressing California Democrats at the Disneyland Hotel. "We must end the war in Vietnam. President Johnson is too emotionally involved, and face-saving is more important to him than peace."

That same month, the FBI issued a directive to its field offices naming Martin as the "primary target" of an operation designed to stop the "rise of a 'messiah' who could unify, and electrify, the militant Black nationalist movement." Bureau officials warned that the Poor People's Campaign could spark riots across the country and began recruiting "ghetto informants" to infiltrate and disrupt planning.

Soon after returning from the Rankin Brigade march, Coretta underwent major surgery to remove fibroid tumors and spent several weeks recuperating. Her sister, Edythe, came to the Kings' home to help care for her. "Martin was home much of that time, but he was not the same person I had known earlier," Edythe recalled. "His conversations and demeanor reflected deep and unresolved pain."

Dagmar Wilson visited Coretta in Atlanta in March, and the two had lunch together. They reminisced about their trip to Geneva in 1962 and the work they had done through Women Strike for Peace in the years since. Coretta said she was still guided by the question that underpinned the campaign against nuclear testing: "What good will freedom be, unless we have a world in which to be free?"

Shortly after Wilson's visit, a florist delivered a bouquet of artificial red carnations to the Kings' house. Coretta admired the flowers but was certain there had been a mistake. In all their years together, Martin had never given her artificial flowers before. She asked him about it as he prepared to leave for the airport. "I wanted to give you something that you could always keep," he said.

On March 28, Coretta was in Washington, DC, speaking at a press conference with the Women's International League for Peace and Freedom. "It takes great strength and courage to receive violence non-violently," she told a *Washington Post* interviewer. When asked about her activism predating Martin's public stance on the war, Coretta declined to take credit. Their shared convictions, she said, were what drew them together. "Before we met each other, we both had similar views," she reflected. "When we met we simply recognized them."

When Coretta returned to Atlanta, Martin was busy preparing for his next campaign. A few days later, he left for Memphis.

AMBUSH

On February 27, 1968, millions of Americans tuned in to *CBS Evening News*, as they did every night. They were used to vivid reports from Vietnam, but tonight would be different. The anchor Walter Cronkite had just returned from the front lines, where he reported on the aftermath of the Tet Offensive—a surprise attack by the Vietcong and North Vietnamese forces on more than a hundred military sites across South Vietnam, launched during the Lunar New Year. Cronkite witnessed brutal urban warfare in Hue, where troops fought street by street and house by house. He left the ancient imperial capital aboard a helicopter carrying the remains of a dozen marines in body bags.

"It seems now more certain than ever that the bloody experience of Vietnam is to end in a stalemate," Cronkite told viewers. Known for his objectivity, he had never publicly voiced an opinion on the war. Now, the most trusted newsman in America was saying the war could not be won. "It is increasingly clear to this reporter," he concluded, "that the only rational way out then will be to negotiate, not as victors, but as an honorable people who lived up to their pledge to defend democracy, and did the best they could."

Skip Johnson was back in Detroit the night the broadcast aired. For him, Vietnam was no living room war. After a year in-country, he knew the conflict was less about winning or losing than about surviving from one moment to the next. Watching the news of the Tet Offensive, Skip thought about the men in his unit—the Sixty-Ninth Armor—and hoped they, too, would make it home.

SKIP WAS NINETEEN YEARS OLD when hc arrived at the division headquarters near Pleiku in January 1967.

It was the dry season in the Central Highlands of Vietnam, and a fine red dust coated nearly everything. In some spots, it collected in mounds several inches deep. When the wind kicked up, it was hard

Skip Johnson in the army

to see or breathe. The dust made for beautiful sunsets—a small consolation for the havoc it wreaked on the tanks' drivetrains, lubricants, and filters. More experienced crewmates assured Skip that the muddy monsoon season would be worse.

The Sixty-Ninth Armor's primary mission was road security, ensuring the safe movement of troops and supplies north on Highway 14 and east toward the coast on Highway 19. "Our job was running road convoys," remembered Thomas Lamar Owens, a tank driver in the unit who grew up in rural Georgia. "We'd run a convoy up from Pleiku to Kontum or Dak To, pick up a convoy and bring it back." To clear foliage and expose potential ambush sites, low-flying air force C-123 aircraft sprayed herbicides—including hundreds of thousands of gallons of Agent Orange. At night, the focus shifted to bridge security, with a tank positioned at each end.

"No task was more disliked by armored soldiers," one army study noted of road security duty. When things went well, it was boring and seemed like a waste of the tanks' firepower. When it went poorly and convoys came under fire, it could feel like "a one-way ride to disaster."

"Tanks were big-ass targets, and going up and down the highway was like being in a shooting gallery," recalled Dwight W. Birdwell, a Cherokee tanker who earned the Medal of Honor for his actions during the Tet Offensive.

Skip tried to absorb everything he could from the older men in his unit. Since the Sixty-Ninth Armor arrived in Vietnam in January 1966, its tankers had been improvising tactics on the fly. The army's field manuals were built for combat in Europe and North Africa—they offered little help for fighting in jungles and swamps. "You'd learn more in the first week in Vietnam than in all of training at Fort Knox," said Barry Davis, the young Californian who trained with Skip in Kentucky and ended up in the same platoon.

One technique Skip learned was the "thunder run," used to clear mines. During the day, two tanks would drive in the same direction, one on each side of the road, with one track on the shoulder and one track on the road. The M48 tanks were heavy enough to trigger mines and survive with only minor damage. Enemy forces planted mines widely and unpredictably, and early in the war, tanks became the army's fastest and most effective way to sweep roads. In Skip's first three months in Vietnam, the Sixty-Ninth Armor detected and disarmed twenty-seven mines and detonated nearly a hundred more by rolling over them. More than eight thousand American vehicles passed safely along the highways to Pleiku under armored escort during that time.

Many of the men had read Bernard Fall, the French war correspondent and Howard University professor who chronicled the French Indochina War. Fall, who had fought in the French Resistance during World War II, first traveled to Vietnam in 1953 and returned several times. His six books and dozens of articles made him the foremost Western expert on the region. Soldiers and senior officers alike looked to his work to understand the challenges and limitations of counterinsurgency—and to realize they weren't the first foreign army to try to secure these roads.

Fall's *Street Without Joy: Indochina at War, 1946–54* (1961) was especially resonant. In it, Fall argued that the French military had overestimated its technological superiority and underestimated the challenges of guerrilla warfare in difficult terrain. One of France's final and bloodiest defeats came on Highway 19, where Groupment Mobile 100—a convoy of infantry and artillery units—was decimated by a Vietminh ambush as it attempted to retreat to Pleiku. A copy of *Street Without Joy* sat on the nightstand of General William Westmoreland, the US commander in Vietnam from 1964 to 1968. The ambush, Westmoreland later said, was "always on my mind."

"One chapter talks about the experiences of a French group as they drove from An Khe up to Pleiku and how that went—or didn't go," recalled Ken Neeld, a member of the Sixty-Ninth Armor who grew up in central Minnesota and Iowa before volunteering for service. "And that's exactly where I ended up stationed when I got over there. So I had no illusions. I knew what I was getting in for. That book was an eye-opener."

As Skip learned minesweeping tactics and the history of French failures along Highway 19, he adjusted to the rhythms of life in a combat zone. Each tank had a four-man crew: driver, gunner, loader, and tank commander. The men lived out of their vehicles and rarely returned to the division's base camp. Skip and his crewmates had canvas tents, but they felt safer sleeping on the tank or in cots alongside it. They would sleep in shifts, each man taking a turn behind the turret with the radio turned on, listening for movement. "The tank was home," said Thomas Lamar Owen. On uneventful days—and there were many—they had time to talk.

"If you have been together as part of a tank crew for any length of time at all, you'll get to know each other," recalled Jack Mountcastle, who served as a platoon leader in the Sixty-Ninth Armor and later became a brigadier general and chief of military history for the army. "You'd listen to guys talk about what it was like growing up on a farm or growing up as a Black kid in Atlanta or Detroit. They aren't just casual acquaintances. It's not like an office or a campus . . . you're together all the time. It's like being a surrogate brother."

Rumbling along the roads in a heavily armored tank—ten feet tall, thirty feet long, twelve feet wide, and weighing fifty tons—it was easy to be lulled into a false sense of security. Mountcastle arrived in Vietnam a few weeks before Skip and remembered his platoon's first enemy contact, in early 1967. The Sixty-Ninth Armor was ambushed by North Vietnamese Army troops equipped with machine guns and RPGs—shoulder-fired rocket-propelled grenades. "At that point, I was in combat for the first time," he said. "And as it has been, I guess, for eternity, young men going into combat are shocked to discover—and it is a deep-seated feeling—that SOB is trying to kill *me*. He wants to kill me. It's that basic." Mountcastle, who had studied history at Virginia Military Institute, later chided himself for being surprised at the intensity of combat. "When that first RPG sailed across a dry rice paddy, past my tank turret, then it was real."

From the moment they arrived in Vietnam, each soldier knew their DEROS (Date Expected to Return from Overseas). They counted down the days in different ways: Some kept pocket calendars or scribbled dates in notebooks; others marked their helmets with a hash for each month completed. But nothing marked a soldier like the first time they were fired upon—the day the war became real.

AMID THE STRESS OF COMBAT and the monotony of daily road security missions, the tankers of the Sixty-Ninth Armor eagerly awaited letters and care packages. Several times a week, helicopters dropped rations, hot meals, and mail into the field. Skip did not receive much correspondence during the first few months of his deployment, so he decided to take a chance and sent a letter to the girl he was sweet on back in Detroit—Katrina Lyn May.

"Have you heard from Skip yet?" One of Skip's friends, who attended Mackenzie High School with Katrina, would swing by her locker every week or so to check in. "Why would I hear from him?" she would reply. Sure, they had gone on a double date before he was drafted, but he was not her boyfriend. It was the spring of her senior year—she was not sitting around waiting for letters from soldiers.

When Skip's first letter arrived, Katrina was surprised. "I don't know what to say," she told her mother. "Say anything," her mom encouraged. "Tell him about the new records that are out. Tell him about what you and your friends did over the weekend." She told Katrina how much her father had appreciated getting mail when he was stationed in the Pacific during World War II. "Just write something," she said, "because anybody that is in the army, in a war that far away from home, needs to hear from anybody at home."

She looked at Skip's letter and smiled at the little frog he had drawn in the corner above the words "I leap for you." She took her mom's advice and began writing. Had he heard "Bernadette" by the Four Tops or the new duet by Marvin Gaye and Tammi Terrell, "Ain't No Mountain High Enough"? Did he know the Tigers were in first place in the American League? Were there other guys from Detroit in his unit?

Skip was delighted to receive Katrina's first letter—and each one that followed during the summer of 1967—even when the news from home was sobering.

IN THE EARLY MORNING HOURS of Sunday, July 23, about a hundred people gathered at a "blind pig," an unlicensed after-hours bar on Twelfth Street near Clairmount Avenue, for a welcome-home party for three Black servicemen who had recently returned from

Vietnam. Police had raided the club multiple times in the prior months—once finding only a children's Halloween party. Just before 4:00 a.m. on that humid July night, a Detroit vice squad busted down the door, stormed the bar, and announced that everyone was under arrest. As officers began shuffling partygoers into paddy wagons, a couple hundred people gathered outside.

"You don't have to treat them like that," shouted Bill Scott, whose dad owned the club, hurling a bottle at a sergeant. Onlookers jeered the police, demanding to know why they were targeting people on the West Side while ignoring house parties in wealthy white suburbs like Grosse Pointe. By 9:00 a.m., the crowd had swelled to nearly ten thousand people.

Over the next five days, Black Detroiters rose up in outrage against the decades of racism, segregation, and police violence that had shaped their lives. The Michigan State Police, National Guard, and US Army joined Detroit's police and fire departments in trying to quell the uprising. Forty-three people were killed, hundreds were wounded, and more than seven thousand were arrested.

"You could hear the tanks rolling up and down Wyoming Avenue," Katrina recalled. "My mom and dad had us playing cards, and I got so tired of playing cards I didn't know what to do. But we knew we couldn't go outside. We had just graduated from high school and had all these plans—what we were going to do, where we were going to go before we went away to college in September. The end of July screwed all that up."

That week, Katrina left the house only to go to her job, at Federal Department Store on Grand River Avenue and Oakman Boulevard. "I was working retail, and nobody wanted to go to work," she said of her one-dollar-an-hour job. "I went to work and made as much as I could." Working near the front of the store, she could hear and see someone firing a rifle from the roof of the building across the street. The smell of smoke wafted through the aisles— evidence of the hundreds of fires burning across the city. Busy day-time streets turned "ghostly empty" as people rushed to get home before the 9:00 p.m. curfew imposed by Mayor Jerome Cavanagh.

Each day, Katrina overheard customers talking about what was happening in the city. "People were burning and destroying and what have you," she recalled. They shared their anger, frustration, and fear—sometimes in hushed tones, more often in bold voices. What struck Katrina most was how often people mentioned Viet-nam alongside their local concerns. "The majority of them were angry about the war more so than anything else," she said.

When Skip read about the riots—first in Katrina's letters, then in the newspapers that reached the Sixty-Ninth Armor in the field—he could picture the storefronts and street corners. He had shopped with his mom on Twelfth Street. Northwestern High School, where National Guard troops and armored vehicles massed, was just a mile or so from the blind pig where the fateful police raid went down. It felt like a cruel irony that a party meant to celebrate three soldiers who had survived the war had ended in calamity. He wondered which of his classmates or friends might have been arrested—or worse.

As his unit drove tanks to and from Pleiku, eight thousand miles away National Guard troops were driving tanks through the streets of his hometown. North Vietnamese propaganda aimed at Black sol-diers made this connection explicit, describing Detroit as a "theater of combat" where American authorities crushed a Black uprising, killing dozens and wounding hundreds. Halfway through his year-long deployment, Skip struggled to reconcile serving his country in Vietnam while Detroit was in flames.

He was not alone. "They say we're fighting to free the people of South Vietnam, but Newark wasn't free. Was Watts? Was Detroit?" asked Private James Barnes, tallying the era's rebellions. "I mean, which is more important, home or here?"

At Camp Pendleton in late July, marines George Daniels and William Harvey discussed the rebellion in Detroit with other young Black marines. They argued that Black men should not be fighting in Vietnam. Planning to request a "captain's mast" to formally raise these grievances with their commander, they were arrested instead, charged with a conspiracy to violate military justice, and court-martialed. Daniels was sentenced to ten years of hard labor; Harvey received six. Both were sent to Portsmouth Naval Prison.

David Parks, the son of the acclaimed photographer Gordon Parks, kept a diary during his tour in Vietnam with a mechanized infantry unit. "Frankly I'm mixed up, the stateside news bugs me," Parks wrote in spring 1967. "On the one hand you have Stokely Carmichael saying Negroes shouldn't be fighting for this country. On the other hand some Negro leaders think just the opposite. I doubt most of them have ever been to war."

Parks, like Skip and thousands of other young Americans, had seen combat. "I think I'm getting a little too casual about death," he wrote. "I can't wait until this bloody mess is over. Time can't go fast enough. Every day you go out looking for someone to kill. And you're disappointed if you don't find a victim. Death as I have seen it here so far is awful."

————

SKIP AND THE OTHER MEN of the Sixty-Ninth Armor confronted the grim reality of war every week in the Central Highlands of Vietnam. In November 1967, they participated in the Battle of Dak To, supporting US Army infantry and airborne units. North Vietnamese soldiers had dug into the hills with an extensive network of bunkers and trenches. Overhead, the sky was crowded with air force F-100 jets, AC-47 gunships, B-52 bombers, and other aircraft. Together, they dropped hundreds of tons of napalm, aimed at killing enemy troops, stripping jungle canopy, and clearing the way for bombing runs. On the ground, fires fueled by napalm burned for more than three weeks amid vicious hand-to-hand combat.

"The Communists seemed bent on staying and fighting to the last man, taking as many Americans as possible with them," wrote the Associated Press war correspondent Peter Arnett. "They fight like they're all John Waynes, three clips each and making every bullet count," one paratrooper said, offering a note of grudging admiration for the enemy's resolve.

The Battle of Dak To—the longest sustained fight of the war to date—raised sharp questions about the US military's overall strategy in Vietnam. American troops fought tenaciously, hill by hill, to control a mountainous region along the borders of Cambodia and Laos. Beyond a few Special Forces camps and an airstrip large enough to accommodate C-130 cargo planes, the sparsely populated highlands held little strategic value and were difficult to defend. After the 173rd Airborne lost more than a hundred men fighting to secure a single hill and the valley below, one paratroop officer remarked, "In a conventional war it would be important, but this isn't a conventional war, so I guess it means nothing."

Lee Lescaze, a correspondent for *The Washington Post*'s Saigon bureau, saw Dak To as a microcosm of the state of the war by late 1967. He questioned the US military's claim that nearly fourteen hundred enemy troops had been killed, noting that reporters on the ground had seen no evidence of graves or corpses to support such a high body count. "Victory and defeat have lost much of their meaning in the battles of Vietnam," he wrote.

Military leaders pushed back. General Westmoreland called Dak To "the beginning of a great defeat for the enemy," and insisted the end of the war was "beginning to come into view." Brigadier General A. R. Brownfield was even more bullish. "We military people are all very optimistic, we see the situation getting steadily better," he told a reporter. The enemy, Brownfield claimed, was on his heels. "We've gone into his base areas. We've burned his rice, captured his weapons and medicine. He's hungry, he's sick and he's hurting. . . . By next year at this time, he's going to be in bad shape."

When military brass offered this upbeat assessment, nearly half a million US troops were stationed in Vietnam, and total American deaths were about to surpass twenty thousand, with more than eleven thousand killed in 1967 alone. A year-end Harris poll found that a majority of Americans still supported the war as necessary to stop the spread of communism in Asia. Another Gallup survey showed that 55 percent of respondents favored increasing US military involvement. Meanwhile, a separate Harris poll found that, by a three-to-one margin, Americans viewed antiwar protests in the prior year as "acts of disloyalty against the boys in Vietnam." The numbers steeled President Johnson's resolve—and served as a sobering reminder of the headwinds facing Coretta and other peace activists.

For Skip and the men of the Sixty-Ninth Armor, thinking about "next year" meant looking forward to going home to family and friends. In the meantime, they focused on their daily assignments and did what they could to keep up morale. When the unit pulled back to a firebase, the men sometimes set up a makeshift volleyball net, and Skip was quick to join the game. "He was always looking for something he could say to lift someone's spirit," Jack Mountcastle recalled. "Always ready to accentuate the positive."

As Christmas approached, Skip thought about his mother and younger brother, spending the holiday without him for the first time. He pictured snow falling softly on the towering Christmas tree set up every year in downtown Detroit, along Woodward Avenue. He remembered the holiday choir concerts he had performed at Northwestern High and Memorial Lutheran Church. Though festive decorations were sparse at their base, Skip and a couple of his crewmates found a small artificial tree and fastened it to the gun barrel of a tank. He smiled as someone snapped a photo—the only known image of him from his time in Vietnam.

In January 1968, the Sixty-Ninth Armor encountered a sharp increase in enemy mining activity. The North Vietnamese had begun placing mines across a wider swath of Highway 19, threatening convoys and supply lines. "Failure to rapidly replace tanks results in a serious drop in the combat power of armor units," the Fourth Infantry noted in its operational report for that month.

Skip spent hours each week inspecting the treads of his tank,

Skip Johnson with two
fellow members of the
Sixty-Ninth Armor in
Vietnam around
Christmas 1967

tapping each connector with a hammer to check for weakness. It
was painstaking work, but any flaw could prove deadly on the road.

THE MORNING OF JANUARY 15 began like so many others in Skip's
tour— his 353rd day in Vietnam. He drove one of the four tanks in
his platoon, escorting a convoy of supply trucks on Highway 14
from Kontum to Dak To. His tank rolled slowly along a dirt road
through a mountain gorge, nestled in the middle of the column.

Suddenly, rockets slammed into the two lead tanks—fired by
North Vietnamese troops lying in wait. Machine gun fire erupted
from both sides of the road. Within seconds, waves of enemy soldiers emerged from the dense jungle, launching a full-scale attack
on the convoy.

Skip accelerated forward to support the burning tanks. He made
it within twenty yards before his own tank threw a track, rendering
it immobile. Without hesitating, he climbed out and joined the

firefight. He had trained for this moment at Fort Knox, but nothing could prepare him for the chaos of the next half hour.

Armed only with his .45-caliber pistol, Skip shot several enemy soldiers rushing his position. When he ran out of ammunition, he returned to his tank, retrieved an M3 submachine gun, and pushed forward, fighting his way toward the other tanks. At one point, he used the stock end of the weapon to fend off an attacker at close range.

"The difference between what Dwight did that day and what the average soldier would do is profound," recalled Jack Mountcastle. "He jumped from tank to tank, using weapons that were left behind by wounded crews. He didn't stop fighting. That's unique. The US Army does not train either draftees or enlistees to do that—not then, not now. There is a great emphasis on teamwork, especially when you are part of a tank crew that's just four people. But what Dwight did went way beyond that. He was fighting as a one-man army for that day."

Just the night before, Skip had been reassigned to a new tank. He knew the crewmates in his old tank were trapped. He had lived in the tank for nearly a year with Bobby Kenneth Allen, a nineteen-year-old from Illinois; Joseph Walter Dudek, a twenty-five-year-old from Chicago; and Michael John Ryan, a twenty-one-year-old from Connecticut. "He was really close to those guys in that tank," recalled Stan Enders, the gunner in Skip's new tank. "He just couldn't sit still and watch it burn with them inside."

Desperate to help, Skip sprinted through the crossfire until he reached the tank. He opened the hatch and pulled one badly burned crewman out of the turret. As he got the man to the ground, an explosion rocked the vehicle. The tank's artillery shells had exploded, killing the men still inside. "When the tank blew up [and] Dwight saw the bodies all burned and black," Enders said, "well, he just sort of cracked up."

Still, Skip kept fighting. He made it back to his immobilized tank, climbed up into the cupola, and began firing the externally mounted .50-caliber machine gun, holding off the attackers until two helicopter gunships arrived to repel the ambush. "He saved the lives of many men," his platoon leader, 1st Lt. Robert T. Wright, wrote shortly after the attack.

"When it was all over, it took three men and three shots of morphine to hold Dwight down," Enders said. "He was raving. He tried to kill the prisoners we had rounded up. They took him away to a hospital in Pleiku in a straitjacket." Skip returned to camp the next day to collect his things. Within days, he was sent back to the States.

January 15 changed everything. Skip was reluctant to talk about what happened, or even what he remembered. "I don't know how many I killed," he later admitted. "I wasn't thinking. I wasn't counting. I was just shooting." Dr. Jonathan Shay, a psychiatrist who did groundbreaking work with Vietnam veterans, described this kind of combat detachment as entering a "berserk" state—borrowing from the Norse term for warriors who fought in a frenzied, trancelike fury. "The berserk state is ruinous," Shay wrote, "leading to life-long psychological and physiological injury if he survives. I believe that once a person has entered the berserk state, he or she is changed *forever.*"

One memory from the frenzy of that day stayed with Skip. He remembered running between tanks, unarmed, when he came face-to-face with a Vietnamese soldier. The man raised his rifle and pointed it directly at him. Machine gun fire rattled in every direction, the air thick with smoke and the explosions of rockets. Skip was close enough to see the man's finger begin to squeeze the trigger. His heart pounding, he closed his eyes, certain the next moment would be his last.

The click of the enemy's gun jamming would haunt him for the rest of his life.

PART 2

AMERICA BELONGS
TO US

Coretta spent the afternoon of April 4, 1968, shopping for Easter clothes in downtown Atlanta with her twelve-year-old daughter, Yolanda. Shortly after they arrived home, the phone rang.

"Coretta, Doc has been shot," Jesse Jackson told her. He urged her to get to Memphis as soon as possible.

As she made arrangements to take the next flight, the children came into the room. They had seen the news on television. "Mommy, when is Daddy coming home?" asked seven-year-old Dexter. "I don't really know," Coretta replied.

After kissing the children goodbye, she headed to the airport with Martin's sister and brother-in-law, as well as Atlanta Mayor Ivan Allen and his wife, who had come to the Kings' home after hearing the news. Just before she reached the gate, Coretta saw Dora McDonald, Martin's secretary, hurrying toward her. The look on Dora's face confirmed Coretta's worst fears. "Mrs. King," the mayor said, his voice formal as the two women embraced, "I have the sad responsibility to inform you that your husband is dead."

It was a moment Coretta had rehearsed in her mind dozens of times since marrying Martin, but that did not make it any easier. That evening, she stayed home, comforting the children and answering calls from family and friends. President Johnson phoned to offer his condolences and announced that Sunday, April 7, would be a national day of mourning.

In the days that followed, Coretta traveled from Atlanta to Memphis to bring her husband's body home, then back to Atlanta to prepare for the visitations, only to return again to Memphis to lead the march Martin had planned in support of striking sanitation workers. After the march, she returned to Atlanta once more for the funeral—all while caring for four young children as a newly widowed mother.

Harry Belafonte accompanied Coretta and the children on the flight back to Memphis and introduced her before the march. "I have never seen such courage, such nobility and dignity as in a black woman called Mrs. Martin Luther King," he said.

Coretta tried to never cry in public. But when she was alone, "the tears would roll down my cheeks in torrents," she recalled. Grief crept in everywhere—the indentation on Martin's side of the bed, his toothbrush still in the bathroom, the scent of his cologne lingering on his suits in the closet.

While Coretta confronted her private sorrow, cities across the country erupted in rage and despair. Black Americans filled the streets in Washington, DC, Chicago, Detroit, and dozens of other cities, protesting a nation that had failed to protect their most beloved leader.

On April 9, the day of the funeral, Coretta—her face veiled in black—held five-year-old Bernice in her lap. Millions of Americans watched the service on television. Vice President Hubert Humphrey attended, offering sympathy on behalf of President Johnson, who remained at Camp David meeting with advisers on Vietnam.

Representative John Conyers of Detroit was among the more than fifty members of Congress, governors, and mayors in the congregation. Just before the funeral, Conyers introduced a bill to create a federal holiday in King's honor. Days later, he joined his colleagues in passing the Civil Rights Act of 1968, which included landmark fair housing legislation—touted by Johnson as a tribute to King.

Throughout the week of mourning, Coretta urged Americans to see the common threads in the causes Martin had fought for. "My husband often told the children that, 'If a man had nothing that was worth dying for, then he was not fit to live,'" she said in a speech at Ebenezer Baptist Church two days after the assassination. "He gave his life for the poor of the world—the garbage workers of Memphis and the peasants of Vietnam."

She refused to view Martin's murder as the act of a lone madman. Instead, she believed it reflected a broader culture of violence that was poisoning the country. "Night after night, the horrors of war, such as the napalming of innocent civilians, were brought into our living rooms through the national news," she later wrote. Americans had grown numb to rising body counts and the sight of villages set ablaze. "To lose great men to assassination and young men and women to the unnecessary violence of war is intolerable," she declared.

Martin's death only deepened Coretta's opposition to the war in Vietnam. On April 27, just weeks after the assassination, she joined more than eighty thousand demonstrators at an antiwar rally in New

York City. Protesters paraded down both sides of Central Park before converging in the expansive Sheep Meadow. Gwen Patton, who had organized in Tuskegee and Atlanta, led a contingent of students marching from Columbia University.

Dressed in black, heart heavy with grief, Coretta stood before the multiracial crowd and explained that she was reading from notes found in her husband's pocket the night he was murdered. Then she read aloud Martin's "Ten Commandments on Vietnam." "Thou shall not believe in a military or political victory." "Thou shall not believe the figures of killed enemies or killed Americans." "Thou shall not believe that the world supports the United States." After each commandment, the crowd erupted in cheers.

Standing behind a phalanx of microphones, Coretta surveyed the thousands of people gathered before her.

Coretta Scott King addresses a peace rally in Central Park's Sheep Meadow on April 27, 1968.

A huge banner declared "Stop the War Madness Now," flanked by signs reading "Veterans for Peace in Vietnam" and "Support the Liberation of Black and Vietnamese People." Undercover officers, disguised as hippies, mingled with the crowd while helicopters circled overhead.

"My husband always saw the problem of racism and poverty here at home and militarism abroad as two sides of the same coin," Coretta told the crowd. She reminded them that exactly one year had passed between Martin's first speech against the war, at Riverside Church on April 4, 1967, and his assassination. Now, despite the enormity of the loss, she insisted, peacemakers stood at the threshold of a new day.

She urged the audience to stay mobilized through the spring. Join welfare mothers for a Mother's Day march, she said. Support the Poor People's Campaign in Washington, DC, on Memorial Day weekend. These fights were inseparable, she argued. "Our Congress passes laws which subsidize corporation farms, oil companies, airlines, and houses for suburbia," she said. "But when they turn their attention to the poor, they suddenly become concerned about balancing the budget and cut back on the funds for Head Start, Medicare, and mental health appropriations." Her voice rising, she vowed to continue the struggle "until the last gun is silent."

To close, Coretta turned to poetry. She said she drew strength from the spirit of Black people and of women who "refuse to be conquered." Then, reading from Langston Hughes's "Mother to Son," she let the crowd hear a mother's resolve:

> Don't you set down on the steps
> 'Cause you finds it's kinder hard.

Don't you fall now—
For I'se still goin', honey,
I'se still climbin',
And life for me ain't been no crystal stair.

Her voice caught slightly on the final lines. Knowing what Coretta had endured in the weeks since Martin's death, the crowd rose in thunderous applause.

The Central Park rally was the largest of dozens of coordinated antiwar protests held that day. In San Francisco, Muhammad Ali—convicted of draft evasion a year earlier and stripped of his heavyweight title—delivered a speech to a cheering crowd. In Philadelphia, the South Vietnamese Buddhist leader Thich Nhat Hanh told demonstrators, "We are not being saved; we are being destroyed." Tens of thousands more marched across the country and around the world, from Cincinnati to Copenhagen, Pittsburgh to Paris, and Seattle to Sydney.

ON MAY 1, Coretta returned to Memphis to dedicate a marble marker in the courtyard of the Lorraine Motel, where Martin had been shot, and to speak at a kickoff rally for the Poor People's Campaign. She joined Ralph Abernathy—who had succeeded Martin as the president of the SCLC—in calling for "poor power." "The resources which are so vital and necessary to carry on the fight against poverty here at home are being used to fight this war 6,000 miles away," Abernathy argued. Phyllis Robinson, representing Black mothers on welfare, charged that Black youth were shortchanged in schools and then "taken by the armed forces to be killed." After the rally, several hundred people began their trek to the nation's capital.

Coretta officially opened the Poor People's Campaign in Washington, DC, on Mother's Day, May 12. More than three thousand people joined the rally, including hundreds of mothers on welfare from Detroit, New York, and other cities who arrived on buses chartered by the National Welfare Rights Organization. Coretta and Ethel Kennedy, the wife of Senator Robert F. Kennedy, led marchers past burned-out buildings in the Shaw neighborhood before speaking at a rally at Cardozo High School stadium, near Howard University. Coretta urged Congress to pass a "freedom budget," including a guaranteed income and robust federal programs to assist people living in poverty. "I must remind you that starving a child is violence," she told the crowd. "Punishing a mother and her family is violence. Discrimination against a working man is violence. Ghetto housing is violence. Ignoring medical needs is violence. Contempt for poverty is violence. Even the lack of willpower to help humanity is a sick and sinister form of violence."

After the rally, demonstrators began erecting A-frame plywood structures and tents on the National Mall. Dubbed "Resurrection City, U.S.A.," the encampment stood for six weeks, growing to nearly three thousand dwellings at its peak. Protesters left the camp several times each week to demonstrate at government agencies and lobby for policy changes related to housing, jobs, health care, and other urgent issues.

When Coretta visited on Memorial Day, the Mall was inundated with mud and deep puddles from a recent storm.

She traded her heels for boots and toured the camp, praising

Coretta Scott King shares temporary shelter from the rain with Juanita and Ralph Abernathy at the Poor People's Campaign march on Washington.

participants for turning the campaign Martin had envisioned months earlier into a reality. She led the crowd in singing "Ain't Nobody Gonna Turn Us Around." Several people reached out to touch her, shouting, "Long live the King."

Coretta addressed a very different audience on June 12, when she became the first woman to speak at Harvard's Class Day. A thousand seniors packed the stately Sanders Theatre an hour early, perspiring in their graduation robes. She opened by referencing Martin—who had originally been scheduled to deliver the address— as well as the assassination of Robert F. Kennedy in Los Angeles just six days earlier. "With all due respect to the office of the President of the United States," she said, "even intense prayer and a new commission of notables will not ease the violence in our lives." She praised the wave of student protests sweeping college campuses and urged the younger generation to keep expressing their righteous indignation about war, racism, and poverty.

"Has not power heard the grim tidings? The anguish from the ghettos, the rural slums, the battlefields?" she asked. "The violence which periodically shocks us is a reflection of the violence to which we have become immune. It is a reflection of the violence our media celebrate." She concluded by calling on President Johnson to stop the bombing in Vietnam. "This war, which is the most cruel and evil war in our history, must come to an end."

While Coretta spoke at Harvard, her longtime ally Dr. Benjamin Spock stood trial with four other antiwar activists in a Boston courtroom. They were charged with conspiring to "unlawfully, willfully, and knowingly commit offenses against the United States" by counseling and aiding men to evade military service and destroy their draft cards. President Johnson had directed Attorney General Ramsey Clark to crack down on draft evasion. Rather than going after student protesters, Clark's strategy was to target Spock as a ringleader—to send a message and intimidate other opponents of the war.

During the monthlong trial, the prosecutor asked Spock why a pediatrician would involve himself in war protests. "What is the use of physicians like myself trying to help parents to bring up children healthy and happy, to have them killed in such numbers for a cause that is ignoble?" he replied. Dressed in a navy-blue suit and a freshly pressed light blue shirt with a high white collar, Spock quipped that he looked more conservative than most men on Wall Street. He told the court that his dissent was motivated by patriotism and a fear that the war "will blacken the reputation of my country for decades, if not centuries to come."

Coretta was en route from Boston to Washington when she saw the news: The jury had found Spock and the other defendants guilty of conspiracy. Each faced up to two years in prison and a five-thousand-dollar fine. Although an appeals court overturned the convictions a year later—ruling that the judge's guidance to the jury had been prejudicial—the highly publicized trial revealed the lengths the White House was willing to go to stifle dissent.

The Washington Post profiled Coretta when she returned to Washington in mid-June for Solidarity Day, the largest demonstration of the Poor People's Campaign. "With her Madonna-like face and serene smile in the midst of her bereavement, she has captured the imagination of the rich and powerful as well as of the poor," the reporters Judith Martin and Carolyn Lewis wrote. "Her public voice is the voice of a trained singer. It builds low from the diaphragm, with liquid resonance. It lingers on vowels." The article emphasized that Coretta had been active in the antiwar movement years before Martin—highlighting her work with Women Strike for Peace and her travel to Geneva as part of a delegation calling for disarmament. In the weeks since Martin's death, the reporters observed, she had moved to a new level of public influence. "Coretta King has become a leader since her husband died," they wrote. "Her speeches show it."

Fifty thousand people gathered at the Lincoln Memorial for Solidarity Day on Juneteenth—on the same steps where, five years earlier, Martin had delivered his "I Have a Dream" speech.

Coretta connected the institution of slavery, the strictures of Jim Crow segregation, and the hopelessness of grinding poverty before turning her focus to Vietnam.

Coretta Scott King addresses the Poor People's
Campaign "Solidarity Day" rally from the steps of the
Lincoln Memorial on June 19, 1968.

"There is hardly a family that has not been affected by the war,"
she said. "If women stood together, even to the point of going to
jail, if necessary, I think it would make a tremendous impact on the
President and policy makers. Women—I urge you to call the President to stop the bombing of Vietnam now in order that a settlement of the war can be negotiated." She supported her emotional
appeal with concrete figures, tallying the cost of continued fighting: "If we stop the war two months sooner, 230 housing units
could be built; one hour could create a new school and housing
center." She called for women to launch a "campaign of conscience"
and to make nonviolence a way of life.

"Solidarity Day" was the final engagement of Martin's that Coretta fulfilled. In the months ahead, she would no longer be speaking
on Martin's behalf—she would be charting her own course.

WORD OF KING'S ASSASSINATION sent shock waves through the military. "When I heard that Martin Luther King was assassinated, my first inclination was to run out and punch the first white guy I saw," said Air Force Staff Sergeant Don Browne. A former Howard University football player who joined the air force in 1959, Browne described himself as "pro-military" when he deployed to Vietnam in November 1967. But the news of King's death crushed him. He wanted to go home, but that was not an option. Instead, he wrote a letter to President Johnson: "I didn't understand how I could be trying to protect foreigners in their country with the possibility of losing my life wherein in my own country people who are my hero, like Martin Luther King, can't even walk the streets in a safe manner."

Days later, Browne confronted some white airmen who were using racial slurs and complaining about seeing King's picture on the TV in the barracks. As a member of an air force police squadron, Browne—along with other Black military police—delivered what he later described as a "physical lesson" on when to not use those words.

The war correspondent Wallace Terry, *Time*'s deputy bureau chief in Saigon, spoke to Browne and thousands of other Black troops while reporting on shifting attitudes about the war. He found that the anger Browne expressed was widely shared. Although the armed forces had made strides in racial integration, King's assassination brought long-simmering tensions to the surface. Black troops reported seeing more Confederate flags flying from barracks and military vehicles. Crosses were burned at Da

Nang and Cam Ranh Bay. Terry wrote that there was "another war being fought in Vietnam—between black and white Americans."

When news of King's death reached the Fifty-Second Artillery Group, they were stationed in Pleiku, traversing the same roads the Sixty-Ninth Armor had helped to secure. Herbert Turner, a Black chaplain with the unit, asked for permission to hold a memorial service in the base chapel. His commander denied the request, saying that "it was better not to make a big thing out of it." In Da Nang, a group of Black soldiers were similarly refused entry at their base chapel. When they tried to gather at the enlisted men's club instead, a white sergeant accused them of inciting a riot and called in the military police. "We are supposed to be American soldiers fighting a war in Vietnam," wrote James Woods, one of the soldiers. "But it seems as though the white man thinks we're still at home."

In the wake of the assassination, Black troops began organizing groups such as the Malcolm X Association, Better Blacks United, De Mau Mau, and Unsatisfied Black Soldiers. These groups fostered cultural pride, expressed opposition to the war, and, in some cases, provided protection from racial violence within the military. More Black servicemen began growing Afros and started wearing Black Power bracelets and insignia. *Time* magazine reported more than four dozen varieties of "dapping" that Black troops used instead of salutes. Speeches by Malcolm X and Muhammad Ali, along with copies of the Black Panther Party's Ten-Point Program, circulated widely among the troops. The Panthers' demands included an end to Black military service and a call to "protect ourselves from the force and violence of the racist police and the racist military by whatever means necessary."

Back in the States, Black soldiers began to draw on civil rights tactics to express their anger and frustration. In the lead-up to the Democratic National Convention in late August, thousands of troops from Fort Hood, Texas, and Fort Riley, Kansas, were ordered to deploy to Chicago to control antiwar and civil rights protesters. The military prepared for the largest domestic airlift of troops in history, with 250 air force C-141 cargo planes on standby.

The night before their scheduled departure, sixty Black GIs staged a sit-in at an intersection in Fort Hood. Most were members of the First Armored Division. More than half had already served in Vietnam, and many had been sent to Chicago just four months earlier for riot-control duty following King's assassination. They were not eager to return.

"We feel that we've done enough for our country," one soldier told *Time* magazine. "The people we are supposed to control, the rioters, are probably our own race. We shouldn't have to go out there and do wrong to our own people. I can't see myself spraying tear gas on my fellow people."

At daybreak, the unit's commander and his staff met with the protesters. Some men ultimately chose riot duty over the threat of military punishment. But forty-three refused to move. When they declined to respond to the morning bugle call, they were placed in the stockade. Each was later court-martialed and sentenced to several months of hard labor, loss of pay, and reduction in rank.

Rudolph Bell, a twenty-year-old private from Detroit, was one of the "Fort Hood Forty-Three." He had already served a year in Vietnam, during which he lived through both the Detroit riots in July 1967 and the Tet Offensive in early 1968. "There I was over there fighting, thinking I was really doing something," he said. "And then I pick up a paper and see tanks in my hometown and my people being shot down. It didn't seem right."

Back at Fort Hood, Bell bristled at the riot-control drills that became part of the weekly routine. He said he did not condone looting or arson, but he understood why people would take to the streets. For him, the sit-in was the clearest, most peaceful way for soldiers to express their beliefs. "How could I fire on my people," he asked, "when, if I hadn't been in the army, I probably would be out there with them?"

While the Fort Hood Forty-Three sat in the stockade, thousands of other army troops, police officers, and Illinois National Guardsmen flooded the streets of Chicago outside the Democratic National Convention. Weeks earlier, Mayor Richard Daley had issued a chilling order: Police were authorized to "shoot to kill any arsonist" and "shoot to maim" any looter. Now, with ten thousand antiwar protesters converging on the city, Daley had the convention arena encircled with barbed wire and put the Chicago police on twelve-hour shifts. On the third night of the convention, demonstrators marched down Michigan Avenue and clashed with officers wielding billy clubs and pepper spray. Television cameras captured the violence in real time. An official investigation, led by the World War II veteran and future Illinois Governor Daniel Walker, would later describe the event as a "police riot."

Inside the convention hall, the twenty-eight-year-old Georgia state legislator Julian Bond was fighting a different kind of battle: to push the Democratic Party toward an antiwar ticket. First, though, he had to secure a seat at the table. Bond had led a multiracial group that challenged Georgia's official delegation, which had been handpicked by segregationist Governor Lester Maddox and the state chairman of the party. Known as the Georgia Loyal Democrats, Bond's group succeeded in securing half of the state's seats. It was a moment of personal and political vindication. Just a year earlier, several of these same party leaders had tried to block Bond from taking his elected seat in the statehouse. Now, *The Atlanta Constitution* declared, Bond had turned the tables. Maddox had famously adopted the axe handle as a symbol of his opposition to desegregation. "Julian Bond has the axe handle now," the editors quipped, "and this time there's a sharp blade on it."

In his speech seconding the nomination of Eugene McCarthy, Bond praised the Minnesota senator for being the Democratic Party's most outspoken opponent of the war. Without McCarthy, he argued, "we would not have had a national judgment on the war in Vietnam—an overwhelming rejection of a war the American people never chose and supported—a rejection of the way we have carried on that war, a rejection of the role of the military in our foreign policy, a rejection of empty slogans and misleading propaganda."

The convention floor erupted again when the Wisconsin delegation nominated Bond for vice president, even though he was seven years younger than the age required by the Constitution. When the CBS reporter Dan Rather asked him what he made of the gesture, Bond used the moment to speak directly to television viewers across the country. He explained that his candidacy was a call to address the urgent issues the convention had failed to confront: "poverty, racism, and war."

Bond returned to these themes again and again, night after night, in speeches to audiences across the country. In the two years following the convention, he gave nearly seven hundred public talks. Though not a fiery speaker, Bond often closed his remarks with a measured but ominous warning, invoking the words of Langston Hughes, Martin Luther King, and James Baldwin. "If this dream is deferred much longer, then an explosion will come," Bond said, "and in the words of the old song, it will be like God giving Noah the rainbow sign; no more water, the fire next time."

As THE 1968 presidential election heated up, Bond's most famous constituent was in high demand. "The hottest political commodity on the market today is Mrs. Martin Luther King Jr.," wrote the esteemed Black journalist Ethel Payne. "Both parties would give a king's ransom to get her on their side." Coretta met with New York Governor Nelson Rockefeller at Spelman College as he pursued the Republican nomination, and she posed for a photo with Vice President Hubert Humphrey, who fed ice cream to her youngest daughter, Bernice. Eugene McCarthy went further: If elected, he said, he would appoint Coretta as ambassador to the United Nations.

Coretta had first met Richard Nixon a decade earlier, during the independence celebrations in Ghana, where he represented the Eisenhower administration as vice president. She found him witty and approachable but never fully trusted him, after the vicious red-baiting he used against the California congresswoman Helen Gahagan Douglas during their 1950 Senate race. Though wary, she welcomed Nixon into her home forty-eight hours after Martin's assassination, when he arrived to pay his respects.

Nixon attended the funeral and walked in the procession days later.

Richard Nixon offers condolences to Coretta Scott
King after Martin Luther King Jr.'s assassination.

Seeking to channel their collective political influence, Coretta
joined the National Committee of Inquiry, a group of prominent
Black leaders who planned to interview all the major presidential
candidates before deciding whether to endorse one. The committee
included John Conyers, Rosa Parks, Stokely Carmichael, Sidney
Poitier, and Harry Belafonte, along with the Southern Christian
Leadership Conference veterans Ralph Abernathy, Hosea Williams,
and Andrew Young.

When the committee met in Gary, Indiana, in October, the
presidential race was tightening. After Humphrey secured the Democratic nomination at the chaotic convention in Chicago, he trailed
Nixon, the Republican nominee, and faced stiff competition from
George Wallace, the segregationist governor of Alabama running as
a third-party candidate. To broaden his appeal and counter Nixon's
and Wallace's "law and order" messaging, Humphrey distanced him-

self from the party's antiwar wing and began touting riot control and increased federal aid for policing. The National Committee of Inquiry declined to endorse any candidate, concluding that none had prioritized the issues most important to Black Americans.

A week before the election, Coretta issued a "qualified endorsement" of Humphrey, calling him the "lesser of the evils" and saying that Martin would have likely made the same choice. Though disappointed that Humphrey had not broken more clearly with Johnson's policies in Vietnam, she argued, "I think his opponents represent too many of the forces in American life that are insensitive and antagonistic to racial and economic justice and peace." Conyers also endorsed Humphrey. "Millions of black people and many other deprived Americans just cannot afford four years of Richard Nixon as President," he warned.

When Nixon won days later, Coretta struck a pragmatic tone. She pledged to "help President Nixon if his policies are right and oppose him where he is wrong." Then she got back to work.

Among the many speeches she gave in the unimaginably difficult months following Martin's death was a keynote address to the Progressive Baptist Association ladies' auxiliary. Speaking over lunch at Washington, DC's Shoreham Hotel, she praised "the greatness of the Black Power movement" for instilling pride and making it easier to teach children "a sense of somebodiness."

There were plenty of reasons to despair, she acknowledged—the assassinations of her husband and Robert Kennedy, uprisings in cities across the country, and the ongoing war in Vietnam. But she drew strength, she said, from the deep roots Black people had in America. "We were here before the Pilgrims," she reminded the audience, referencing the arrival of the first enslaved Africans in the

English colonies in 1619. "We shed our blood on the battlefields. We helped to build the cities and highways; we tilled the soil. We're part of all that helped make America great."

It was love for America, not hatred, that motivated her to fight against the war. "We're proud of our African heritage," she concluded, "but America belongs to us."

HONOR

f I ask you to marry me, would you say yes?"

Katrina raised an eyebrow. "Are you asking?"

Skip smiled at her playful reply. "If I ask you to marry me, would you say yes?"

She wasn't about to let him off the hook that easily. "Are you *asking?*"

"Never mind," Skip said, grinning as he left the kitchen and walked toward the back of the house, where Katrina's parents, Leroy and Jessalyn, were watching television. A few minutes later, he returned.

"That's okay," he said. "I asked your mother, and she said yes."

"Well, I guess you're marrying my mother, then," Katrina replied. "You better ask her husband."

While Skip had been in the other room, Jessalyn had taken his hand and quietly placed a ring in his palm. It was the one her husband had given her in 1947, after returning from army service in the Pacific during World War II. When Skip slid it onto Katrina's finger, it caught her completely off guard. "It blew my mind," she recalled.

The past three months had been a whirlwind for both of them. After the ambush in Dak To, Skip was flown back to the United States. He spent a couple of weeks recovering at a military hospital in California before returning home to Detroit. He rejoined his mother and younger brother, who had moved out of the Jeffries Homes into a small house on Pacific Avenue, in the city's northwest section.

One of the first things Skip did was call Katrina. "It was a cute little romance," she recalled. They ate at the A&W and Daly drive-ins, went bowling, and saw *Planet of the Apes* at the local movie theater. Some nights, they would hang out on the mezzanine level of the Detroit Metro airport, shooting pool and watching television until after midnight.

Though they had exchanged dozens of letters over the past year, it was not until those first few months of 1968 that they really got to know each other. "When we started dating, I realized he was a nice guy," Katrina said. "He was always nice, he was funny, and he was silly. It just went from there."

One night, while they were out dancing, Skip began singing along to the Delfonics' "La-La Means I Love You." Katrina had not known he sang—let alone that he had been in the choir at Northwestern.

"You been hiding that from me?" she said.

"I thought you knew," Skip replied.

If Katrina was not already in love, that sealed it. She was eighteen years old when Skip proposed in March 1968.

Katrina and
Skip, c. 1968

Skip was twenty and eager to begin the next chapter of his life. In the two years since graduating from high school, he had been through basic training, learned to drive and fire an M48A3 tank, watched from afar as his hometown burned, and survived his deployment in Vietnam.

Across the country, scenes like this played out again and again— young veterans going from battlefield to living room in a matter of days. "The adjustment period when I got back was really strange," remembered James Gillam, a Black soldier in the Fourth Infantry Division. "I had less than forty-eight hours, maybe seventy-two hours between the last time somebody tried to kill me" and being back in Ohio.

A 1990 Veterans Administration study would later reveal that Black and Hispanic Vietnam combat veterans experienced more severe mental health and reintegration challenges than their white peers. But in 1968, when Skip returned home, military officials and the VA offered little to help veterans transition back into civilian life. Making matters worse, the second edition of the *Diagnostic and Statistical Manual of Mental Disorders* (*DSM*-II), published that January by the American Psychiatric Association, had removed the "gross stress reactions" diagnosis—a label previously applied to World War II and Korean War veterans. With that change, doctors lacked even the clinical language to diagnose the trauma Vietnam veterans were experiencing.

Many came home with the same stories: waves of anger, crushing guilt, and nightmares that left them drenched in sweat. Some refused to talk about the war at all, even as it stalked their every thought.

"I been livin' with Vietnam ever since I left," Reginald "Malik" Edwards, who served as a marine in Da Nang before joining the Black Panthers, told Wallace Terry. "You can't get rid of it. It's like that painting of what Dalí did of melting clocks. It's a persistent memory."

Thomas Brannon, who served with the Fourth Calvary Regiment, put it bluntly: "Once you've fought in Vietnam you can't stop thinking about it. Once you've been in combat, once you've heard guys screaming for their momma, guys pissing on themselves, you can never get it out of your life."

"When Skip came home from Vietnam he was different," recalled his friend Eddie Wright. "I noticed it, all jumpy and nervous and he had to be doing something all the time. But mostly he was the same fun-time guy."

Whenever his buddies asked for war stories, Skip would fall silent and change the subject. His cousin, Tom Tillman—who had also served in Vietnam, in the air force—was not sure what to make of those moments, or of the mementos Skip brought home. "The one thing I thought was kind of strange and unlike him was the pictures he brought back," Tillman said. "He had a stack of pictures of dead people, you know, dead Vietnamese. Color slides." After that, Tillman learned to avoid the topic of the war altogether.

Skip and his cousin spent much of 1968 looking for work. "We went around to place after place looking for a job and got doors slammed in our face," Tillman recalled. "When he got out of the service, people gave him a lousy break. Nothing happened decent to him."

Their experience was all too common for Black and working-class veterans. "The big question is still what will happen to the Negro grunt," noted a *New York Times* series on Black troops, "whose skills with the M-16 rifle and the M-79 grenade launcher are hardly marketable. If historical patterns prevail, he will find employers much less interested in him than front-line commanders were."

"The Army was supposed to teach them a trade in something—only they didn't," said Herb DeBose, a Black lieutenant who commanded hundreds of working-class soldiers recruited under Project 100,000. "No skills before. No skills *after*."

For Willie Thomas, who returned to St. Louis after serving in a military intelligence unit in Vietnam, unemployment made him question both his service and his place in America. "It gave you a feeling like you didn't have a country," he recalled, "because you know you came home to very few job opportunities, along with the hatred, it didn't give you a lot to look forward to." *The Wall Street*

Journal reported that "even black senior officers with a wealth of managerial experience cannot find jobs in the civilian community worthy of their abilities."

By 1971, the unemployment rate for Black veterans under the age of twenty-four—young men like Skip—was 21 percent, compared to 14 percent for white veterans and 11 percent for non-veterans of the same age across racial groups. "If the average Vietnam veteran was catching hell, the average African American veteran was catching more hell," said Ron Bradley, who returned home to the Bronx after serving in the Ninth Infantry Division.

Against this backdrop, Skip clung to the future he was building with Katrina. As the country reeled through another turbulent year, they drew even closer. Skip called her immediately on April 4, when he saw the television bulletin that King had been shot. "I was shocked, but not surprised," Katrina recalled.

A couple of weeks earlier, she had gotten word that a friend's brother had been killed in combat near Quang Tri. Ronald Dobbs, a private first class in the Third Marine Division, had been a year ahead of her at Mackenzie High School. He was the first person she knew who died in the war. His funeral in Detroit took place just days before King's service in Atlanta. "It was crushing to all of us," she said. "I don't think he was in the service eighteen months before he was killed in Vietnam. That made me even more angry."

Blocks away, the father of Marine Private First Class Monzie Durrel Edmonds—one of Skip's classmates at Northwestern—mourned his son, who had been killed in action in Thua Thien. "It really hurts," he told the *Michigan Chronicle.* "This is a bitter time in our lives, the hardest thing we have ever known. Why continue to riddle the bodies of our sons with burning iron?"

For Katrina and others, King's assassination and the deaths of friends and classmates in Vietnam blurred into a single, searing memory of 1968. Too many lives lost, too soon. "That was a trying time," she remembered.

Skip turned twenty-one that May, finally old enough to vote. He read about the turmoil of the Democratic National Convention in the pages of the *Michigan Chronicle* and took pride in seeing Congressman John Conyers—his representative and the speaker at his high school graduation—rising on the national stage. Conyers's endorsement of Humphrey mattered to Skip, but he wondered whether any politician could heal the wounds Detroit—and America—had suffered that year.

ON A CRISP autumn morning, just before the November election, a car pulled up in front of Skip's house.

"What did you do?" his mother whispered, watching two military policemen stride up the walkway.

"I didn't do nothing, Ma. Honest," he said.

The men were more polite than the MPs Skip remembered from Fort Knox, but still brisk and formal. They asked a series of questions about his whereabouts since discharge—wanting to know if he had been arrested or gotten in trouble with the law.

"I've been staying out of trouble, looking for work," Skip replied. "I'm getting married in a few months."

Not long after they left, the telephone rang. A voice Skip didn't recognize introduced himself as a colonel from the Department of Defense, calling from Washington, DC.

"Sergeant Johnson," the man said, "it is my pleasure to let you know that, based on the recommendation of the Secretary of the Army and the Secretary of Defense, President Johnson has conferred the Medal of Honor to you for your courageous actions in Vietnam."

The colonel asked if Skip and his family could come to Washington for the ceremony, where the president would present the award in person.

Skip hung up the phone, stunned. The army had not contacted him in months. He had gone out of his way not to talk about what happened that day in Dak To. Now, he was being summoned to the White House to receive the nation's highest military honor.

On November 19, Skip accepted the Medal of Honor alongside four other recipients: Sammy Lee Davis, a freckle-faced sergeant from Indiana; Angelo Liteky, a Roman Catholic priest and captain

Skip Johnson, along with four fellow servicemen,
is awarded the Medal of Honor by
Lyndon B. Johnson on November 19, 1968.

in the 199th Infantry Brigade; James Taylor, a first lieutenant from San Francisco; and Gary George Wetzel, a twenty-one-year-old specialist fourth class from Milwaukee who lost his left arm in combat. While their stories differed, each had risked his life to save fellow American soldiers.

"Other brave men will be called upon to perform other brave acts before the search for peace yields a settlement at the conference table," President Johnson said. "But men like these have brought us the distance that we have traveled, and men like these will see us the rest of the way."

With his presidency nearing its end, there was a note of melancholy in Johnson's voice. He alluded to the many Medal of Honor ceremonies held in the East Room and echoed a line President Truman once delivered during a similar ceremony honoring World War II service members: "I want to remind you of what another President said upon another occasion: That 'I would rather be able

Skip Johnson with his mother, Joyce Alves, and his brother, David

to have that blue band around my neck for the Congressional Medal of Honor than to be the President of the United States.'"

Among the two hundred family members and dignitaries in the audience were Katrina; Skip's mother, Joyce Alves; his younger brother, David; his cousin Tom Tillman; and his grandparents.

They listened closely as the commendations were read. "Specialist Johnson's tank threw a track, and he became immobilized," said Secretary of the Army Stanley Resor. "Realizing that he could do no more as a driver, he climbed out, armed only with a pistol. Despite intense hostile fire, Specialist Johnson killed several enemy soldiers before he had expended his ammunition." Resor continued, detailing how Skip fought with courage and determination, before concluding, "Specialist Johnson's conspicuous gallantry at the risk of his life is in keeping with the highest traditions of the military service and reflects great credit on himself and the United States Army."

The commendation was brief—just over 350 words, delivered in under two minutes. But for Skip's family, it was the first time they had heard in detail what he had endured in Vietnam. For Skip, it was the first time anyone had tried to capture—in public, no less— what happened on the day that changed his life.

After the ceremony, Joyce approached Skip in the receiving line and noticed tears rolling down his face. "Honey, what are you crying about?" she asked softly. "You've made it back." Skip took a moment to compose himself before stepping forward to speak with the press.

"I'm thrilled and proud," he told a reporter from the *Michigan Chronicle*. "I guess this isn't an everyday thing." The article noted that while the army encouraged him to reenlist and offered him a recruiting position, Skip had other plans. He hoped to enroll at Highland Park Junior College. "What I really want is a career in computer programming," he said.

From the White House, Skip and the other medal recipients traveled to New York City, where they were honored guests in the studio audience of *The Ed Sullivan Show*. Dusty Springfield sang "Son of a Preacher Man," and the Muppets performed a skit. Skip was especially excited to see one of his favorite singers, Nancy Wilson. Dressed in a floor-length white evening dress, Wilson sang a haunting rendition of "Face It Girl, It's Over":

> *What's the use in hanging on*
> *While he slowly slips away from you . . .*
> *Well, the time has come, I know, for our last goodbye*
> *Guess I'll have to go on living, when it's easier to die.*

After Wilson's sorrowful ballad, Sullivan asked the honorees to stand and be recognized.

One person missing from the Medal of Honor ceremony was Skip's stepfather, Brenton Alves. A migrant farmworker from Jamaica, Alves had been deported in 1956 for entering the country without legal status and had been living in London ever since. Joyce's petition to reunite the family had been denied at the time because, as an unemployed mother, she could not demonstrate financial support. His absence lingered as a quiet sorrow within the family.

But after Skip received the Medal of Honor, he asked officials if anything could be done to bring his dad home. With his new visibility, the wheels of bureaucracy began to move. The Detroit immigration office revalidated Joyce's original petition, and the State Department approved a permanent visa. On December 24—after twelve years away—Brenton Alves returned to Detroit. A photo of the reunited family ran in the *Detroit Free Press* and other newspapers.

"His return was my Christmas present to my mother," Skip said. "Getting the medal was the proudest moment of my life, but this is the happiest."

Alves was also able to attend Skip and Katrina's wedding, on January 18, 1969. Katrina's grandfather escorted her into Unity Baptist Church, and her father walked her down the aisle. "My father couldn't wait to tell people about his hero son-in-law," Katrina remembered. More than three hundred people attended the cere-

Twelve years after his deportation from the United States, Skip Johnson's stepfather, Brenton Alves, reunites with his family.

mony and the reception at the London Inn Motel, including Congressman John Conyers, who had gone to high school with Katrina's mother. President Johnson and former Michigan Governor George Romney sent congratulatory notes. A local bakery even crafted a replica of the Medal of Honor in confectioners' sugar.

Skip wore a black tuxedo, and Katrina chose a simple white satin A-line gown with long sleeves and a beaded collar. Her bridesmaids wore burgundy velvet dresses. "My mom and I went dress shopping at this little shop out in Dearborn," she recalled. "Some girl had just canceled her wedding, and we got my dress, three bridesmaids' dresses, and a matron of honor dress for two hundred bucks."

Katrina's seven-year-old brother, who served as a junior usher, was crestfallen when he realized his big sister would be moving out.

"I'm married to Skip—I have to go home with him," she explained.

"You've been here all this time," her little brother protested as the newlyweds loaded the moving van. "You might as well stay."

The day after their wedding, Skip and Katrina returned to Washington, DC, as official guests for President Nixon's inauguration. "We did sightseeing and went to one of the inaugural balls," Katrina said. "Basically, that was our honeymoon."

When Skip returned to Detroit, he was celebrated across the city. Local politicians, business leaders, and community groups clamored to associate themselves with him—the first person from Michigan to receive the Medal of Honor during the Vietnam War. The city even temporarily renamed Washington Boulevard "Dwight Johnson Boulevard" in his honor. At first, Skip was flattered by the attention. "It's really ironic that it took winning this medal to really get me going in life," he told *Jet* magazine.

After repeated overtures from military officials, Skip reenlisted for a three-year term as an army recruiter. Instead of going to college to study computer programming as he had hoped, he spent the following months visiting Detroit-area schools, encouraging young people to consider military service. One newspaper described him as "a living recruiting poster."

WHILE SKIP WAS WORKING TO get young men into the military, thousands of other soldiers were openly questioning the war. When Joe Miles, a student activist from Washington, DC, arrived at Fort Jackson, South Carolina, in January 1969, he was struck by the level of political consciousness among other Black GIs. They greeted each other with raised fists and spent their downtime talking about Black Power.

Looking to build on this energy, Miles began organizing informal meetings in the barracks. Soldiers gathered to listen to tapes of Malcolm X's speeches and discuss the war and racism. "People were really listening," Miles recalled. "Malcolm was getting into everybody's mind and doing all kinds of things to them. . . . It was like Malcolm had been made for this kind of audience and we were ready for him."

About fifteen men showed up the first night. By the second meeting, three dozen soldiers packed into the room, listening to recordings of "Message to the Grassroots" and "The Ballot or the Bullet." Malcolm's voice echoed off the concrete floor. "You remember Dien Bien Phu," he urged, reminding them how Vietnamese soldiers had defeated the better-equipped French army. He praised decolonization movements in Asia and Africa and argued that Black Americans faced a similar form of internal colonization. "I'm not a Republican, nor a Democrat, nor an American, and got sense enough to know it," he declared. "I speak as a victim of America's so-called democracy."

"Malcolm X laid his rap so clear and so plain that anyone could understand it," said Andrew Pulley, a Black soldier from Chicago. "We realized as GIs we were being oppressed and exploited more so than any other group of people in the country because we are asked to risk our lives for something we don't believe in."

When a first sergeant announced that no more than eight people could meet inside the barracks—citing concerns about the spread of upper respiratory infections—the men took their meetings outside. Soon, more than a hundred soldiers, including Black, Puerto Rican, and white troops, were gathering regularly to share their views on the war.

Many of them had already served in Vietnam and spoke candidly about how their experiences had changed their thinking. Robert Mall, who fought in Pleiku and Dak To with the 173rd Airborne Brigade, recalled that he initially believed in the war. "I figured it must be the right thing or else we wouldn't be here," he said. By the end of his tour, he felt betrayed. "I can't really see where the Vietnamese are going to come charging under the Golden Gate Bridge," he joked. "I've heard no argument whatsoever that makes any sense why we're in Vietnam. It's a civil war which is strictly the Vietnamese's business."

The group began calling themselves GIs United Against the War in Vietnam. In a statement addressed to fellow soldiers, they wrote: "We, as GIs, are forced to suffer most of all in the Vietnam fiasco. . . . We are forced to fight and die in a war we did not create and in which we don't believe." Determined to stay within legal bounds, they studied the Uniform Code of Military Justice and framed their actions as an exercise in free speech. They petitioned Fort Jackson's commanding general, James Hollingsworth, for the right to hold open meetings to discuss the war, civil rights, and the rights of soldiers. "It is our right to think, and to speak out against an unjust war, to demonstrate our opposition if that is necessary," they declared. "We are citizens of America even if the Army would like to forget it, and these rights are guaranteed to us by the Constitution of the United States."

The army disagreed. After a GIs United meeting on the night of March 20, officials arrested a group of soldiers on charges including "breach of the peace," "inciting to riot," and "disrespect to an officer," placing them in the stockade. The GI Civil Liberties Defense Committee, a New York–based group supporting antiwar soldiers, took up the case of the "Fort Jackson Eight." National magazines and newspapers covered the arrests, and their stories spread through a growing network of antiwar coffeehouses near military bases—places like UFO, near Fort Jackson in Columbia, South Carolina; the Oleo Strut, near Fort Hood in Killeen, Texas; and Mad Anthony Wayne's, near Fort Leonard Wood in Waynesville, Missouri.

After two months of legal maneuvering and mounting public pressure, the army dropped the charges. The men were released from the stockade and given less-than-honorable discharges rather than face trial. Matilde Zimmerman, national secretary of the GI Civil Liberties Defense Committee, called the decision "the most important victory to date of the GI antiwar movement."

In response to rising dissent within the ranks, the army issued a five-page directive in May 1969. It instructed commanding officers that soldiers, like civilians, retained the "right to express opinions on matters of public and personal concern." Underground newspapers and protest activity were to be tolerated, so long as they did not interfere with military discipline, morale, or operational effectiveness. Surveying the widening defiance, *The Washington Post* observed that "the military reservation is fast becoming the newest battleground for youthful rebellion."

OPPOSITION TO THE WAR weighed heavily on Skip's mind as he began to work as a military recruiter. One of his first assignments was to visit his alma mater, Northwestern High School. Like many other Black high schools, Northwestern had grown more militant in recent months. In late February 1969, students hoisted a red, black, and green liberation banner on the school's flagpole and repainted the World War II–era cannon out front in the same Black nationalist colors. They declared that Northwestern would now be known as Malcolm X High—a proposal the school board quickly dismissed. Skip worried that the students, just a few years younger than he was, would boo him and call him an "Uncle Tom." He was relieved when their reception was more curious than confrontational.

Still, not everyone was welcoming. One student sent a letter to the editor of the *Michigan Chronicle* expressing concern. "We object to the Army using Sgt. Johnson and his brave deeds to entice black youth to enlist," the letter read. "He is being used to make an evil war appear good, glamourous, heroic, and palatable to the black community." The writer urged peers to read what Martin Luther

King had said about Vietnam. Even when school audiences greeted him warmly, Skip could sense a quiet unease among many students.

The mood was more celebratory on February 18, 1969, when the Detroit Chamber of Commerce hosted a fifteen-dollar-a-plate banquet in his honor at Cobo Hall. More than twelve hundred people attended. Skip sat at the head table alongside eight other Michigan veterans—all white—who had earned the Medal of Honor in previous wars. He listened as dignitaries including Detroit Mayor Jerome Cavanagh, Michigan Governor William Milliken, General William Westmoreland, and Ford Motor Company President Semon Knudsen praised his valor. With Detroit and the nation still reeling from war, riots, and racial strife, the speakers tried to fold Skip's story into a broader narrative of unity and hope.

Not only was Detroit "honoring Sgt. Johnson," Mayor Cavanagh said, "but through him the other American servicemen who have fought so bravely and steadfastly." Governor Milliken, refer-

Civic tribute to Skip Johnson on February 18, 1969, cosponsored by *The Detroit News* and the Greater Detroit Chamber of Commerce

encing the city's recent riots, warned that a house divided cannot stand. "We are aware that the American position abroad and the commitments that Dwight Johnson fought to honor will not be secure unless we can keep our own house in order," he said. "I can assure you that we are determined to work together to make your fight worthwhile."

General Westmoreland, who had commanded US forces during Skip's tour in Vietnam and now served as chief of staff of the army, offered a sweeping assessment of the war. Sergeant Johnson had earned a "special permanent place in the annals of history," he declared. "Acts of great bravery are common in Vietnam," Westmoreland argued, and because of them, "we are in a position of undeniable strength on the battlefield. Therefore, and fortunately, our negotiators can talk at the table in Paris from a position of strength." His optimism was increasingly out of step with public opinion; the latest Gallup poll showed that a majority of Americans believed the United States had made a mistake in sending troops to Vietnam.

Skip was seated next to Harold Furlong, a seventy-five-year-old obstetrician from Pontiac, Michigan. Half a century earlier, during World War I, Furlong had crawled across an open field in Bantheville, France, and single-handedly taken out four German machine gun nests. He understood the burden Medal of Honor recipients carried. When asked if he had any advice for the soldier at his side, Furlong said simply, "He's a marked man, much more is expected of him now."

After more than an hour of tributes, Skip rose and approached the microphone. The room fell silent. Katrina, seated with the wives of the other speakers, could see how nervous he was. Young

Black men raised in the projects didn't often make it into venues like this—much less to the podium.

"Only God and myself know how I feel tonight," Skip said. He spoke so quietly that even those at the head table had to lean in to catch his words. "From the bottom of my heart, thank you, Detroit." When he stepped away, the crowd stood in applause.

MORATORIUM

Coretta stood before a crowd of nearly thirty-five thousand gathered at the outdoor Sylvan Theater in Washington, DC, on October 15, 1969. "I see this war as an enemy of black and poor people," she told them. "More than 40,000 of our people have given their lives as sacrificial lambs to a godless cause." She added that her eldest son, just days shy of his twelfth birthday, had already decided he "will not give his life on such a sacrificial altar."

The air was cool and crisp, the sky fading into a brilliant autumn sunset. Coretta's voice—measured, resolute—carried across the slope leading up to the Washington Monument, amplified by loudspeakers. Vietnam was not just a distant war, she warned—it was unraveling "the very fabric and fiber" of the country. "The only solution is to bring the boys home and bring them home now," she declared, as the crowd erupted in applause.

At twilight, she led a candlelight march to the White House. Dressed in a black overcoat and white hat, she moved steadily at the

Coretta Scott King leads a march to the White House as part of the
Moratorium to End the War in Vietnam on October 15, 1969.

front of the procession, her silhouette bobbing gently in the glow of
flashlights.

Marshals lined the route, guiding the hushed crowd up Seven-
teenth Street and along Pennsylvania Avenue. When a Justice Department official suggested that buses be used to block the marchers
and divert them down Constitution Avenue, Mayor Walter Washington refused. "Are you prepared to tear gas Mrs. King when she
climbs over the front of one of the buses?" he snapped. When
Coretta reached the White House, she lit a large candle, while
around her, the marchers softly sang "This Land Is Your Land" and
"We Shall Overcome."

The windows of the White House were dark, though President
Nixon was inside. Press Secretary Ron Ziegler noted dryly that the
president was "obviously aware" of the protest and the sea of can-

dles flickering in the night breeze. "It will probably be his worst day in office to date," *The Globe and Mail* opined. "Hundreds of thousands of his countrymen publicly demonstrated their dissatisfaction with the slow progress of what Mr. Nixon not more than a month ago considered one of his glowing achievements—moves toward ending the War in Vietnam."

Coretta's candlelight march was the centerpiece of a national Moratorium to End the War in Vietnam, held on October 15. More than two million people participated in rallies, vigils, memorials, and teach-ins across the country—at college campuses, in churches, and in public squares. These were not radicals but ordinary citizens, fed up with a war that seemed endless. It was the largest cascade of dissent in American history.

Mass protests do not emerge from thin air. They require months of organizing and, just as crucially, a figure who can galvanize people into action. Coretta was that force. In the eighteen months since her husband's assassination, she had crisscrossed the globe, urging world leaders and everyday Americans to join the cause for peace. Each speech, every stop on her calendar, and the media coverage that followed gave her another chance to shift public opinion.

CORETTA BEGAN 1969 with an eleven-day trip to Italy and India to receive humanitarian awards. She met with Pope Paul VI at the Vatican and was hosted by Indian President Zakir Husain and Prime Minister Indira Gandhi. "If mankind wishes to survive, it must begin traveling the road to peace," Coretta said during a speech in Verona, Italy. "I pray this spirit will pervade the Vietnam peace talks."

After arriving in India, she listened to a recording of President Nixon's inaugural address and was struck by moments that suggested antiwar activists were making inroads at the White House. "For the first time, because the people of the world want peace, and the leaders of the world are afraid of war, the times are on the side of peace," Nixon had said. "The greatest honor history can bestow is the title of peacemaker. This honor now beckons America." Coretta hoped his words were more than empty platitudes.

On February 5, she was back in Washington, DC, where she led five hundred people in a march from the Metropolitan African Methodist Episcopal Church to the Justice Department. Carrying a bouquet of purple chrysanthemums, Coretta was joined by several prominent religious leaders: Rabbi Abraham Heschel of the Jewish Theological Seminary in Manhattan; Rev. Richard John Neuhaus, pastor of St. John the Evangelist Lutheran Church in Brooklyn; Rev. William Sloane Coffin, the Yale University chaplain who had been arrested the prior year for aiding draft resisters; and Rev. Richard Fernandez, director of Clergy and Laymen Concerned About Vietnam, the antiwar religious group sponsoring the rally. Once again, Coretta stood out—not only as the sole woman and the only Black person among the rally's leaders, but as the activist who most powerfully bridged the peace and civil rights movements.

Outside the Justice Department, Coretta told the crowd that Americans needed the wisdom to admit that "we are not the world's policeman." She rejected the false choice between continuing the Vietnam War and supporting domestic programs. "I do not want guns—with or without butter," she declared. "I want our vast resources used to rescue black people from slow death and systematic self-destruction."

That afternoon, Coretta and the religious leaders met at the White House with Henry Kissinger, President Nixon's national security adviser. The group pressed Kissinger on the disconnect between Nixon's lofty rhetoric and his administration's lack of a clear path toward peace. They called for amnesty for imprisoned draft resisters and exiled military deserters, and questioned the harsh sentences handed down to the Presidio Twenty-Seven, a group of soldiers who staged a protest in the army stockade in San Francisco. Reverend Coffin said Kissinger gave the group a "very respectful hearing" but remained noncommittal on every point they raised.

By the time Nixon entered the White House, US military involvement in Vietnam had already stretched across multiple presidencies. With each new administration, the war expanded in both scale and futility. On the campaign trail, Nixon promised that "new leadership will end the war and win the peace in the Pacific," but he was deliberately vague about how he intended to do so. In the early weeks of his presidency, as American combat deaths neared the total from the prior year's Tet Offensive, his administration offered little clarity about either military strategy or the peace negotiations underway in Paris between US officials, the North and South Vietnamese governments, and representatives from the Vietcong. American citizens were left to wonder why hundreds of US troops were still dying each week.

Sensing this frustration, Coretta joined the religious leaders in penning an open letter to Nixon, urging him to make a clear public statement on America's intentions in Vietnam. "We fear the time is approaching, Mr. President, when we must declare your Administration accountable for the continued suffering and death in Vietnam," the letter stated. Clergy and Laymen Concerned About

Vietnam followed up with a full-page advertisement in *The New York Times*, arguing that Nixon bore responsibility "for what is happening in Vietnam—and for what is not happening in Paris" at the negotiating table. In the months that followed, Nixon escalated military pressure, authorizing covert B-52 bombings of North Vietnamese bases in Cambodia.

On March 14, Coretta traveled to London, where she became the first woman to preach during Sunday service at St. Paul's Cathedral, whose history traced back to the first church founded on the site in 604. Her two oldest children—thirteen-year-old Yolanda and eleven-year-old Martin—accompanied her, along with her sister, Edythe Bagley, and assistant Bernita Bennette. Coretta had listened to Martin speak at St. Paul's in 1964, shortly before he received the Nobel Prize. As she slowly ascended the stairs to the elevated pulpit and looked out at the three thousand people filling the ornate cathedral, she was comforted by the sight of her loved ones and felt Martin's spirit with her.

"For too long, we have seen the ministry of the church as a mission to the individual," she said. "The mission of the church must be to set at liberty those who are oppressed." Citing the British economist Barbara Ward, Coretta described a "revolution of rising expectations" heralding a new era. The thirty billion dollars a year America spent on the Vietnam War, she said, could instead be used to cure disease or raise people out of poverty. Instead, it was used to create captives. "We must release the captives whether they are in Vietnam, South Africa, or South America," she said. She likened napalm, defoliates, and nuclear weapons to the seven deadly sins, concluding, "Ultimately the power of the spirit is greater than the power of the sword."

When Coretta returned home from London, she turned her attention to the first anniversary of Martin's death. Thousands of people gathered for memorial services across the country, including in Memphis, Washington, DC, Boston, Selma, Chicago, Nashville, and dozens of other cities. In New York, two dozen women met at daybreak in Foley Square in Lower Manhattan and placed 312 crosses in the small park—one for each American soldier killed in Vietnam the previous week.

In Atlanta, Coretta visited Martin's grave at South View Cemetery with her four children, Martin's father, his sister, and other relatives. She placed a red-and-white flower cross on the marble tomb, then paused for a photo with a group of schoolchildren who had traveled from New Orleans for the memorial. A couple hundred people held a vigil downtown at the Georgia State Capitol, some carrying signs that read "Make King's Dream a Reality—End War, Poverty and Racism."

Despite the national outpouring of grief and remembrance, President Nixon remained at the Winter White House, his vacation home in Key Biscayne, Florida. His adviser and speechwriter Patrick Buchanan advised against visiting "the Widow King" in Atlanta, arguing that it would "outrage many, many people who believe Dr. King was a fraud and a demagogue and perhaps worse." Buchanan warned that there would be "no long-run gains and considerable long-run risks in making a public visit." He concluded that there were "thousands of other ways and means to communicate the president's beliefs with black Americans without paying tribute to a figure who alienates and angers so many whites." Instead, Nixon sent Robert Finch, Secretary of Health, Education, and Welfare, to Atlanta to deliver a note of sympathy to Coretta.

On Easter Sunday, Coretta attended services at Ebenezer Baptist Church with Daddy King and other family members. Afterward, Ralph Abernathy, Martin's successor as president of the Southern Christian Leadership Conference, led a "Black Easter" march to nearby Hurt Park. The protest was one of several large GI-civilian antiwar demonstrations held that weekend, with tens of thousands taking to the streets of New York, Chicago, Los Angeles, San Francisco, and Seattle.

Two dozen soldiers from Fort Gordon traveled from Augusta to join the Atlanta march. A twenty-one-year-old GI who had recently returned from Vietnam said he was especially worried because his younger brother was still there. "I can't accept what the Army is doing," he said. "Killing is not right. My father's a mortician and death is very final." One soldier from Fort Jackson made the two-hundred-mile journey to Atlanta to rally support for the Fort Jackson Eight and GIs United Against the War. "Let us save America by ending the war in Vietnam," Abernathy shouted at the rally.

Coretta was in constant motion through the winter and spring of 1969, building bridges between antiwar activists and broader social movements. Twenty-five hundred people filled Yale's Woolsey Hall, where she praised student activists who "dare to struggle to right wrongs," adding that "there is nothing wrong in a stance against war and unadulterated racism." Speaking just before Julian Bond at the annual meeting of the American Orthopsychiatric Association, she warned that America's spending on war was mortgaging the future of Black and working-class children. "We cannot give a few-billion-dollar plan the pompous exaggerated title of an antipoverty program," she said. "A coat of paint on a crumbling house is not radical reconstruction."

A couple of months later, Coretta joined Jesse Jackson as a featured speaker at the National Beauty Culturists' League's fiftieth annual convention in Philadelphia. The group's president, Katie E. Whickam—a successful New Orleans entrepreneur and SCLC committee member—had been holding voter registration workshops at her business, Katie's School of Beauty Culture and Barbering, for more than a decade. After introducing Coretta as "the queen of the black women of the world," Whickam took her seat as Coretta addressed the thousand-person audience. She encouraged them to follow Whickam's lead and "engage in social and political action and education." "After all," Coretta added with a smile, "who talks to more women than a beautician?"

Returning to themes that had animated her recent speeches, she criticized the misplaced priorities of both the Nixon and Johnson administrations. "What kind of country are we living in," she asked, "that can spend $33 billion to put a man on the moon but cannot feed people? What kind of country can spend billions of dollars on an unjust and immoral war in Vietnam but can only spend a pittance to fight a war against poverty?"

IN A YEAR when opposition to the war surged, no one reached a broader cross section of Americans than Coretta. Her tireless efforts paid off. Beauticians, psychiatrists, nurses, and college students joined young radicals, housewives, senior citizens, and GIs at Vietnam Moratorium protests on October 15, 1969. "America has confronted its conscience," the journalist Robert Hey wrote in *The Christian Science Monitor* after the largest antiwar demonstrations in the nation's history. "What, it has asked, should we do about Vietnam?"

Coretta answered that question from the stage at the Sylvan Theater in DC. The only option, she declared, was to end the war now. "The war has destroyed the hopes of black and poor Americans and Americans in general," she said. It had damaged the nation's standing abroad, giving potential allies in Asia, Africa, and Latin America little reason to trust America's intentions. "They surely see us not as promoters of freedom and democracy, but as the purveyors of violence and militarism," she warned.

As the sun set, marshals distributed tens of thousands of candles. Protesters held them in cupped hands, shielding the flames from the brisk autumn wind.

Inside the White House, William Watts, a young assistant to Henry Kissinger, was working on a draft of the president's upcoming address when he caught sight of Coretta leading the flickering river of marchers. He stepped outside toward the gate—and spotted his wife and children among the demonstrators, candles glowing in their hands. "I felt like throwing up," Watts said. "There they are demonstrating against me, and here I am inside writing a speech."

President Nixon, too, was drafting his remarks—scribbling, as always, on yellow legal pads. "Don't get rattled—don't waver—don't react," he wrote in the margins.

If the march shook President Nixon, it propelled Coretta. Writing in *The Chicago Defender* after the protest, Ethel Payne called her the "most prestigious leader of the opposition and the country's most important woman." The Moratorium drew extended coverage on nightly television news, with both CBS and NBC airing hour-long specials. *The New York Times*, *The Washington Post*, *Life*, and hundreds of local newspapers featured images from the march, most placing Coretta prominently at the center of the outpouring of dissent. *Newsweek* declared October 15 "a day destined to go down in history," while *Time* noted that the protests demonstrated "a diversity and spread unknown in the earlier landmark protests against the war," bringing "new respectability and popularity" into the movement. "Nixon cannot escape the effects of the antiwar movement," *Time* concluded. "Unless he can assert new leadership and rally much of the nation in some unforeseen way, Nixon's time-table for a withdrawal from Viet Nam will surely have to be speeded up."

The power of the Moratorium lay in the extraordinary breadth of participation. Two miles northeast of the White House, Howard University students rallied outside Frederick Douglass Hall. "There is not now and can be no justification for black participation in the war in Vietnam," declared the student leader Irving Ray. "Our fight is here. . . . America is the black man's battle ground." In Baltimore, faculty at Morgan State University canceled classes, and student leaders echoed the sentiment: "Our black brothers in Vietnam are becoming increasingly aware that this brutal war is nothing more than racial genocide."

Students in the Philadelphia area canvassed the suburbs, knock-ing on doors and saying, "Hello, ma'am. I'd like to talk with you before I die in Vietnam." At Stanford University, students boarded commuter trains to hold teach-ins with businessmen en route to San Francisco. Bankers in New York participated in a daylong ser-vice at Trinity Church, near Wall Street. In Youngstown, Ohio, seventy-six crosses were arranged neatly in a park—one for each local man killed in Vietnam. Nearly three thousand people gath-ered outside a federal courthouse in Lexington, Kentucky, to read the names of the state's war dead. "This is my son," a middle-aged woman said sadly into the microphone after reading one name. "He was killed last week."

While the New York Mets and Baltimore Orioles faced off in game 4 of the World Series, protesters handed out antiwar pamphlets to fans entering Shea Stadium. Overhead, two skywriting planes etched a peace symbol into the sky. One demonstrator held a sign reading "Bomb the birds, not the peasants."

In Lexington, Massachusetts, protesters rallied on the Battle Green, where the first shots of the American Revolutionary War were fired. Massachusetts Governor Francis Sargent, who had fought with the Tenth Mountain Division in Italy during World War II, addressed the crowd. When a group of pro-war teenagers heckled him, Sargent shouted back, "Listen to me, I know the war, and you never will know war. This war is costing America its soul."

Newspapers tallied Moratorium march estimates from across the country: Albuquerque (three thousand), Boston (one hundred thousand), Burlington (four thousand), Denver (thirty-five hundred), Detroit (twelve thousand), Minneapolis (ten thousand).

Even Whitney Young, the executive director of the Urban League—who had previously criticized the Kings' antiwar activism as a distraction from civil rights—changed his mind. His daughter joined fellow students at Bryn Mawr College in a hunger strike to protest the war. Young called Vietnam a "moral and spiritual drain" and admitted, "Dr. King was probably more right than I was, because it is hard to separate the war from domestic problems in terms of the resources of the country and the manpower."

Still, most moderate and liberal politicians remained reluctant to publicly denounce the war or align themselves with the peace movement. Senators who called for an immediate withdrawal of troops and an end to bombing—like George McGovern of South Dakota, Frank Church of Idaho, William Fulbright of Arkansas, and Harold Hughes of Iowa—were the exception, not the rule.

Conservative politicians, on the other hand, were vocal critics of the Moratorium. "We have a right to suspect that at least some of those who arrange the parades are less concerned with peace than with lending comfort and aid to the enemy," said California Governor Ronald Reagan. Virginia Governor Mills Godwin called the protests a "travesty upon the sacrifices of patriotic Americans." Arizona Senator Barry Goldwater, newly returned to the Senate, said the demonstrators "are playing into the hands of the people whose business it is to kill American fighting men." A spokesman for the far-right John Birch Society went even further: "We feel the moratorium is an act of treason."

Americans who supported the war expressed their views in symbolic acts: leaving porch lights and car headlights on during the day, affixing miniature US flags to mailboxes and car antennas, and wearing red, white, and blue clothing. In New York City, police and firefighters defied Mayor John Lindsay's order to lower flags on public buildings to half-staff in recognition of a national day of mourning over the war. "On city flagpoles, the national emblem was going down and up with bewildering speed," noted *The New York Times*.

PRESIDENT NIXON INSISTED he would remain unmoved by the Moratorium, arguing that the two million or so Americans who protested on October 15 represented a minority view on the war.

His aim, he said, was "to bring the war in Vietnam to an end in a way that will be a lasting peace."

But that goal seemed distant as the war's toll mounted during Nixon's first year in office. While military leaders touted high enemy "body counts" and favorable "kill ratios," more than eleven thousand American troops were killed in 1969—pushing total US combat deaths in Vietnam past the number lost in the Korean War. In February, on the first anniversary of the Tet Offensive, the People's Army of Vietnam (PAVN) and Vietcong staged coordinated attacks on US military bases in Saigon, Da Nang, and other sites across South Vietnam.

In July, US commanders ordered repeated assaults on Hill 937, a lone peak near the border with Laos in central Vietnam. Dozens of American troops were killed and hundreds wounded fighting their way to the summit—only to abandon it days later. The mountain held little strategic value, and soldiers openly questioned the logic of a strategy that yielded such high casualties. "Have you ever been inside a hamburger machine?" nineteen-year-old Sgt. James Spears asked a reporter, searching for words to describe the battle. "We just got cut to pieces by extremely accurate machine gun fire."

Life magazine published the final letter of a young soldier who died at Hamburger Hill. "You may not be able to read this," he wrote to his parents. "I am writing it in a hurry. I see death coming up the hill." The letter appeared in the June issue of *Life* alongside portraits of 241 US soldiers killed in one week of combat—a visual chronicle of the anguish that touched cities and towns across the country.

While Nixon recognized that the war needed to end, he was determined to end it in a way that protected his political future. He attempted to thread this needle in a televised address to the nation on November 3, 1969. "Let us all understand that the question before us is not whether some Americans are for peace and some Americans are against peace," he said. "The question at issue is not whether Johnson's war becomes Nixon's war. The great question is: How can we win America's peace?" Nixon briefly reviewed how the Eisenhower, Kennedy, and Johnson administrations had approached foreign policy in Southeast Asia. He then reiterated his commitment to "Vietnamization"—a plan to gradually reduce the number of US combat troops while expanding equipment and training so South Vietnamese forces could take on a larger share of the fighting.

The president expressed sorrow over having to sign eighty-three condolence letters that week to the families of US troops killed in Vietnam. While acknowledging the right of protesters to voice dissent, he insisted, "I would be untrue to my oath of office if I allowed the policy of this Nation to be dictated by the minority who hold that point of view and who try to impose it on the Nation by mounting demonstrations in the street."

Most Americans, he claimed, supported continuing the fighting. "And so tonight—to you, the great silent majority of my fellow Americans—I ask for your support," he said. "Let us be united for peace. Let us also be united against defeat. Because let us understand: North Vietnam cannot defeat or humiliate the United States. Only Americans can do that."

The next day, Nixon proudly welcomed reporters, photographers, and television cameras into the Oval Office, where supportive telegrams were stacked on his desk—a show of public approval, he said, for his Vietnam policy. As his poll numbers climbed, Nixon bragged to aides, "We've got those liberal bastards on the run now, and we're going to keep them on the run."

The president had barely finished his speech before reporters began calling Coretta for her response. "It is hard to escape the impression that President Nixon is trying to end the massive opposition to the war rather than seeking to end the war itself," she argued. She said the president's speech strengthened her resolve and would serve as further motivation for the second Moratorium rally, scheduled for mid-November in Washington, DC.

Amid Justice Department reports that the Weathermen—a militant faction of Students for a Democratic Society—were planning to vandalize Washington's business district, Coretta said that the protests would be peaceful. "These predictions of violence remind me of the civil rights march in 1963," she said. "There was so much talk of violence then, but it never occurred." She contended that government officials were spreading rumors of violence to intimidate people and suppress turnout. "If the government can keep people away, then they can say that people are satisfied and that they won't really want to end the war."

ON NOVEMBER 15, 1969, half a million people rallied in Washington, DC, the climax of three days of antiwar protests in the capital and across the country. The front pages of *The New York Times* and *The Washington Post* declared that the demonstration was larger than the March on Washington for Jobs and Freedom six years earlier. Young marchers carried wooden coffins bearing the names of US war dead, followed by banners reading "Silent Majority for Peace" and "We're here because we love our country." Three drummers beat a solemn funeral cadence. Thousands of marshals—trained in nonviolence by Pennsylvania Quakers—lined the route, linking arms when radical contingents carrying Vietcong flags tried to break through the march lines. Several hundred paratroopers with rifles stood in formation in the inner courts of the Justice Department and Pentagon, prepared for large-scale violence that never materialized.

Coretta marched to the Washington Monument alongside Minnesota Senator Eugene McCarthy, National Welfare Rights Organization Director George Wiley, and New York Senator Charles Goodell, the most prominent antiwar voice in the Republican Party.

Nixon had spent the prior week on Capitol Hill, praising congressmen who supported his Vietnam policy and cajoling those who did not. Goodell knew that opposing the president on the war would almost certainly cost him his political career.

Coretta Scott King walks arm in arm with antiwar advocates,
including Senators Charles Goodell and George McGovern,
at a march to the Washington Monument.

"We are not here to break a President," Goodell said. "We are here to break the war and begin the peace." A Korean War veteran, Goodell had initially supported the war in Vietnam. But conversations with his young congressional staffers—many of whom were weighing whether to flee to Canada—changed his mind. "We are told that a United States pullout would result in a bloodbath in South Vietnam," he said at the rally. "What in the world has been going on for the last six and a half years if not a bloodbath?"

Coretta stepped to the podium wearing a white wool coat and black hat to keep warm on the crisp fall day. "We have been told we cannot afford the humiliation of withdrawal," she said. "I feel that even less can we afford the humiliation of pursuing a war for ignoble ends." The crowd erupted in cheers as she concluded her remarks. If these antiwar voices were not yet the majority, Coretta was determined they soon would be.

President Nixon, for his part, insisted publicly that the protests had no influence on his foreign policy. He made sure reporters knew that, while the largest demonstration in the capital's history was underway, he was inside the White House watching college football. That afternoon, he even called Ohio State coach Woody Hayes to congratulate him on the Buckeyes' 42–14 victory over Purdue.

Privately, the massive antiwar protests Coretta led in the fall of 1969 unsettled Nixon and disrupted his plans. "He was totally absorbed," recalled Daniel Ellsberg, a military analyst at the Pentagon. "Every 10 minutes he was calling the Situation Room and finding out what was going on, getting reports from the U-2s on crowd size." Nixon and his advisers closely monitored public opinion, seeing strong public support as essential to their negotiating leverage with Hanoi. That July, Nixon and Kissinger warned North Vietnamese leaders they would face "measures of great consequence and force" if they failed to accept American peace terms by a November 1 deadline. Kissinger oversaw a group of Pentagon and National Security Council advisers who drafted plans—codenamed "Duck Hook"—to escalate the war through intensified aerial bombing, the mining of North Vietnamese harbors, and, potentially, the use of "tactical" nuclear weapons. Nixon envisioned these as "savage, punishing blows" that would bring the conflict to a decisive close—which is why he cared so deeply about public opinion.

"In the weeks remaining before November 1, I wanted to orchestrate the maximum possible pressure on Hanoi," Nixon wrote in his memoirs. "I was confident that we could bring sufficient pressure to bear on the diplomatic front. But the only chance for my ultimatum to succeed was to convince the Communists that I could depend on solid support at home if they decided to call my bluff." With the immense, highly publicized Moratorium protests on October 15 and November 15 bookending that deadline, Nixon acknowledged that the chances of widespread public backing "were becoming increasingly slim." By year's end, 58 percent of Americans said they believed the United States had made a mistake sending troops to fight in Vietnam.

Coretta had achieved a monumental victory. She was the most visible leader of the two largest protest days in American history, giving countless ordinary citizens the courage to confront their own government. More work lay ahead to end the war and bring home the 475,000 US troops still stationed in Southeast Asia.

"NOBODY'S A
HERO FOREVER"

t was the week of Thanksgiving 1969, and Skip and Katrina had much to be grateful for. Beyond Skip's accolades, the couple had welcomed their first child, Dwight Christopher, in July. In October, they signed the mortgage on their first home, a modest bungalow on Allonby Street and Schaefer Road in northwest Detroit. A new decade—and new possibilities—lay on the horizon.

They were also thankful for simple things, like sitting down to dinner together. After months of banquets and formal receptions in Skip's honor, the comfort of a home-cooked meal at their own table felt like a celebration.

That chilly November evening, Katrina worked to settle the baby while Skip turned on the nightly news. Back at Fort Knox, he had entertained his army buddies with a deadpan impression of CBS anchor Walter Cronkite's famous sign-off: "And that's the way it is." But there was little to laugh about these days. The war dominated every broadcast.

Like millions of Americans, Skip was horrified to learn about the massacre of hundreds of unarmed Vietnamese civilians in the hamlet of My Lai, carried out by US troops. The freelance journalist Seymour Hersh broke the story on November 12, just days before the second massive Moratorium protest in Washington, DC. While the army opened an investigation, television and newspaper journalists tried to make sense of the atrocity.

On November 24, CBS correspondent Mike Wallace interviewed Paul Meadlo, a twenty-year-old private who admitted he and others had followed orders from platoon leader Lieutenant William Calley to round up and shoot villagers.

WALLACE: You're married?

MEADLO: Right.

WALLACE: Children?

MEADLO: Two.

WALLACE: How old?

MEADLO: The boy is two and a half and the little girl is a year and a half.

WALLACE: Obviously, the question comes to my mind . . . the father of two little kids like that . . . how can he shoot babies?

MEADLO: I don't know. It's just one of them things.

WALLACE: How many people do you imagine were killed that day?

MEADLO: I'd say about 370.

Meadlo estimated that he personally killed between ten and fifteen people at My Lai and told Wallace that he could still see the faces of the women and children in his dreams. "It's been on my conscience and it's going to stay on my conscience for the rest of my life." The day after the massacre, Meadlo stepped on a mine that blew off his right foot. He believed it was divine retribution.

"I raised my son to be kind and thoughtful," Meadlo's mother told Wallace, speaking from the family's farmhouse in rural Indiana. "I sent them a good boy and they made him a murderer."

Watching the interview on television, Skip felt a knot form in his stomach. He, too, had nightmares. Fragmented memories of the firefight in Dak To replayed in his head. The dull click of the enemy's gun misfiring still startled him awake. While the men he killed during the ambush had been armed soldiers, he understood what it meant to do things that could not be undone, to see things that could not be unseen.

Skip's hometown newspaper drew connections between the My Lai massacre and violence against Black Americans. Brutality against civilians was "business as usual," wrote the *Michigan Chronicle* columnist Bill Black. Americans outraged by atrocities in Vietnam, he argued, needed to understand the history of lynchings, the "Red Summer" of 1919, the bombing of the Sixteenth Street Baptist Church in Birmingham, and the murders of civil rights activists Medgar Evers and Vernon Dahmer. In Detroit, Black wrote, "the stench remains" from the death of four-year-old Tanya Blanding—killed when the Michigan National Guard fired a barrage of bullets into her parents' apartment during the 1967 riots—as well as the killings of three Black teenagers at the Algiers Motel by police officers. "Listen," Black concluded, "to the silence of the more than 39,000 Americans, black and white, who have died in this terribly dirty war that all the bombs, napalm and M-16s in the world can never win."

In the months before and after the My Lai story broke, news leaked that the United States had been conducting bombing campaigns in Cambodia and Laos—both sovereign and officially neutral countries—since the mid-1960s. Furious at the disclosure, the Nixon administration initiated a program of illegal surveillance targeting members of both the press and the government. Then, in April 1970, President Nixon's announcement that American ground troops were invading Cambodia prompted intense backlash from Congress and the antiwar movement. Thousands of college students staged protests on campuses across the country. On May 4, National Guardsmen killed four unarmed students and wounded nine others at Kent State University in Ohio. Eleven days later, at Jackson State University in Mississippi, police opened fire on a group of students gathered in front of a dormitory, injuring a dozen people and killing a twenty-one-year-old prelaw student and a seventeen-year-old high school student.

Coretta joined seventy-five thousand demonstrators who jammed the Ellipse behind the White House to express their outrage at the eruptions of state violence at home and abroad. "Our society is critically ill when the president of the United States can escalate and expand an illegal, immoral and unjust war," she told students at Morgan State College later that month. "Our country is close to becoming a fascist state where no redress is permitted."

Days later, Skip read a report in the *Michigan Chronicle* that the first soldier from Detroit had been killed in Cambodia. Everett

Brocks, a twenty-seven-year-old staff sergeant, had enlisted in the army in 1964 and planned to end his military career after his latest tour. His vehicle struck a mine not long after crossing the Cambodian border. He left behind a wife and two young sons.

ALL OF THIS MADE Skip feel increasingly uneasy about his job as a military recruiter. He tried to throw himself into fatherhood. He would wake up early with baby Christopher and drive to visit his mother and mother-in-law. "He was the best dad," Katrina remembered. "Just a big kid at heart."

Still, Katrina noticed changes in her husband in the months after the My Lai massacre was reported. "Skip had always been an easygoing, happy-go-lucky type," she recalled. "Nothing ever seemed to bother him, then eventually everything started to bother him." He would wake up screaming and sometimes vomit in his sleep. His daily behavior became erratic. "We'd be watching television, and he'd get into a really quiet mode," she said. "Then he'd get angry and almost just lose it. It was frightening, although I was always more afraid for Skip than I was of him."

After the initial wave of adulation for the Medal of Honor, Katrina began to worry that Skip was being used. "It was a dog and pony show," she said of the banquet circuit. The Ford Corporation, the American Legion, the Lions Club, the Rotary, politicians, and businessmen all wanted to bask in the reflected glory of the medal. "Dwight was a hot property back in those days, I was getting calls for him all over the state," recalled Charles Bielak, a civilian information officer in the army's Detroit recruiting center. Friends and acquaintances mistakenly assumed the honor came with a financial windfall, expecting Skip to pick up the check at dinner or lend them money. "People were trying to suck him dry," Katrina recalled.

Going out for a meal or a drink could be an ordeal—an experience shared by other Medal of Honor recipients. "It makes you a target for every jealous freak around," said Ken Stumpf, who received the Medal of Honor a couple of months before Skip. "If I walk into a bar with 10 guys there, and I say hello to nine of them, the one fellow I missed will sure as hell get hot about it and start something." Gary Wetzel, who stood beside Skip at the White House ceremony, later told a reporter, "Sometimes I wish I hadn't won the Medal."

Skip was reluctant to talk about what he was experiencing, even with Katrina. "My husband was sick at the time, mentally and physically," she recalled. She encouraged him to see a doctor and to tell his army recruiting commanders that he needed help. When he did, he felt his concerns were dismissed. "He was reaching out, asking for help, but the people he was asking were too busy trying to display and exploit him," she said. "The military refused to believe he needed help because they wanted him to be their token hero."

Skip began missing work and speaking engagements. "It got so I had to pick him up myself and deliver him to a public appearance," recalled Bielak, his recruiting colleague. "I had to handcuff myself to the guy to get him someplace. It was embarrassing. I couldn't understand his attitude." At one point, Skip bought a cast from a novelty store and claimed he had fractured his arm—just to have an excuse to avoid his recruiting job. "He didn't know how to break away," Katrina said.

AMID THE JOYS and strains of caring for their baby boy, Katrina came to a painful realization: The funny, caring man she fell in love with was no longer there. "He had turned from a loving husband and father into a real demon," she said. "He became a person I never knew." Once, after a minor argument, Skip lunged at her in a fit of rage.

The next day, Skip checked himself into the hospital at Selfridge Air Force Base, outside Detroit. Doctors diagnosed him with bleeding ulcers and transferred him to Valley Forge Army Hospital in Pennsylvania in September 1970. The hospital sprawled across multiple acres, with several miles of corridors connected by arcades and sheltered walkways. Oak floors creaked as veterans in wheelchairs and wounded soldiers on crutches navigated the mazelike facility.

"The first day Dwight arrived here, the hospital's sergeant major brought him to us," recalled Specialist Herman Avery, who headed the ward where Skip was initially assigned. "It was the first time the sergeant major ever did that. We got the message. This guy was something special."

The next day, the sergeant major had Skip change out of his hospital-issue blue denims into an army dress blue uniform and took him to shake hands at a Freedoms Foundation event at the Medal of Honor Grove, adjacent to Valley Forge National Park. Skip was livid. He said if that ever happened again, he would go AWOL.

Skip spent a month at Valley Forge before returning to Detroit in mid-October on a thirty-day convalescent leave. Not long after he got back, he walked into the offices of the *Michigan Chronicle*. Aretha Watkins, the assistant managing editor who regularly covered veterans' issues, recognized him immediately. Skip spoke haltingly, sharing details of his illness, his financial struggles, and his frustration that, after nearly two years as a recruiter, he remained a sergeant (E-5)—the lowest ranking in Detroit's recruiting command. He shared his hope to take computer programming courses so he would have marketable skills when his army enlistment ended. Despite all the backslapping and promises of job offers from businessmen, nothing had materialized. "I tried calling a Ford official last week," he told Watkins. "At first, he didn't remember who I was."

The Medal of Honor, he said, now felt like an albatross. "When they gave it to me," Skip said, "a white officer told me that in the very near future I would be sorry I ever received it."

He buried his face in his hands. "I just can't explain it," he said softly. He felt as though the city and country that once exalted him no longer cared. "As we talked, I got the impression he believed himself to be merely a paper hero, especially to his people," Watkins recalled. "He was a deeply troubled, deeply confused, deeply depressed young man." After several minutes, Skip stood up to leave. He said he could not put his problems into words—but he would "put it down on paper" and return to the *Chronicle* office.

It was a feeling shared by many Vietnam veterans. "We came back totally fucked up in the head," the army combat photographer Stephen Howard told the journalist Wallace Terry. Howard tried group counseling at Walter Reed Medical Center, but with three dozen veterans in each session, he never felt truly heard. The VA hospital in Baltimore gave him two aspirin and told him to go to bed and call back in the morning.

"This psychological thing, we try to suppress it, but it kills us quicker than if somebody just walked up to you and put a bullet in your head," Howard said. "It eats away at your inner being. It eats away at everything that you ever learned in life. Your integrity, your word, all that you have."

A 1981 VA study found that 70 percent of Black veterans who experienced heavy combat were suffering long-term stress reactions. The study also found that simply being in Vietnam was as psychologically stressful for Black soldiers as direct combat was for many white troops.

When Skip did not return to Valley Forge after thirty days, he was considered absent without leave. He mostly stayed home with Katrina and Christopher, dodging calls from the army. A few times a week, he drove to the Jeffries Projects where he had grown up to play basketball with teenagers after the bell rang at Northwestern High School.

"He'd be down there five minutes and the kids would come around and say, 'Hey man, ain't you Dwight Johnson?'" recalled Skip's cousin Tom Tillman. "Skip was something special. He had that medal, and they were proud of him. We had all lived in the project and had been on welfare, just like the kids there today, and we were like heroes because we have broken out of there. We had made it to the outside world. He was a big man down there with the kids."

His mother, who had moved out of Jeffries a couple of years earlier, worried about the older crowd that began sidling up to her son. "They were strung out on drugs, and they just seemed to be hanging around Skip for his money," she said. One night she asked him if he was using heroin. "Ma, I'm not taking a thing," he said, pulling up his sleeves to show there were no needle marks on his arms.

Since Skip was neither at the hospital nor reporting for his recruiting job, the army withheld his pay. Bills began to pile up, and Skip and Katrina fell behind on their $160 monthly mortgage. At first, they had felt welcomed as one of the few Black families in their northwest Detroit neighborhood, but that changed. Several neighbors turned hostile, including one who burned a cross on their front lawn. As Thanksgiving 1970 approached, the optimism that had filled Skip and Katrina's home just a year earlier had given way to despair.

Skip returned to Valley Forge Army Hospital on his own volition in January 1971. The army dismissed the AWOL charge and reinstated his back pay. He began seeing an army psychiatrist, and because he was a Medal of Honor recipient, the division chief was assigned to his case.

"Subject is bright, his Army G.T. rating is equivalent of 120 I.Q.," the psychiatrist noted in his early observations. Skip did not volunteer much at first. "He related he grew up in a Detroit ghetto and never knew his natural father," the doctor wrote. "He sort of laughed when he said he was a 'good boy' and did what was expected of him. . . . In general, there is evidence the subject learned to live up to the expectations of others while there was a build-up of anger he continually suppressed."

Doctors prescribed Maalox and a bland diet to address Skip's ulcers. Their preliminary analysis: "Depression caused by post-Vietnam adjustment problem." As Skip gradually opened up, he expressed regret about reenlisting as a recruiter. He felt the army had made promises about education, job training, and promotions—none of which had materialized. What hurt most, he said, were the Black militants who protested his visits to Detroit high schools, calling him an "electronic nigger"—an army robot sent to recruit Black teens to fight and die in Vietnam.

"Since coming home from Vietnam the subject has had bad dreams," the psychiatrist wrote. "He didn't confide in his mother or wife, but entertained a lot of moral judgment as to what had happened at Dakto. Why had he been ordered to switch tanks the night before? Why was he spared and not the others? He wondered if he was sane. It made him sad and depressed."

Skip told the psychiatrist that his memories of the ambush were fragmented, but one image remained vivid: coming face-to-face with the Vietnamese soldier who pointed a rifle at him. "He can remember the soldier squeezing the trigger but the gun jammed," the psychiatrist wrote. "The subject has since engaged in some magical thinking about this episode. He also suffers guilt over surviving it, and later winning a high honor for the one time in his life when he lost complete control of himself."

During one session, Skip asked, "What would happen if I lost control of myself in Detroit and behaved like I did in Vietnam?"

By LATE MARCH 1971, Skip was back in Detroit. He had been granted a three-day pass from Valley Forge—and never returned. One afternoon, he bumped into Eddie Wright, a friend from the Jeffries Homes.

"Hey, man, where've you been?" Wright said.

"I just got out of Valley Forge on a pass," Skip replied.

"How things going there?"

"They got me in the psycho ward," Skip said. "They think I'm crazy."

By this point, Skip and Katrina were nearly a year behind on their mortgage payments, and the bank had begun foreclosure proceedings. Skip changed their unlisted phone number to avoid calls from the army and bill collectors. When officials could not reach him, the army contacted Ford Motor Company, which had loaned Skip a Thunderbird and another car indefinitely. "One day they came after them like they were repossessing them," Katrina recalled. The army believed the inconvenience might pressure Skip to return to the hospital. Instead, he cashed a fifteen-hundred-dollar army check for back pay and bought a 1967 Mercury for $850.

One afternoon, in the waiting room of a doctor's office while taking his mother to an appointment, Skip ran into Ronald Turner, a Black veteran who had recently joined the Detroit Police Department.

"Very happy to meet you, brother," Turner said. He told Skip that he recognized him from the paper.

"Thanks, brother, just don't ask me anything about the medal," Skip replied. "I don't even know how I won it."

He was tense at first but relaxed when he learned that Turner had also served in Vietnam. He seemed to appreciate the chance to let his guard down. Skip said he felt "disenchanted and resentful" about the way the army had treated him.

"Ever since I won the medal, they put me on the hero's path as an inspiration to Black kids," Skip explained. After several recruiting visits to high schools, he said, he "had begun to feel that what he was saying and doing was not in the best interests of Black people." He told Turner that people on the street called him a "traitor" and that he received dozens of critical letters from "my people."

Skip said he suspected the army psychiatrists had ulterior motives. "He said he felt this was their way of shutting him up or discrediting anything he might say to other soldiers that might be critical of the government," Turner later recalled. He offered to connect Skip with a lawyer or journalist who might be able to help. "The guy seemed so full of pressure, so troubled and tense that you almost feel it," Turner said.

WHILE SKIP STRUGGLED, Detroit became the epicenter of veteran antiwar activism in early 1971. More than a hundred veterans came to the city for the three-day Winter Soldier Investigation, organized by Vietnam Veterans Against the War, where they testified about witnessing and participating in atrocities during the Vietnam War. The name "Winter Soldier" alluded to the Revolutionary War pamphleteer Thomas Paine, who condemned "summer soldiers and sunshine patriots" who "shrink from the service of their country" in times of crisis.

The opening statement was delivered by William Crandell, a stocky redhead who had served as a first lieutenant in the 199th Infantry Division. He captured the sense of betrayal many veterans felt. Rather than bringing peace to the region, "we have set all of Indochina aflame," he told an audience of more than five hundred activists, citizens, and journalists gathered in a hotel ballroom. "We went to guarantee the right of self-determination to the people of South Vietnam and our testimony will show that we are forcing a corrupt and dictatorial government upon them" and that "our strategy and tactics are permeated with racism." America, he lamented, "is being torn apart by what we are doing in Vietnam."

Michael Hunter, a twenty-four-year-old Black veteran from Morristown, New Jersey, testified that he had participated in the shooting and killing of Vietnamese civilians and wounded Vietcong prisoners, and had mutilated the bodies of dead Vietcong soldiers. "I was ordered to shoot him, and I shot him," Hunter said, describing how he killed a Vietnamese child from a hundred yards away in a "free-fire" zone, where GIs were instructed to shoot anything that moved. James Duffy, who sat alongside Hunter on a panel of army First Air Cavalry veterans, said this was "common policy" in the war zone. "Kill anything you want to kill, any time you want to kill it, just don't get caught," Duffy said.

Several of the speakers referenced the My Lai massacre and the trial of 1st Lt. William Calley Jr., which also took place in the early months of 1971. On March 29, a jury of six military officers convicted Calley of the premeditated murder of twenty-two South Vietnamese civilians. Of more than two dozen officers and soldiers charged for their roles in the massacre and cover-up, Calley was the only person convicted.

Jan Barry Crumb, cofounder and first president of Vietnam Veterans Against the War, said one of the principal reasons for organizing the Winter Soldier Investigation was "to prove that war crimes in Vietnam did not start with My Lai." The Vietnam War Crimes Working Group—a secret Pentagon task force created in the wake of the massacre—later uncovered more than three hundred substantiated allegations of massacres, torture, mutilations, rapes, and other atrocities.

Congressman John Conyers joined Senator George McGovern in calling for a congressional investigation into the charges presented at the hearings. "I consider these men patriots of the highest order," Conyers said of the veterans who testified. "Our servicemen are coming home and telling us what it is really like," he continued. "It would seem that the massacre at My Lai forms only a part of the grossly brutal and immoral way we have supposedly tried to bring peace and freedom to the Vietnamese."

Even the *Detroit Free Press*, which questioned the credibility of some of the veterans' testimony, described the Winter Soldier hearings as "an outcry by young men who are haunted by an experience in which they and their country have been entrapped."

Dr. Robert Jay Lifton, a research psychiatrist at Yale, had been thinking about the issues raised in Detroit since his service as a psychiatric officer in the air force during the Korean War. His study of the psychological consequences experienced by atomic bomb survivors in Hiroshima, *Death in Life*, earned him a National Book Award in 1969. Lifton was intrigued by the work of Vietnam Veterans Against the War and wanted to better understand the problems many veterans faced—guilt, rage, and internalized violence. He and half a dozen professional colleagues were invited to participate in informal "rap group" meetings with veterans at the group's New York office.

"They said the shrinks could join, provided that we joined as peers," recalled Dr. Chaim Shatan, who partnered with Lifton. "They knew more about the war than we did, and we knew more about what makes people tick." The veterans found solace in talking with others who had similar experiences. "The rap groups became known as the place where you could tell your story, even the most horrible parts, and other people would listen," recalled the army veteran Arthur Egendorf, who later earned a PhD in psychology from Harvard and supported other veterans in their healing.

Motivated by what they heard, Lifton and Shatan began pushing to have veterans' traumatic experiences recognized by the broader medical community.

When Lifton spoke at the Winter Soldier hearings, he emphasized that the Vietnam War presented unique psychological challenges for returning veterans. The absence of clear battle lines and a definable enemy made it difficult to measure success or experience a sense of heroism. As a result, returning veterans struggled to find meaning in what they had done in Vietnam. He and his colleagues had begun using the term "post-Vietnam syndrome" to describe the unique psychological effects they observed among young veterans.

"When one comes back to the society, it is quite clear that one does not return a hero, either in others' eyes or one's own eyes," Lifton argued in his testimony. "Both the veteran and the larger society see in him the taint of this filthy, unnecessary, immoral war."

On April 23, more than seven hundred veterans gathered in Washington, DC, to express their disillusionment, hurling the medals and ribbons they had earned in Vietnam onto the steps of the US Capitol. Bronze Stars and Purple Hearts caught in the sunlight before glittering to the ground. Veterans spoke the names of friends killed in the war—some shouted in fury, others wept. "It was a disservice to my country," said twenty-five-year-old Joseph Triglio, a former air force sergeant. "As far as I'm concerned, I'm now serving my country." The protest was part of another weekend of massive antiwar demonstrations, with more than 200,000 people marching in the capital and 150,000 rallying in San Francisco.

John Kerry, then a twenty-seven-year-old US Navy veteran, had participated in both the Winter Soldier Investigation and the medal protest. On the eve of the DC rally, he addressed the Senate Foreign Relations Committee, describing the anguish he had witnessed in Detroit. "The country doesn't know it yet, but it has created a monster," Kerry warned. "A monster in the form of millions of men who have been taught to deal and to trade in violence, and who are given the chance to die for the biggest nothing in history; men who have returned with a sense of anger and a sense of betrayal which no one has yet grasped." Speaking on behalf of thousands of veterans who had turned against the war, Kerry declared, "We are angry because we feel we have been used in the worst fashion by the administration of this country."

DAYS AFTER THE MEDAL PROTEST, on April 28, Skip took Katrina to the emergency room at Highland Park General Hospital to have an infected cyst removed. When the admitting office clerk asked for a twenty-five-dollar deposit, Skip promised to pay it the next day. He felt embarrassed not to have the money—an unexpected car repair had pushed their already strained finances to the breaking point.

With Katrina in the hospital, Skip went home despondent. That night, he called a friend from his old army tank unit. "I have a story I'm writing, and I want you to peddle it for me," he said. "It starts out like this: Sgt. Dwight Johnson is dead, and his home has been wiped out."

The next day, Skip brought Christopher to visit Katrina. She told him that hospital staff had been pestering her about the twenty-five-dollar admission fee. Skip promised he would be back later that evening—with the money, her bathrobe, and her curlers. Katrina kissed him goodbye.

Skip dropped their son off with family, then met up with his friend Eddie Wright. He asked Eddie to drop him off at a friend's house—someone, he said, who owed him money. But instead of going inside, Skip walked through the yard, crossed the street, and slid onto a stool at the Sip 'N Chat Lounge, where he ordered a Johnnie Walker and a Pabst.

After finishing the drinks, Skip walked around the corner and into the Open Pantry Market. He asked the store owner, Charles Lee Van Landeghem, for a pack of cigarettes. When the register opened, Skip pulled a .22-caliber pistol, told Van Landeghem to step aside, and reached for the cash. Van Landeghem pulled a gun from beneath the counter and fired.

"I first hit him with two bullets, but he just stood there, with the gun in his hand, and said, 'I'm going to kill you,'" Van Landeghem told the *New York Times* reporter Jon Nordheimer. "I kept pulling the trigger until my gun was empty."

The next morning, Katrina was in her hospital room watching *Kelly & Company*, a local talk show on which she and Skip had once been guests during happier times. A nurse entered and turned off the television. She told Katrina that her parents and brother were here to see her.

Still recovering from surgery, Katrina was helped into a wheelchair and pushed down the hall to the visiting room. Her father was weeping. Her mother could not speak.

"I thought they were coming to tell me about my grandfather," Katrina recalled. "He lived with us at the time and had been very sick."

After a few silent moments, Katrina's younger brother told her the truth: Skip had been shot the night before. He died in the early morning hours in the emergency room at Detroit General Hospital.

The first person Katrina called was Frank Galt, the army liaison she had spoken with during the difficult months of Skip's decline.

"I'm so sorry," Galt said.

Sadness, grief, and anger came quickly—and stayed for years. Katrina, just twenty-one, was now a widow. And Christopher, not yet two, had lost his father.

Those closest to Skip struggled to make sense of the loss. "I think he went into that store as a form of suicide because he had so much guilt about the medal," Katrina later said. "Not only that the guys who were in his old tank died, but that he came home and nobody else did."

Her father, who used to sit up late joking with Skip, saw echoes of military training in the attempted robbery. "They say he shot somebody at the store, well, that's what they taught him to do and that is exactly what got him the medal."

Eddie Wright was one of Skip's first friends—and the last to see him alive. In the aftermath, he could only offer a memory from the turbulent months after Skip returned from Vietnam and received the Medal of Honor, unraveling under its weight.

"It's changed my life so much I don't know if I'll ever get my head straight again," Skip told him. "But I know this. Nobody's a hero forever."

MAKING THE PEACE

L et us declare that the war in Vietnam is over," Coretta said. "Let us declare that the wars on poverty, hunger and repression are in force." It was April 24, 1971, and nearly three hundred thousand people stood shoulder to shoulder in front of the US Capitol, spilling down the National Mall toward the Washington Monument. Some climbed into trees for a better view.

Like Coretta, many in the crowd had marched in the Moratorium protests two years earlier. That dramatic show of force had yielded results. With each passing month, more average citizens and members of Congress were demanding an end to the war. By then, even President Nixon could not ignore the shifting tide of public opinion.

"The war presents a very serious problem," Nixon told Kissinger in April 1971. "The war has eroded America's confidence up to this point. The people are sick of it, and so therefore, our game here must be to deal with it." Nixon's plan was to use monthly troop withdrawals to buy time until his reelection campaign the follow-ing year. And in some ways, it was working. By spring 1971, there were 267,000 US troops in Vietnam, down from a peak of more than 530,000 in 1968. Nixon said there would be fewer than 200,000 by the end of the year.

At the same time, revelations of covert operations in Cambodia and Laos deepened the credibility gap Nixon now faced—just as Johnson had before him. Sixty-seven percent of Americans believed the Nixon administration was not "telling the public all they should know about the Vietnam war." Unable to trust the president, Co-retta and her fellow demonstrators sought to keep the pressure on—demanding that Nixon follow through on his promise to withdraw all US troops from Southeast Asia.

When Coretta looked out from the speaker's platform, she could see, in the hazy distance, the Lincoln Memorial—where Martin delivered his "I Have a Dream" speech at the March on Washing-ton in 1963. Folk singers Peter, Paul and Mary had already asked the crowd to remember Dr. King when they performed "Blowin' in the Wind," the same song they had sung at that earlier civil rights march. Now, Coretta invoked that history as a challenge. She called on the president and the nation to honor her slain husband by with-drawing US troops by August 28, the eighth anniversary of the March on Washington. "We must force our government to stop the bombing now, to get out now," she said. "I urge you the people to make the peace."

Coretta was heartened by the visible and vocal presence of sol-diers, veterans, and their families at the rally. Soldiers in partial uni-form led the march, carrying banners that read "Fort McClellen GIs—U.S. Out of Asia Now" and "GIs of Fort Hood, Tex. Want

Peace Now." Two Black Vietnam veterans walked through the crowd collecting draft cards and war medals. Several Gold Star mothers marched with the medals their sons had received posthumously. When a reporter asked a Black father whose son had been killed in Vietnam why he was marching, he said, "There is no way to bring my son back, but maybe we can save others."

Reflecting on the events of the previous day—when hundreds of veterans threw their medals and ribbons on the steps of the Capitol—navy veteran John Kerry told the crowd that it was the Nixon administration's continuation of the war that provoked the act. "They forced us to return our medals, they denied us the integrity those symbols supposedly gave our lives," he said. He reminded the audience that the effort to end the war—and to prevent "more Vietnams"—required lasting dedication. "This is not the struggle of one month, or one year or one war," Kerry declared. "It's a contribution we must make for the rest of our lives." Coretta admired the veterans' protest, saying "they had a very powerful influence."

George Wiley, director of the National Welfare Rights Organization and a marcher alongside Coretta at the Moratorium rally, amplified her message. He urged the crowd not to "forget about the other war" at home against poverty and racism. "Too many of you out here are not ready to take up the course of fighting repression against blacks and poor people here at home," he said.

Wiley's exhortation was music to Coretta's ears. Two days shy of her forty-fourth birthday, she had spent more than half her life fighting racism, poverty, and war. At every rally and in each interview, Coretta made it clear: Ending the war in Vietnam was only part of the battle. Bringing the troops home meant little if those veterans returned to a country that denied them, along with their families and fellow citizens, access to decent jobs, housing, health care, and education. She called on Americans to confront the full cost of war.

"Our nation's preoccupation with building up the military in the name of national defense has led to a disastrous neglect of the real social needs of the people of our country," she said. "While we have spent billions on tanks, planes, and antipersonnel mines, our cities are dying of bankruptcy, our universities have become prisons, and millions of American lives are monitored as in a police state."

The FBI took note, as they had with all her antiwar activities. In May 1968, a month after Martin's assassination, a memo to Director J. Edgar Hoover had warned that Coretta was trying "to tie the anti-Vietnam war movement to the civil rights movement" in a speech she planned to give in Los Angeles. The following year, agents urged the House Un-American Activities Committee to investigate her for organizing the antiwar candlelight vigil outside the White House. When her memoir, *My Life with Martin Luther King, Jr.*, was published in October 1969, FBI agents read and annotated it. "The book, being a widow's epitaph, depicts a saintly couple, with saintly children, surrounded by saintly associates," one memo noted derisively. Another agent wrote that Coretta's "selfless, magnanimous, decorous attitude is belied by her actual shrewd, calculating, businesslike activities."

In early 1971, the FBI intercepted a letter Coretta wrote to Ruth Gage-Colby, a leader in several organizations including Women Strike for Peace and the National Peace Action Coalition. Coretta wrote that "this war has ravaged our domestic programs" and pledged to speak at the April 24 rally, adding, "I think this is the single most important thing that I could do at this time toward fulfilling my husband's dream.'"

After the rally in DC, Coretta returned to Atlanta in late April to continue building the Martin Luther King Jr. Center. She envisioned the King Center as a place to institutionalize the philosophy of nonviolent social change and as a home base for her activism in the years to come. As she shifted her focus to organizational development and fundraising, tensions arose with ministers and staff at the Southern Christian Leadership Conference, the organization Martin had cofounded and led. Some disparaged her both privately and to the press, calling her "uppity," "Queen," and "Black Jackie"— a sarcastic nod to the widowed former First Lady Jacqueline Kennedy.

"When I experienced the attacks on my attempts to build the Center, it felt like backstabbing, plain and simple," Coretta later wrote. "At the root of their problems with me, I think, was that I appeared to them to be a strong woman, not one to be pushed aside." She tried to steer clear of public disputes, focusing instead on daily work that lay ahead.

EACH MORNING, Coretta took time to read the newspaper after getting the children off to school. On May 1, the front page of *The Atlanta Constitution* carried a UPI story titled "Medal of Honor GI Killed." Two days later, *The Atlanta Journal* featured an AP article that began, "Why did Michigan's first black Medal of Honor winner die as an armed robber?" It noted that the fallen hero left behind a young wife, Katrina, and an eighteen-month-old son, Dwight Christopher. At the end of May, Jon Nordheimer's deeply reported story on Skip Johnson's death ran on the front page of *The New York Times* and in hundreds of newspapers across the country.

For Coretta, the story was yet more evidence of the war's devastating toll on veterans and their families. She understood that Skip's life had been shaped by the Detroit neighborhood where he was raised and the lack of job opportunities that awaited him when he came home. She also knew Katrina needed support as she navigated single parenthood and grief, and that Christopher deserved to grow up in a country free from brutality. While her calls for a nonviolent society could sometimes be perceived as abstract ideals, they were rooted in the real lives of people impacted by the economic, political, and social structures she sought to change.

She maintained a frenetic travel schedule through the summer of 1971, making these points again and again to different audiences. In commencement addresses at Northeastern University in Boston, Bates College in Maine, City College of New York, Roosevelt University in Chicago, and Hunter College in Manhattan, Coretta praised young people for helping to change the world. "In many ways American students have now, with all their innocence and open generosity, become the prodding conscience to those in power and those aspiring to it," she said. At each stop, she warned that unchecked technological advances risked dehumanizing society, and urged graduates to resist what Martin had called the "thingification" of people.

Coretta's critiques of the war took on new resonance in June, when *The New York Times* began publishing excerpts from a top-secret report titled "The History of the United States Decision-Making Process on Vietnam Policy," later known as the Pentagon Papers. Daniel Ellsberg, a forty-year-old RAND Corporation analyst who had grown disillusioned with the war, copied the forty-seven-volume, seven-thousand-page report and leaked it to the press. The documents revealed decades of failed foreign policy decisions and provided damning evidence that multiple presidential administrations had misled the American people about the extent of US involvement in Southeast Asia. *The Washington Post* described the government's arrogance and contempt for public opinion as "chilling."

Eager for anything that might change the subject, President Nixon gave a speech days later announcing a new "War on Drugs." Calling drug abuse "America's public enemy number one," he specifically singled out GIs and young veterans as a focal point of the initiative. "It is essential for the American people to be alerted to this danger," he said, "to recognize that it is a danger that will not pass with the passing of the war in Vietnam which has brought to our attention the fact that a number of young Americans have become addicts as they serve abroad, whether in Vietnam, or Europe, or other places."

The military soon announced that all US service members would be required to undergo urinalysis—unofficially dubbed Operation Golden Flow—before they would be allowed to board planes home. By fall, army labs were conducting more than seven thousand urine tests every day. Soldiers who failed the tests were subject to military discipline and required to remain at foreign bases for detoxification.

While drug use was common among soldiers in Vietnam—fueled by the stress and boredom of war and the easy availability of marijuana and heroin—experts found no evidence of widespread addiction among returning troops. That did not stop politicians and journalists from using the specter of drug abuse to deflect attention from the war. "Addicts instead of the war itself and the way we are fighting it become the locus of evil," argued the psychologist Robert Jay Lifton. Senator Thomas Dodd went so far as to blame the My Lai massacre and other atrocities on illegal drug use. "Marijuana—The Other Enemy in Vietnam," read a headline in *U.S. News and World Report*, while *Newsweek* ran a cover story warning of a "Heroin Plague" spreading across the country. "Once confined to black urban ghettos, heroin addiction has come to invade the heartland of white middle-class America," *Time* magazine warned. "The specter of highly weapons-trained, addicted combat veterans joining the deadly struggle for drugs is ominous."

As media outlets spread the image of the drug-addled veteran, Black and working-class veterans trying to readjust to civilian life were increasingly ensnared by the criminal justice system. By 1978, one in four people incarcerated in state prisons had served in the military, with Black veterans making up a third of those imprisoned former service members. For many, the War on Drugs had become a War on Veterans.

IN THE SUMMER OF 1971, the novelist Alice Walker interviewed Coretta for *Redbook* magazine. The twenty-seven-year-old Walker had first met Coretta nearly a decade earlier, when she was a first-year student at Spelman College. Coretta had welcomed Walker and a group of students preparing to travel to the Helsinki Peace Festival into her home. "At that time she seemed to be the only Black woman in Atlanta actively and publicly engaged in the pursuit of peace," Walker wrote. Despite the brevity of the visit, she remembered Coretta as "bright-eyed" and "bubbly" and was delighted to find that the family's furniture was plain rather than ostentatious. She next saw Coretta at Martin's funeral. Now, sitting again in the Kings' home, Walker remarked on Coretta's transformed countenance and demeanor.

"The first thing I noticed was that her eyes have changed—they are now reserved, almost cool," Walker wrote. "And she is tense, perhaps because she has been written about so often and because she is bored with it." Reporters often described Coretta's speaking style as deliberate and measured, though Walker sensed there was more to it. "When she talks she seems very calm and sure, though not relaxed," she observed. "She is careful that her precise meaning is expressed and understood. Her voice is quite different from the way it sounds when she gives speeches—it is softer and not as flatly Southern." Listening to Coretta's caution and precision, Walker found an unexpected "fragility and formality." "Perhaps it's necessary," she mused, "when faced with overwhelming publicity, to guard one's private person so vigilantly that even a smile no longer comes easily."

As the women talked, Coretta seemed to relax. She leaned back in a camel-colored swivel chair, a large portrait of Martin adorning the wall behind her desk.

"Periodically Martin and I would have these discussions about my being so involved in my singing and speaking and being away from home so much," she confided to Walker, smiling slightly at the memory. "We always agreed that when both of us were under a lot of pressure to be away from home, I would be the one to curtail my activities." She said Martin, too, found it difficult to be away from the family as often as the movement required.

Coretta Scott King sits at her desk in her Atlanta home.

Walker gave Coretta a copy of her first novel, *The Third Life of Grange Copeland*, and expressed admiration for Martin's gentleness. "When he was assassinated in 1968 it was as if the last light in my world had gone out," Walker said. Coretta's face grew thoughtful. The hour allotted for the interview had long passed. "It was such a good feeling that Martin gave me—from the first time I met him," Coretta said. "I miss this now very much. Since his death I've had to struggle on alone, and I can appreciate now more than ever how important it is to have somebody to share things with, to have someone who cares, someone who is concerned."

When *The New York Times* interviewed Coretta in January 1972, she described her role as "an evolving one." In addition to her responsibilities as a mother of four, she was raising money for the King Center—which she called "my fifth child"—and campaigning to establish Martin's birthday, January 15, as a national holiday. Nearly four years after his assassination, she saw the stewardship of Martin's legacy as a vital way to institutionalize nonviolent social change. "It will be 50 years before he will be properly recognized in this country," she said.

At the same time, Coretta knew she deserved recognition in her own right as a leader and activist. The title of the *New York Times* article referred to her as the "widow of Dr. King," as did many other news stories of the era. "How well I understood the power of my husband's name and what he represented!" Coretta later wrote. "But sometimes I wondered how and when people would look beyond the name and see me as a woman of substance and commitment, working for the Cause each day of her life."

As the 1972 election approached, the work continued. "My main focus was ridding our nation of Richard Nixon and his reactionary policies on race, war, and poverty," she wrote. In speeches, organizing work, and coalition building, she kept showing up for organizations and people who shared these goals.

ACROSS POLITICAL ORGANIZATIONS, churches, and college campuses in the spring of 1972, Coretta delivered a consistent message: Systemic injustice must be fought—and nonviolence was still the most powerful tool. In March 1972, Coretta attended the National Black Political Convention in Gary, Indiana, where several thousand civil rights activists and Black Power leaders gathered for three days to draft a national agenda. In his welcome address, Gary Mayor Richard Hatcher declared, "We shall shun like the plague, any political party which does not demand the immediate return of every American boy from the distant Southeast Asian lands." Coretta spoke on a panel on the development of Black political power in the seventies, alongside the writer Amiri Baraka, Congressman William Clay (D-Missouri), Congressman Charles Diggs (D-Michigan), Mayor Hatcher, and Manhattan Borough President Percy Sutton. In Gary, Coretta met Betty Shabazz, Malcolm X's widow, for the first time—a meeting that marked the beginning of a lasting friendship.

After the second day of the convention, Coretta performed at a fundraising concert held at a local high school with Harry Belafonte, Isaac Hayes, the comedian Dick Gregory, and others. "This is a historic event," she said after receiving a standing ovation from delegates. "We are here on very serious business. What we do at this convention will be judged by future generations of the black liberation struggle."

Despite significant ideological disagreements, the delegates produced a fifty-page *National Black Political Agenda* that became a touchstone for Black politics in the years ahead. In addition to calling for an immediate end to the war in Vietnam, the document demanded a "guaranteed suitable job for every employable worker," an increase in the federal minimum wage from $1.60 per hour to $3.13 per hour, and a guaranteed minimum annual income of $6,500 for a family of four, with cost-of-living increases. Delegates proposed that these programs be funded by shifting federal spending from defense to social programs.

Coretta increasingly immersed herself in policy details, criticizing what she called the "topsy-turvy morality" of Internal Revenue Service regulations. "Our present tax and welfare structure is such as to encourage the wealthy to speculate and the poor to vegetate," she argued. "If a rich man wants to speculate, he is encouraged by preferential capital gains and loss provisions which give him a 25% cushion against losses and take less than half as much on his nominal earnings. But if a poor man on relief took a part-time job, he had to pay a 100% tax on his earnings in the shape of a dollar-for-dollar reduction in his relief allowance." Coretta argued that changing these policies was vital to building a peacetime economy that would benefit ordinary Americans, including veterans and their families.

Building a peaceful and prosperous America remained a deeply personal mission for Coretta. Two weeks after the National Black Political Convention, she brought her two daughters—sixteen-year-old Yolanda and eight-year-old Bernice—to the "Children's March for Survival" in Washington, DC, to protest President Nixon's childcare and welfare policies. More than thirty thousand demonstrators, including thousands of children, marched, skipped, and dawdled around the Ellipse south of the White House. Some carried signs that read "Nixon's dogs eat better than our children." Many others wore buttons and held placards featuring a cartoon drawn by a local nine-year-old, showing the president turning his back on two children beside the misspelled phrase "Nixon dosen't care." Jesse Jackson, the feminist activist Gloria Steinem, Congresswoman Bella Abzug, Congressman Ron Dellums, and Senator Eugene McCarthy spoke at the rally, as did John Kerry, representing Vietnam Veterans Against the War.

Speaking at Ebenezer Baptist Church in April, Coretta emphasized the importance of Black participation in the 1972 elections. She said her ideal presidential candidate would guarantee a minimum annual income for all Americans and work to eliminate "systemic violence" against Black and poor people. A lack of jobs for those eager to work, a welfare system that treated recipients like criminals, and persistent childhood hunger were all forms of violence, she argued—ones that must be opposed as vigorously as the war in Vietnam. "This is the most violent period in the history of mankind, America is the greatest purveyor of violence," she told an audience at Trinity Baptist Church in Los Angeles, echoing a theme from Martin's "Beyond Vietnam" speech. "An alternative to it must be found."

In her many speeches, Coretta occasionally sparred with audience members who believed the ideals of peace and love she and Martin championed were outdated. Speaking at Cheyney State College in Pennsylvania, one student argued that the times demanded more militancy and less nonviolence. "I disagree totally," Coretta replied sharply. "Martin wrote five books, you ought to go back and read them." Elsewhere, she contended that "militancy without purpose is unproductive" and that lasting change required a long-term battle within the system. She reminded audiences that in his fight against racism, poverty, and war, Martin was "the most militant of militants."

In May 1972, the *Washington Post* investigative journalist Jack Anderson confirmed what Coretta and many Black activists had long suspected: The FBI was spending millions of dollars to systematically surveil Black leaders. "Our study of the secret files indicates that the investigation has been heavily one-sided," Anderson wrote. "Only the most extreme white racists have come under FBI scrutiny, but almost every black leader in the country has an FBI dossier in his name. Even congressmen and Nixon-Agnew supporters, if they're black, are regarded with suspicion by the FBI." Anderson reported that Martin and Coretta topped the FBI's list of Black "subversives." Newspapers across the country picked up the story, one of several exposés Anderson published in the weeks following the death of FBI Director J. Edgar Hoover, who died, on May 2, at age seventy-seven. The Nixon administration so feared and loathed Anderson that two of the president's fixers, E. Howard Hunt and G. Gordon Liddy—among the so-called White House Plumbers— plotted to assassinate him before their arrest in connection with the Watergate burglary.

Even as the country was reeling from revelations about FBI surveillance, Nixon's actions sparked a fresh wave of outrage. Later that month, protests erupted on more than a dozen college campuses after Nixon ordered the mining of Haiphong Harbor and other major North Vietnamese ports. Representative John Conyers sponsored a House resolution declaring the action an impeachable offense and joined seven congressional colleagues in placing a two-page ad in *The New York Times* with the headline: "A Resolution to Impeach Richard M. Nixon as President of the United States." Coretta, speaking to graduating seniors at Simmons College in Boston and Goucher College in Baltimore, argued that the roots of radicalism were not found in student protests but in the corridors of power. "If FBI and congressional investigators want to find the well-springs of radicalism, they should not look on the campus . . . they should look into the White House and into the marble halls of Congress," she said. "Policies made there have radicalized more young people than a million books by revolutionaries." She told the students that she understood their disillusionment and anger at the "gangrene of Vietnam."

After weeks of speculation about her presidential pick, on May 18 Coretta endorsed Senator George McGovern, with whom she had appeared at several antiwar rallies in previous years. His platform—calling for an immediate withdrawal from Vietnam, a reduction in defense spending, and a one-thousand-dollar guaranteed minimum income for the poor—aligned closely with her core values. But McGovern's campaign, hampered by factionalism within the Democratic Party and an early controversy over his choice of running mate, failed to generate the momentum needed to unseat the incumbent. Nixon won reelection in a landslide, claiming more than 60 percent of the vote and carrying every state except Massachusetts.

On the subject of the war, Nixon could credibly claim that he had delivered on his promise to draw down US troops in South Vietnam. In August, *The New York Times* reported that by the end of the year, "Mr. Nixon will have reduced the authorized ceiling from 549,500 to 27,000 during his term in office—a reduction of 95 per cent." At the same time, Nixon refused to stop bombing raids over North Vietnam until a peace settlement was finalized. The antiwar movement had succeeded in pushing the president toward disengagement, but with fewer troops on the ground and a sharp decline in US casualties, public outrage faded. "In 1965, the American people knew there was a war, and we had to convince people it was wrong," one activist remarked. "In 1972, people know the war is wrong, but we have to convince them that there is a war."

A week before the election, Nixon expressed confidence that a ceasefire with Saigon was imminent. In a press conference announcing progress on the negotiations, Henry Kissinger declared, "Peace is at hand."

ON JANUARY 15, 1973, Coretta and her children laid a wreath of red and white carnations at Martin's grave in Atlanta, marking what would have been his forty-fourth birthday. Congressman John Conyers and members of the Congressional Black Caucus used the occasion to announce new legislation calling for a national observance of King's birthday.

The following week, Coretta sat near the back of Washington, DC's National City Christian Church for the funeral of former president Lyndon B. Johnson, a man with whom she and Martin had shared a complicated and often fraught relationship. "He believed in America—in what America could mean to all of its citizens and what America could mean to the world," President Nixon said in his eulogy. Rev. Billy Graham praised Johnson's commitment to the Great Society and his efforts to help the poor, before noting that "it was his destiny to be involved in a tragic war." The soprano Leontyne Price, whose brother, George B. Price, served in Korea and Vietnam and mentored a generation of Black army officers, sang "Take My Hand, Precious Lord" and "Onward, Christian Soldiers." When reporters asked for her thoughts, Coretta acknowledged Johnson's role in passing landmark civil rights legislation, but added pointedly that "it would be hypocritical to pretend that one can forget a war that still goes on."

On January 27, two days after Johnson was laid to rest, US Secretary of State William Rogers and North Vietnamese Foreign Minister Nguyen Duy Trinh signed a ceasefire agreement in Paris. The last US combat troops left South Vietnam on March 29, 1973, bringing to a close what was, at the time, the longest war in American history.

The human cost was staggering and would take years to fully come into focus: More than fifty-eight thousand Americans were killed, alongside over two hundred thousand South Vietnamese soldiers, more than one million North Vietnamese and Vietcong troops, and at least five hundred thousand civilians across Vietnam, Cambodia, and Laos. The ceasefire itself proved tenuous, as North Vietnamese troops, tanks, and artillery began moving south. "Vietnam Peace Hope Dim," read the *New York Times* headline on the day of the US troop withdrawal.

While many cheered the end of the war, Coretta focused her energy on a different question: What kind of country would America be when the soldiers came home? "If we could solve the unemployment problem most of the social problems we have could be solved," she argued. In the face of rising inflation and a growing backlash against civil rights initiatives, she saw guaranteed employment as one way to tamp down racial resentment—especially among white workers who viewed workers of color as economic threats. In 1974, Coretta cofounded the National Committee for Full Employment/ Full Employment Action Council to push for legislation that would ensure jobs for all Americans.

"This nation has never honestly dealt with the question of a peacetime economy and what it means in terms of the development within the country," she said in 1975. "We've had much greater employment during times when we've been engaged in war. . . . We recognize that in the urgency of the unemployment crisis there must be immediate solutions, jobs must be provided immediately by the government."

Coretta recognized that the military was part of the employment market—and an increasingly important one for Black and working-class Americans. At the end of the war, Black Americans made up 11 percent of the civilian population but accounted for more than 18 percent of the army's enlisted ranks. On July 1, 1973, after years of deliberation, the military draft ended and the army transitioned to an all-volunteer force. In the months that followed, recruiting data consistently showed that Black volunteers were over-represented in the new system, sometimes comprising more than 30 percent of new enlistees. By 1980, one in every three army GIs and one in five marines were Black.

"The rising number of blacks in the Army tends to reinforce arguments made by critics of the all-volunteer military concept who said it would lead to either a poor man's army or a black man's army or both," reported *The Washington Post* in August 1973. Recruits were guaranteed meals, medical and dental care, housing, clothing, and a starting salary of around three hundred dollars a month. Those who enlisted in armor, infantry, or artillery received additional combat bonuses. With inflation high and civilian jobs scarce, military service became an increasingly attractive option. In cities like Detroit, recruiters found that economic necessity was the driving force for many young people choosing to enlist.

The sociologist Peter Moskos believed these trends said as much about America as they did about the military. "It is a commentary on our nation that many black youths, by seeking to enter and re-main in the armed forces, are saying that it is even worth the risk of being killed in order to have a chance to learn a trade, to make it in a small way, to get away from a dead-end existence, and to become part of the only institution in this society that seems really to be integrated," Moskos contended.

"Our armed forces are the exception that proves the rule," argued the *Black Enterprise* publisher and army veteran Earl Graves. "Most Americans with decent economic prospects in civilian life, by far, prefer these to a military career."

When Clifford Alexander became secretary of the army in 1977—the first Black person appointed to the role—he said he favored the volunteer system over the draft. But, he emphasized, "you have to ask why there is almost 40 percent unemployment among black teenagers before you ask why they enlist or why they re-up."

The challenge, Coretta understood, was to ensure that the civilian labor market welcomed Black and working-class Americans as enthusiastically as the military did. The stakes of supporting ordinary Americans—including tens of thousands of returning Vietnam veterans—were cast in sharp relief by the death of Skip Johnson in Detroit.

RESTORED TO HONOR

R ev. Carl Hort had known Skip since he was a child, as an altar boy and Explorer Scout at Faith Lutheran Memorial. Hort, a World War II veteran, understood the dangers of combat and had spoken to Skip about military life before he deployed to Vietnam. He hoped this day would never come.

"We can never judge another person; we cannot probe a man's mind deeply enough," Hort said to the three hundred mourners who filled the modest church for Skip's funeral on May 5, 1971. The pastor asked the congregation to pray for Skip's soul and said that the young veteran was not in his right mind on that fateful night when he walked into the convenience store with a gun. "This man did not know what he was doing."

An army honor guard and a contingent of JROTC cadets from Northwestern High School, Skip's alma mater, flanked the flag-draped coffin.

Katrina and Skip's mother sat in the front row, trying to maintain their composure, each attended to by nurses. Outside the church,

Skip Johnson's funeral
service at Faith Memorial
Lutheran Church in Detroit

neighborhood residents paid their respects, lining the road for several blocks under a sparkling spring sky, from the Jeffries Projects to Faith Lutheran.

"I really couldn't believe it," said Barry Davis, the auburn-haired veteran who served with Skip in the Sixty-Ninth Armor and flew from California to attend the service. "I even went to the store where he got shot, I just couldn't believe the whole thing. I guess maybe what he experienced in Vietnam was a burden, something we can't comprehend how it affected him later."

The next day, Katrina and Skip's family members flew to Washington, DC, for a private ceremony at Arlington National Cemetery. A seven-man detail from the Third Infantry Regiment, the Old Guard, honored the Medal of Honor recipient with a twenty-one-gun salute. A member of the unit played taps before a soldier presented Katrina with the folded flag. Skip was laid to rest in the northeast section of the cemetery, a shaded area not far from the memorial to President Kennedy and President William Howard Taft's grave site.

"I was walking in a fog," Katrina said of attending the funeral and burial. The previous week had been chaotic. After her surgery and the news of Skip's death, she and Christopher went to stay at her parents' house. She was inundated with phone calls. A man reached out saying he was Skip's biological father—one of dozens of scammers who asked her for money. Several local police departments called trying to close cases, speculating incorrectly that Skip may have been responsible for them. "I did a lot of hanging up on people," Katrina recalled.

Katrina, now a twenty-one-year-old widow and single mother of a toddler, tried to keep herself busy, working while going to college part-time. When she allowed herself to think about Skip's return from the war, she felt furious. "They kept pushing him to be some kind of monument," she later said. "They never let up. They just wanted a hero to sit at the head table. Now that it's all over they may be almost glad. They will say, 'See, we told you so. He was nothing but a nigger after all.'"

Space was tight with seven people living in her parents' single-story ranch home. Katrina and little Christopher shared one bedroom, while her two brothers and grandfather shared another. The cramped quarters brought small moments of levity amid the grief. "I'd wake up in the middle of the night and couldn't turn over," Katrina remembered. "I'd open my eyes and my baby brother is on one side. He'd gotten up and gotten Chris and brought him into the bed, too, so I'm laying between the two of them. One had their feet in my face and other one's got their feet in my back. So, I would politely get up and go in the kitchen and start cooking something. And before I could get the bacon out of the package, there they were, sitting at the table." Katrina found an apartment so she and Christopher could move out by the end of the summer.

Katrina had always enjoyed reading newspapers and watching the evening news, but now anything related to the war just made her mad. "After Skip died, I wouldn't even stand up for the national anthem, because I was so angry and bitter," Katrina recalled. "We are in a war that doesn't even really concern us. I was mad at the government for a long time."

Her aunt worried about the toll this was taking on Katrina. One day she pulled her aside and said, "Baby, I know you're angry, but you're going to have to get over being mad about everything." It did not come easily, but Katrina took the advice.

"I just let it go," Katrina remembered. "I prayed and I let it go. It wasn't going to bring him back. It wasn't going to stop the hardship that my son may have had to go through. I just got over it."

ACROSS THE COUNTRY, people who had never met Skip found meaning in his story. After a Memorial Day parade in Middletown, Connecticut, Korean War veteran Raymond Dzialo encouraged the crowd to care for the "war living" who struggled upon returning from Vietnam. "There are thousands of war veterans who are equally as hopeless as Dwight Johnson," Dzialo said. Veterans found job training and drug treatment lacking, he argued: "We are thankless for the duty they have performed." Dzialo, who had read about

Skip's death in the newspaper days earlier, said the lack of support he encountered after the war was a stain on America's pride. "We must honor the war living with jobs, with respect, with care, with thanks, and above all, with love."

The psychiatrists Robert Jay Lifton, Chaim Shatan, and their colleagues were also keenly interested in Skip's story. The year before, they had begun leading group therapy sessions in New York City, organized by Vietnam Veterans Against the War. Listening to the men describe their emotions in these "rap groups," the psychiatrists identified feelings of alienation, guilt, rage, and depression as common among many veterans. They hoped to identify enough shared characteristics to establish a medical diagnosis and improve the treatments available for returning soldiers. For them, Skip became a high-profile example of the war's psychological toll.

"The dying of Congressional Medal of Honor winner Dwight Johnson on the floor of a grocery store has the impact of a modern tragedy," they wrote in a June 1971 letter to the editor of *The New York Times*, following the paper's report on Skip's death. They sought to assign a new clinical language to a phenomenon as old as war itself—the ancient Greeks called it "divine madness," it was "soldier's heart" in the Civil War, "shell shock" in World War I, and "combat fatigue" in World War II and the Korean War. Introducing the phrase "post-Vietnam syndrome," the psychiatrists said Skip's struggles echoed what they were hearing in their weekly sessions with veterans.

"When soldiers are hailed as heroes by a grateful nation, they receive absolution from society for both killings and the atrocities they have committed," Shatan said. "But today's vets return piecemeal, without victory parades, to an ambivalent nation. They return to an administration that does little to care for their wounds, much less to further their educations and even less to find them work." The psychiatrists noted the lack of economic opportunities for veterans, especially Black veterans, as a factor that exacerbated their feelings of abandonment and scapegoating by the country they served.

When Shatan traveled to Detroit in 1972 for a conference, he met with Katrina and other members of Skip's family. He was convinced that Skip's story might have unfolded differently if his symptoms had been properly diagnosed and treated.

Lifton and Shatan discussed "post-Vietnam syndrome" widely over the next several years, lobbying for its recognition by the psychiatric community. They spoke at professional conferences, veteran advocacy meetings, and with journalists, and shared their findings in academic articles and books. They regularly cited Dwight Johnson as "the first public acknowledgment of the existence of a Post-Vietnam Syndrome" and questioned government figures suggesting that "psychiatric casualties" among Vietnam veterans were lower than those from World War II or Korea. Lifton compared Skip's story to that of the veteran and actor Audie Murphy, who earned the Medal of Honor and numerous other awards for valor in World War II but struggled with insomnia and depression in the years that followed. "No soldier ever really survives a war," Murphy said.

In 1973, Shatan organized the National Planning Conference on Emotional Needs of Vietnam Veterans, which led to the creation of the National Veterans Resource Project—a coalition of veterans, psychiatrists, and religious leaders working to raise visibility around veterans' needs. They began lobbying the American Psychiatric Association (APA) to have the combat stress experiences of veterans recognized by the medical community.

Skip's story helped to personalize the struggles of veterans more broadly. In 1980, thanks to Shatan and Lifton's advocacy, the third edition of the *Diagnostic and Statistical Manual of Mental Disorders* (*DSM*-III) officially recognized post-Vietnam syndrome as post-traumatic stress disorder (PTSD). Shatan later estimated that the twelve-year absence of a suitable clinical diagnostic category for veterans' experiences—the American Psychiatric Association had removed "gross stress reactions" from the *DSM*-II in 1968—"saved the government hundreds of millions of dollars" in medical claims.

THE PLAYWRIGHT RICHARD Wesley was editing *Black Theatre* magazine and working at the New Lafayette Theatre in New York when he read about Skip's story. He understood it in the context of other young men he knew from Howard University and his hometown of Newark who had served in Vietnam. "You were constantly hearing about people who were killed, running into people who were wounded physically and psychologically," Wesley recalled. "There was no escaping it. The war was with me even if I wasn't physically present."

When New York's New Phoenix Repertory Company commissioned him to write a play, he developed *Strike Heaven on the Face*, a drama based on the story of Dwight Johnson that debuted in 1973. The play's title referred to lines from *Macbeth*: "Each new morn new widows howl, new orphans cry, new sorrows strike heaven on the face." Wesley saw the toll of the war as a tragedy unfolding on the streets of Newark, Detroit, and countless other American cities and towns. "I started asking around—I wanted to know what was going on in these guys' heads," Wesley recalled.

One veteran described being in a firefight in Vietnam one morning, getting his discharge papers, and being back in civilian life in New Jersey twenty-four hours later. It was a common and disorienting experience shared by many of the men Lifton and Shatan spoke with in developing the post-Vietnam syndrome diagnosis. Wesley dedicated *Strike Heaven on the Face* to Skip and to two of the playwright's friends who were killed in the war: Leon Earl Bell, a marine corporal who was killed in Quang Tri, and David Gregory, an army private first class who died of gunshot wounds in combat a month before he was due to return to Newark.

The Shakespearean contours of Skip's life reminded Wesley of another fallen hero, Ira Hayes, the Native American acclaimed as one of the six marines who raised the US flag on Mount Suribachi during the Battle of Iwo Jima. Hayes struggled after the war with the trauma of combat and alcoholism. Wesley was nine years old when Hayes fell into an irrigation ditch and froze to death on the Gila River Reservation near Sacaton, Arizona. As a child, Wesley could not understand how a war hero could meet such a tragic end. "Dwight Johnson became my generation's Ira Hayes," Wesley suggested. "It felt like history repeating itself a generation later with another soldier of color."

Wesley's play brought pivotal moments in Skip's life to the stage for the first time, exploring both the honor and the overwhelming burden of receiving the Medal of Honor. "This is too much," Skip's character thinks at one point. "The VFW . . . these bastards wouldn't even spit on me if it wasn't for this medal . . . usin' me, a victim, as some kinda goddamn patriotic symbol . . . Come to the ghetto, bastard, an' talk that credit to his race shit." *Strike Heaven on the Face* gave the final words to Skip's widow. "My son's gonna know the truth about his father," she says. "He gonna know about those dreams an' nightmares an' the time he woke up screamin' out to a world that didn't give a damn about him. My son gonna know the hell his dad went thru fightin' in a war he ain't supposed to have had nothin' to do with . . . They took my man from me an' drove him to his death, far as I'm concerned. I'll never forget that an' neither will his son."

Like Wesley, the writer Tom Cole drew inspiration from reading about Skip's death in *The New York Times*. Cole wrote *Medal of Honor Rag*, a taut, two-character one-act play that imagined an extended dialogue between a Black war hero, fictionalized as Dale Jackson, and a white psychiatrist at the Valley Forge Army Hospital. The play debuted in Boston in 1974 before opening at the Folger Theatre in Washington, DC, Off-Broadway at Theatre de Lys in New York City, and at Philadelphia's New Foxhole Café in 1976.

Cole saw the play as a way to address the "overwhelming psychological burden" of Vietnam veterans. "In this conflict," he said, "there were no parades or ceremonies to redeem the returned warrior, to say 'We forgive you; you are now once again a son, a husband, a father, and not a killer.'"

Reviewers often took as much space retelling Skip's story as they did discussing the play itself, emphasizing its ripped-from-the-headlines power. One critic described it as "a succinct and moving dramatization of an actual tragedy," while another called it "eloquent in its barely suppressed rage." In his review, titled "Death of a Hero," the *New York Times* critic Clive Barnes wrote, "The facts remain the facts—this man died for us all, and whether you want to call him Jackson or Johnson, the man's story is intact and terrible."

The play was produced in London, Los Angeles, Detroit, Fort Bragg, and more than a dozen other cities and towns in the years ahead. In 1982, PBS broadcast a film adaptation of *Medal of Honor Rag* on its *American Playhouse* series. "It was more frightening than dramatic to live it," Katrina remarked when a reporter asked her about the film.

Millions of people encountered Skip's story in the decade after he was killed. As Americans struggled to make sense of Vietnam, his courage and his suffering became a touchstone for veterans and underscored the need to talk honestly about the war. "A long and degrading war has made Americans desperate for heroes," Robert Jay Lifton wrote in March 1973, as hundreds of returning prisoners of war were celebrated as part of Operation Homecoming. "We would better serve returning prisoners, and other Vietnam veterans as well, with attitudes of openness, truthfulness and recognition of the extent to which all Americans fighting this war have been victimized no less than their assigned enemies."

THE END OF THE WAR arrived without much fanfare in cities like Detroit. "Peace came Saturday and Black Americans hardly noticed," the *Michigan Chronicle* columnist Bill Black wrote in early 1973, after the Paris Peace Accords were signed, finalizing plans for the withdrawal of the remaining American combat troops. The physical and psychological wounds inflicted on veterans left little to celebrate. "The young Black Viet vets came home to the sound of silence," he continued. "Or the scorn of their contemporaries who considered them fools for answering the calls to the colors. And to unemployment compensation lines. And to ghettoes that had deteriorated even more in their absence." Questioning the phrase President Nixon used to describe the accords, Black asked, "Peace with honor? For whom?"

In a nationally televised speech on August 8, 1974, President Nixon resigned from office due to the Watergate scandal, including the program of illegal surveillance he launched after the release of the Pentagon Papers. "The President and his aides became increasingly enmeshed in the snare of lies and half-truths they had themselves created," Congressman John Conyers wrote. Conyers went further than most of his congressional colleagues in proposing an article of impeachment based on the president's false and misleading statements regarding the existence and scale of bombing operations in Cambodia—actions that disregarded Congress's constitutional power to declare war. He drew a direct connection between the Watergate crimes and the ways President Nixon flouted the Constitution in his handling of the Vietnam War. The article of impeachment sought to set a precedent for punishing presidents who violated Congress's authority to initiate war. Congress ultimately voted down this article in favor of charges that garnered bipartisan consensus, shifting attention away from the administration's foreign policy decisions and military activities.

On April 29, 1975, as North Vietnamese forces closed in on Saigon, President Gerald Ford ordered the evacuation of US personnel and thousands of Vietnamese civilians. "This action closes a chapter in the American experience," he said. Ford urged Americans to "close ranks" and "avoid recrimination about the past." The editors of *The Chicago Defender*, among others, defied the president's plea. "Now that the curtain of surrender has come down on a useless civil war, the implications are crystal clear that American interference was indefensible, unwise and unrewarding," the editors wrote. "Our military commitment in Indochina has left U.S. foreign policy with a disastrous legacy."

As the war came to an end, Katrina fought for a different kind of legacy. When Dwight died, the VA denied her request for full war widow's benefits. "They said he did not die in service," Katrina recalled. This meant she received one hundred dollars a month—the standard compensation for widows of soldiers who suffered "nonservice"-related deaths—instead of three hundred dollars, the amount that would have been provided if he had been killed in combat. "There were people thinking I had gotten a big windfall as the widow of a Medal of Honor recipient, asking me for money," she said. "I had to tell them that wasn't true." The financial strain was tremendous. There were months when she could not make ends meet, Christmases when she could not afford presents. "My son has suffered more than anyone else," she recalled. "How do you tell a kid he can't go to the circus because we don't have $5? But that's the way it's been."

Katrina chose to fight the decision. As a single mother, the money would certainly help—but it was more than that. She wanted to prove that Skip's death was related to his experiences in Vietnam. Katrina's mother worked at the VA and connected her to James Pellegrini, who directed the Detroit chapter of Disabled American Veterans. Working with Pellegrini, Katrina appealed the VA's decision in 1974 and pursued the case for more than two years. They argued that Skip was suffering from post-Vietnam syndrome, which was exacerbated by his reenlistment as an army recruiter.

"The Army used Mr. Johnson to motivate other blacks, not honoring him for what he did, saving lives by killing the enemy, but using him," Pellegrini testified before the Board of Veterans' Appeals in Washington, DC. "He was exposed to white middle class society and used by it—exploited. This destroyed Mr. Johnson." Katrina said Skip "hated appearing in public" after receiving the Medal of Honor. "Each time someone recognized him on a street he would turn his back and hide his head." She recalled that he intentionally got into a car accident in hopes of missing the testimonial dinner in his honor at Cobo Hall, with Mayor Jerome Cavanagh, Governor William Milliken, General William Westmoreland, and an audience of more than twelve hundred people awaiting him. The psychiatrist Bruce Danto, director of Detroit's Suicide Prevention Center, reviewed the medical records and testified that he believed Skip's actions were consistent with a victim-precipitated homicide. "Johnson's criminal behavior was an effort to get himself killed," Danto said.

In March 1977, the Board of Veterans' Appeals ruled in Katrina's favor, finding that Skip was mentally incompetent when he was killed and that the robbery attempt was a direct result of his military experience. "He began to feel helpless and not in control of the situation," the board wrote. "He began to feel that he was being made a fool of, being used, becoming a freak in a side show, and he felt he could not trust anyone." The board concluded that by persuading him to be a recruiter, the army had worsened his mental health. "He felt ill-prepared for and uneasy about public speeches and appearances," they noted. "He constantly had to relive the battle and consequent death of his buddies." The board described army officials asking Skip to make a public appearance shortly after checking into Valley Forge Army Hospital for psychiatric help as a particularly egregious example of neglect for his mental state and well-being. In sum, the board found that, at the time of his death, Skip was "completely confused, bitter, distrustful and depressed, and his feelings of inadequacy and helplessness were so overwhelming that he could no longer make a rational decision."

The decision received international news coverage and ensured that Katrina would receive retroactive benefits to 1974, when she had filed the appeal.

The money was welcome, though it hardly compensated for what she had lost. "It took me six years to prove that he was suffering, that he was actually active duty when he died," she recalled. "They gave me three thousand dollars. That's all his life was worth—three thousand dollars. It was comical."

Still, Katrina believed there was something more at stake. "For

Katrina May, c. 1977

those who felt he did something dramatically wrong, this should change their minds," she said when the decision was announced. "For those of us who looked upon him as a hero, it will make them feel better." The front page of the *Michigan Chronicle* ran a large photo of Skip, smiling in his army uniform, with the headline: "Restored to Honor."

As the first successful VA benefits appeal regarding post-Vietnam syndrome—soon to be formally recognized and codified as post-traumatic stress disorder (PTSD)—Katrina and Skip's case opened the door for thousands of other veterans and their families to have their military experiences more accurately recognized, supported, and compensated.

IN 1982, with *Medal of Honor Rag* scheduled to air on PBS, the *Detroit Free Press* theater critic Lawrence DeVine interviewed Katrina. She said she had seen the play at the Theater Company in Detroit a couple of years earlier and was planning to borrow a videocassette recorder to tape the program.

She described what life had been like in the decade since the tragedy. "My parents, our family have been great in seeing us over the rough times," she said. "Without Skip things never quite meet; it's like a chain that's not quite strong enough to pull hard enough to make it clamp." Dabbing at tears, Katrina said that twelve-year-old Christopher looked exactly like Skip and had inherited his great sense of humor. He was ridiculous and silly—just like his dad before he went to war. "It's been hard," she said, "but we've made it."

EPILOGUE

F ellow citizens, we cannot escape history," Coretta told a crowd of three thousand people at Detroit's Ford Auditorium. "No personal significance or insignificance can spare one or another of us. The fiery trial through which we pass will light us down in honor or dishonor to the latest generation. We, even we here, hold the power and bear the responsibility."

It was early February 1972, and Coretta was in Detroit to perform Aaron Copland's *A Lincoln Portrait* with the city's symphony orchestra. As she had done twice before in Washington, DC, Coretta narrated the excerpts from President Abraham Lincoln that Copland wove into the orchestral work.

The audience understood how poignant it was for Coretta to speak Lincoln's words. She had weathered the battles of the civil rights movement and persevered after her husband's assassination. Her calls for peace helped galvanize millions of Americans to oppose the war in Vietnam. She urged her fellow citizens to fight for each other—and for the soul of their country. When she read from the Gettysburg Address, delivered by Lincoln to dedicate Soldiers' National Cemetery after the Civil War's deadliest battle, the echoes between the past and present were impossible to ignore.

"That from these honored dead we take increased devotion to that cause for which they gave the last full measure of devotion," she intoned. "That we here highly resolve that these dead shall not have died in vain. That this nation, under God, shall have a new birth of freedom—and that government of the people, by the people, for the people, shall not perish from the earth." Coretta, too, wanted to ensure that those who lost their lives during—or because of—the Vietnam War, Skip Johnson among them, did not die in vain.

BECAUSE CORETTA UNDERSTOOD that America is shaped by its past, she was able to see the future. She foresaw fundamental truths that can help us better understand the present and navigate the years to come. First, she recognized that the legislative gains of the civil rights era were incomplete—and could be rolled back by determined politicians and ambivalent voters. This is why she worked so hard to build bridges between the peace and civil rights movements: She saw that a larger consensus would be needed to produce and sustain changes to the country's values and priorities.

"Unless our work for peace succeeds, our work for civil rights will be meaningless," she said upon returning from Geneva in 1962. Martin's Nobel Peace Prize two years later brought "joy mixed with panic" for Coretta, because she understood that they both bore a tremendous responsibility to live up to the award. Her consistent emphasis on defeating war, racism, and poverty may have seemed idealistic, but it was also exceedingly practical—

focused on how these larger forces shaped everyday life for ordinary Americans.

One of the early issues that rallied Coretta and Women Strike for Peace was the discovery of strontium 90, a harmful radioactive isotope, in samples of children's baby teeth. The babies drank milk from cows that had eaten grass contaminated by fallout from atomic bomb testing. "It is very nice to drink milk at an unsegregated lunch counter—but not when there's Strontium 90 in it," Martin remarked in Boston in April 1965, one of the many moments when Coretta influenced his thinking.

Coretta fought for the things that she believed would make life better for average citizens—jobs, education, health care, housing, and food. The Vietnam War drew precious resources away from these needs, which is why she opposed it with every fiber of her being.

The second way Coretta saw the future was in terms of the prevalence of war in American society. Speaking in 1968, she told an interviewer that the experience of living through World War II, the Korean War, and the threat of nuclear war during the Cuban Missile Crisis and the Cold War was formative. "We really had been a generation of one war after another," she said. When Coretta urged Americans to rally for peace, it was not only to end the wars in Southeast Asia—it was also to bring an end to this cycle of war. She anticipated, correctly, that this larger goal would require ongoing vigilance. Since the end of the Vietnam War, in 1975, US armed forces have deployed to at least two dozen countries in situations of military conflict, including wars and interventions in the Persian Gulf (1990–1991), Iraq (2003–2011; 2014–2021), and Afghanistan (2001–2021).

Coretta consistently voiced her opposition throughout these

decades of perpetual war, linking foreign policy decisions to domestic concerns. At a 1983 march to the Lincoln Memorial commemorating the twentieth anniversary of the March on Washington, she said, "We must demand justice in Harlem and in the Bronx, but also in the Philippines. We must demand justice in the barrios of Los Angeles, but also in El Salvador." When the UN Security Council's deadline for Saddam Hussein to withdraw Iraqi forces from Kuwait—January 15, 1991—coincided with Martin Luther King's birthday, she urged those who had supported her husband and the civil rights movement, as well as those who had rallied against the Vietnam War, to oppose the war against Iraq "with the same fervor." Celebrating the King holiday in 2003, during the early years of the "War on Terror," she drew on Martin's words, telling a packed crowd at Ebenezer Baptist Church that "wars are poor chisels for carving out peaceful tomorrows."

After Coretta died, on January 30, 2006, President George W. Bush and three former US presidents—Jimmy Carter, George H. W. Bush, and Bill Clinton—joined civil rights luminaries at her funeral outside Atlanta. Her children Yolanda, Martin, and Dexter, all middle-aged now, sat together in the front row of the church, while Bernice sat onstage, waiting to deliver the eulogy. "I don't want us to forget that there's a woman in there," Clinton said, gesturing toward the coffin. "Not a symbol, a real woman who lived and breathed and got angry and got hurt and had dreams and disappointments."

Several speakers referenced Coretta's life and politics to critique the Bush administration's prosecution of the War on Terror. Carter alluded to Bush's secret authorization for the National Security Agency to eavesdrop on American citizens without warrants, calling it an echo of the FBI's wiretapping of Coretta and Martin. "We know now there were no weapons of mass destruction over there" in Iraq, said Rev. Joseph Lowery, before questioning why there were billions of dollars available for war, "but no more for the poor." In an editorial, Rev. Jesse Jackson said the president's praise for Coretta at the funeral would ring hollow when the country was expected to spend more than one hundred billion dollars that year fighting wars in Afghanistan and Iraq. "President Bush will pay tribute to Mrs. King, no doubt," Jackson wrote, "but she'd much prefer he pay tribute in his budget than in his words."

After the funeral, a motorcade carried the coffin to the King Center, the institution Coretta founded as a living memorial to her husband and the philosophy of nonviolent social change. Her coffin was placed in a temporary crypt until a new family tomb could be constructed, where she would lie next to Martin.

Third and finally, Coretta saw the future in terms of the racial and class demographics of the volunteer military. She recognized, earlier than most, that the military was part of the labor market—and an important one for Black and working-class Americans. When civilian jobs are scarce, military service and the pay and benefits it provides become especially appealing. In the fifty years since the end of the Vietnam War, Black Americans have continued to volunteer for duty and to reenlist at higher rates than the general population.

In 2024, for example, Black Americans made up 13 percent of the civilian population but 17 percent of active-duty service members across all branches. The numbers are even higher in the army, where Black soldiers comprised 23 percent of active-duty enlisted personnel and Black women accounted for 36 percent of all enlisted women.

The volunteers who step forward for military service today—of all racial and ethnic backgrounds—have much in common with Skip Johnson: young, working-class men and women from Rust Belt cities and rural towns, for whom military service is more promising than the alternatives. Coretta fought for these same Americans decades ago.

Coretta consistently said she opposed war but supported warriors. For her, this meant holding politicians accountable when they rushed headlong into foreign military conflicts—and building a peacetime economy with full employment that did not rely on military stimulus to fuel the labor market.

"The unemployed are not pawns to be sacrificed in some economic chess game," Coretta testified at a congressional hearing on jobs and inflation in 1975. "There are not enough hospitals and there is not enough medical care provided for people," she contended. "There are not enough public schools. There are not enough teacher aides or nursing aides. If we built more hospitals we could put a lot of people to work just building hospitals." She argued that focusing on these areas of human need would benefit all Americans—including soldiers, veterans, and their families.

In 1967, as public opinion for President Johnson's war plans waned, his supporters established the National Committee for Peace with Freedom in Vietnam, which launched a letter-writing campaign and organized demonstrations to "Support Our Boys in Vietnam." President Nixon bolstered this strategy, framing any opposition to the war as an attack on the country's soldiers. Since Vietnam, "support our troops" has become a litmus test for patriotism across the political spectrum.

Coretta was suspicious of the way the phrase "support our troops" could be used to silence dissent and make average citizens feel they had no right to question foreign policy decisions. Even worse, she understood that many people who claimed to support the troops in the abstract did precious little to support the actual men and women who volunteered for military service. By linking the military to the civilian labor market and advocating for soldiers and veterans alongside other workers, Coretta articulated a bold, expansive vision for what it means to support the men and women fighting the country's wars.

A SIMILAR REVOLUTION in values took place within Veterans Affairs, spurred in part by Skip Johnson's tragic death. While the psychologists Robert Jay Lifton and Chaim Shatan used Skip's story to personalize post-Vietnam syndrome and successfully pushed for PTSD to be added as a diagnostic category, other veterans' advocates lobbied for policies and resources to better support the nation's returning troops.

Senator Alan Cranston (D-California), for example, introduced a bill in 1971 to establish special counseling programs to help Vietnam veterans readjust to civilian life. The bill passed the Senate but died in the House Committee on Veterans Affairs—a pattern that repeated throughout the decade. The obstacle was in part generational: The House committee was dominated by World War II and Korean War veterans, who did not believe Vietnam veterans deserved a separate program. Olin "Tiger" Teague (D-Texas), a D-Day veteran who chaired the committee at the time, typified this view.

Shad Meshad, an army psychiatrist who served in Vietnam, re-called lobbying Teague, who wore his combat awards—including a Silver Star, Bronze Star, and two Purple Hearts—to the meeting and roared, "How could you little wimps be sick? How could you be traumatized?"

Finally, in 1979, the legislation passed the House on its fifth at-tempt, thanks to political horse-trading. The Senate committee members gave their House counterparts authority to select future VA hospital construction sites in exchange for their support. Max Cleland, a Vietnam combat veteran who lost both legs and an arm in the war, was then head of the Veterans Administration. In the first two years, he oversaw the rollout of more than a hundred vet centers across the country, where Vietnam veterans could receive individual counseling, benefits assistance, and job referrals, and participate in rap groups. In Detroit, the *Michigan Chronicle* regu-larly featured updates on services at the local vet center—just a short drive from the home Skip and Katrina tried to build together after the war.

While the bureaucracy of the VA remained overwhelming, within its hospitals, psychiatrists such as Sarah Haley and Jonathan Shay worked to understand and support the unique experiences of Vietnam veterans. "The VA fought it tooth and nail," Haley said of her efforts to publish a groundbreaking paper on veterans who re-ported atrocities. "I took so much flak from colleagues because I spent time listening to veterans' stories."

At the Boston VA, Shay counseled veterans with PTSD, weaving stories of Achilles and Odysseus into therapy sessions. He used an-cient Greek tales of guilt, anger, loss, and betrayal to explore how war damages the spirit as well as the mind. "One of the things the veterans appreciate is the sense that they're part of a long historical context," Shay said, "that they are not personally deficient for having become injured in war." He introduced the term "moral injury" to describe the betrayal of what is right by people in positions of legitimate authority. This framework helped doctors better understand and treat veterans grappling with the pain of having performed, witnessed, or failed to prevent actions that violated their values.

Shay went on to work with veterans from the wars in Iraq and Afghanistan and advised military officers on how ethical and competent leadership can reduce or prevent moral injury. "Until we end wars, we will need men and women to do the military work of collective security that allows the establishment of peace," Shay wrote. "In the face of this necessity, we must protect these soldiers with every strength we have, and honor and care for them when inevitably they are injured by their service."

Skip Johnson's story—arguably the first high-profile case of psychological injury among Vietnam veterans—captured national attention just as medical professionals were beginning to confront the less visible wounds of a different kind of war. The strides the VA, psychiatrists, and military leaders have made in recognizing and treating PTSD and moral injury in the decades since are part of Skip's enduring legacy.

WHEN I HAD LUNCH with Katrina in February 2024, the waitress had just cleared our plates when Katrina's son, Christopher, joined us. "Matt and I were having a conversation about your dad," she said by way of introduction. Katrina had mentioned several times how much Christopher looked like Skip, and the resemblance was indeed unmistakable. The comparison carried a sense of loss—Skip never made it to his fifties. "I imagine that's what your dad would have looked like if he lived to be your age," Katrina said at one point.

After he sat down, Christopher started talking about his work as a long-haul truck driver—what warehouses had quick unloading times, the speed traps on the border between Michigan and Ohio. I was driving from Detroit to Cleveland later that evening and appreciated the tip. His eyes lit up when he told me about the time he was working for a courier service, making a delivery to the VA hospital in Battle Creek, Michigan. "I was just driving and I'm lost, and I came to a screeching halt, because I'm on this street," he said, showing me a picture on his phone of a street sign reading "Dwight Johnson Drive." "And it freaked me out. When I went inside and told the nurses, they didn't believe me at first, but I showed them a picture and said, 'That's my dad!'"

After Katrina, Christopher, and I said our goodbyes, I decided to drive to Battle Creek to see the street named for the hero whose story had brought me to Detroit. As I drove west along I-94, past cornfields dried in the winter chill, I thought of the vast number of American families whose loved ones lost their lives in the Vietnam War—more than fifty-eight thousand names recorded on the Vietnam Veterans Memorial in Washington, DC, and hundreds of thousands more, like Skip, whose lives were irreparably changed by it.

The sun was beginning to set by the time I reached Battle Creek.

I parked my car, zipped up my coat, and walked alongside the brick buildings of the VA hospital until I reached my destination. Barely a tenth of a mile long, Dwight Johnson Drive takes only a few minutes to walk, back and forth. This modest road is a memorial to a life—and to so many lives—taken too soon.

ACKNOWLEDGMENTS

This book would not have been possible without a lot of help.

Thank you to Katrina May for sharing her memories and stories with me. When I first reached out, I told her I wanted to tell a fuller version of Skip's story—and that hers was an important part of the history of the Vietnam War era. In our interviews, phone conversations, and text exchanges, she was consistently kind, generous, and funny. After reading the full draft manuscript, she said, "You hit the nail on the head." It made me as happy as any book review I've ever received.

Thank you to William Black, Barry Davis, James Luoma, Jack Mountcastle, Ken Neeld, Thomas Lamar Owen, and Harrison Picard for sharing their memories of serving in the Sixty-Ninth Armor in Vietnam. Their perspectives gave me invaluable insight into what Skip experienced during the war.

Thank you to Rachel Klepper, Evan Rothman, and Jennifer Lamm for assisting with archival research.

Thank you to my colleagues at Dartmouth—and especially to Dean Elizabeth Smith, former President Phil Hanlon, and President Sian Beilock—for supporting my research.

I'm also grateful to the archivists and librarians at the Schomburg

Center for Research in Black Culture, the National Archives, the Lyndon B. Johnson Presidential Library, and the George A. Smathers Library at the University of Florida for their expertise and generosity.

Thank you to Jeanne Theoharis for talking through ideas with me and sharing research materials while we worked on our respective books.

Thank you to the team at Viking for helping bring this book into the world. This project grew out of months of conversations with executive editor Ibrahim Ahmad. We explored many different ways to approach this history before deciding to tell it through the lives of Coretta Scott King and Skip Johnson. In many ways, it was the most challenging and rewarding book I have written. Thank you for embracing the project from its earliest stages and helping me find the heart of the story. Thank you to editorial assistant Elizabeth Pham Janowski for guiding this book through production; to Greg Villepique for his careful copyediting; to Laura Starrett, Melissa Churchill, and Susan VanHecke for their thoughtful reads of the book; and to IndexingPros for indexing the book.

Thank you to the publicity and marketing team, including Yuleza Negron, Carolyn Coleburn, and Chantal Canales, for helping this book reach readers; to senior production editor Chelsea Cohen for her logistical skills; to Linda Friedner for her meticulous legal review; to Dave Litman for the striking cover; to Meighan Cavanaugh for the beautiful interior design; and to Brian Tart, Andrea Schulz, Rebecca Marsh, Mary Stone, and Bridget Gilleran for their support of this book.

Thank you to my literary agent, Michelle Tessler, for seeing the potential in this project and supporting me throughout the process.

Thank you to my mom, Diane Delmont, for teaching me the importance of history. I'm deeply grateful for the love, time, and energy she dedicated to being a parent. She passed away in 2023. She was loved.

Finally, thank you to Jacque Wernimont, Xavier, and Simone for their love—and for making the woods of New Hampshire our home.

NOTES

PREFACE

xiii **typical newspaper headline:** "Vietnam Hero Collapses Under Glory Strain," *St. Louis Post-Dispatch*, June 9, 1971.

xiv **"God must have listened":** Katrina May interview, February 12, 2024.

xv **"He looks so young":** Katrina May interview, February 12, 2024.

xv **"I was never just":** Barbara Reynolds, "The Biggest Problem with 'Selma' Has Nothing to Do with LBJ or the Oscars," *Washington Post*, January 19, 2015; Jeanne Theoharis, *King of the North: Martin Luther King Jr.'s Life of Struggle Outside of the South* (The New Press, 2025), 20.

xvi **"I wish I could say":** Jonathan Eig, *King: A Life* (Farrar, Straus and Giroux, 2023), 448–49.

xvi **"What kind of country":** Len Lear, "Mrs. King Tells Beauticians to Enter Political Arena," *Philadelphia Tribune*, August 9, 1969.

xvi **"She came to help":** Fern Shen, "Hollywood Joins Hospital Workers to Press Johns Hopkins to 'Pay a Living Wage,'" *Baltimore Brew*, May 11, 2014.

xvii **"Sometimes we win":** Coretta Scott King, *Coretta: My Life, My Love, My Legacy* (Henry Holt and Co., 2017), 183.

xvii **"Look here, we've got":** David Halberstam, "The Second Coming of Martin Luther King," *Harper's Magazine*, August 1, 1967, 49.

xviii **"We had never seen":** Coretta Scott King interview, Ghana trip, Alden and Allene G. Hatch Papers, George A. Smathers Libraries, University of Florida.

xix **"I don't know":** Coretta Scott King, "Freedom Concert: The Story of the

Freedom Movement in Narrative, Song, and Poetry," box 23, folder 3, Alden and Allene G. Hatch Papers, George A. Smathers Libraries, University of Florida.

xix **The story appeared:** Michael Posner, "LBJ Gives 5 Medals of Honor," *Atlanta Constitution*, November 20, 1968; "Florida Priest, 4 Others Get Top Medal," *Atlanta Journal*, November 19, 1968.

xx **"Many of our young men":** Coretta Scott King interview, box 22, folder 8, tape 24, Alden and Allene G. Hatch Papers, George A. Smathers Libraries, University of Florida.

PART 1

CHAPTER 1: CORETTA

3 **crowd of eighteen thousand:** Raymond Daniell, "U.S. Assailed on Vietnam Policy Before 17,000 at a Garden Rally," *New York Times*, June 9, 1965; Arnold Abrams and Robert Mayer, "18,000 Cheer in NY at Viet Peace Rally," *Newsday* (Hempstead, NY), June 9, 1965.

4 **"Mrs. Martin Luther King":** "Emergency Rally on Vietnam," *New York Amsterdam News*, June 5, 1965.

4 **"Have you often wondered":** Coretta Scott King, "Highlights," *Emergency Rally on Vietnam: Madison Square Garden Rally*, June 8, 1965, album.

4 **State Department confirmed:** John Finney, "Johnson Permits U.S. Units to Fight if Saigon Asks Aid," *New York Times*, June 9, 1965.

5 **one of nearly a thousand:** "Viet Critics Maintain Barrage," *Christian Science Monitor*, June 10, 1965; Abrams and Mayer, "18,000 Cheer in NY at Viet Peace Rally."

5 **was "completely opposed":** Jack Langguth, "Taylor Supports Pace of Bombings," *New York Times*, June 8, 1965.

5 **"throwing bombs in Vietnam":** Scott King, "Highlights."

6 **"Too many men":** Scott King, "Highlights."

6 **Rustin knew as well:** Coretta Scott King, *Coretta: My Life, My Love, My Legacy* (Henry Holt and Co., 2017), 20–21, 78.

6 **The crowd rose:** Bayard Rustin, "Peace and Civil Rights, Our Common Ground," *Emergency Rally on Vietnam: Madison Square Garden Rally*, June 8, 1965, album.

7 **Freedom songs and chants:** Abrams and Mayer, "18,000 Cheer in NY at Viet Peace Rally"; "Rally, March Hit Viet Policy," *Press and Sun-Bulletin* (Binghamton, NY), June 9, 1965.

7 **He began carrying:** Edythe Scott Bagley, *Desert Rose: The Life and Legacy of*

Coretta Scott King (University of Alabama Press, 2012), 17–26; Scott King, *Coretta*, 10.

7   **"If you look"**: Scott King, *Coretta*, 10.

8   **burned to the ground**: Scott King, *Coretta*, 7–11.

8   **Obie Scott never showed fear**: Scott King, *Coretta*, 7–11.

8   **"He had the ability"**: Scott King, *Coretta*, 9.

8   **"If another child"**: Coretta Scott King, interviewed by Renee Poussaint, 2002, National Visionary Leadership Project interviews and conference collection, American Folklife Center, Washington, DC.

8   **"Hearing young people"**: Coretta Scott, "My College Aims," box 23, folder 4, Alden and Allene G. Hatch Papers, George A. Smathers Libraries, University of Florida.

9   **"Pacifism felt right"**: Scott King, *Coretta*, 28.

9   **"Do you then"**: Coretta Scott, "Senior Paper," December 19, 1950, box 23, folder 4, Alden and Allene G. Hatch Papers, George A. Smathers Libraries, University of Florida.

9   **"free souls who"**: John Clark, "Sincerity, Earnestness, Youth Mark Wallace," *Pittsburgh Courier*, July 31, 1948.

10   **fiery speeches from**: "Afro Camera Records Highlights of Progressive Party's Convention," *Baltimore Afro-American*, July 31, 1948; "Seen and Heard at the Progressive Party Convention," *Baltimore Afro-American*, July 31, 1948; "Negroes Play Prominent Role at New Party's Convention," *Chicago Defender*, July 31, 1948; Mark Hyman, "List of Negro Candidates at New Party Convention," *New York Amsterdam News*, July 24, 1948; W. H. Lawrence, "'Wallace or War' Keynotes Progressive Party Conclave," *New York Times*, July 24, 1948.

10   **"Jim Crow must go"**: Shirley Graham, "Shirley Graham's Keynote Speech, 1948," W. E. B. Du Bois Papers (MS 312), Special Collections and University Archives, University of Massachusetts Amherst Libraries; David Stein, "'This Nation Has Never Honestly Dealt with the Question of a Peacetime Economy': Coretta Scott King and the Struggle for a Nonviolent Economy in the 1970s," *Souls* 18, no. 1 (January–March 2016), 83; Lawrence, "'Wallace or War' Keynotes Progressive Party Conclave."

11   **used homespun pragmatism**: "Peace Big Issue, Keynoter Asserts," *New York Times*, July 24, 1948.

11   **"After watching Robeson's performance"**: Scott King, *Coretta*, 28–29; Jacqueline Trescott, "The New Coretta Scott King: Emerging from the Legacy," *Washington Post*, January 15, 1978.

11   **"The party was"**: Scott King, *Coretta*, 28.

12   **"He doesn't look"**: "Transcript of CSK interview," box 22, folder 4, tape 3,

Alden and Allene G. Hatch Papers, George A. Smathers Libraries, University of Florida.

12   his "intellectual jive": "Transcript of CSK interview."

12   "You have everything": Scott King, *Coretta*, 35.

12   "I saw that my views": Scott King, *Coretta*, 35–38.

13   "The language made": Scott King, *Coretta*, 46.

13   "The system was operated": Scott King, *Coretta*, 60.

15   "I felt very much": Scott King, *Coretta*, 54.

15   "I love being your wife": Scott King, *Coretta*, 97.

16   "We decided it was": Marjorie Hunter, "Arms Race Opposed," *New York Times*, November 22, 1961; Alvin Shuster, "Close-up of a 'Peace Striker,'" *New York Times*, May 6, 1962.

16   "The girls are only": Dennis Hevesi, "Dagmar Wilson, 94, Anti-Nuclear Leader," *New York Times*, January 24, 2011.

17   "women known through their husbands' reputations": Milton Bracker, "50 Women Striking for Peace Fly to Geneva to Present Views," *New York Times*, April 2, 1962.

17   "I go to Geneva": "'Human Survival Is Problem': Mrs. M.L. King," *Pittsburgh Courier*, April 7, 1962; "'Women for Peace' Air Views at UN Conference," *Chicago Defender*, April 11, 1962.

17   accompanied Martin on journeys: Jonathan Eig, *King: A Life* (Farrar, Straus and Giroux, 2023), 183, 211–13.

18   Dean received the women: "Women Pacifists in Geneva," *Des Moines Tribune*, April 5, 1962; "Zorin, Dean Hold Geneva Summit . . . with 90 Mothers," *Boston Globe*, April 5, 1962; "Mrs. King, Others Plead Against Test," *Atlanta Daily World*, April 3, 1962.

19   "It's all rather reminiscent": Shuster, "Close-up of a 'Peace Striker.'"

19   "The women are disappointed": "Mrs. King Home from Geneva," *New York Amsterdam News*, April 14, 1962.

19   a "private war": David Halberstam, "Our G.I.'s Fight a 'Private War' in Vietnam," *New York Times*, November 4, 1962.

21   offering "strong encouragement": "Welcome All, Even Reds Peace Group Head Says," *Boston Globe*, December 14, 1962.

21   "Peace Among Nations": "An Appeal to Negro Women," *California Eagle*, May 23, 1963.

21   no way of contacting: Scott King, *Coretta*, 104–5.

21   "bringing our nation": Martin Luther King Jr., "Letter from Birmingham Jail," *Ebony*, August 1963.

22   "I have a dream": Martin Luther King Jr., "Speech at the Great March on Detroit," June 23, 1963, in *A Call to Conscience: The Landmark Speeches of*

Dr. Martin Luther King Jr., ed. Clayborn Carson and Kris Shepard (Warner Books, 1984).

22 **hoped for a hundred thousand:** Scott King, *Coretta*, 113–14.

23 **as many as 250,000:** Scott King, *Coretta*, 114.

23 **"The list was endless":** Scott King, *Coretta*, 114–15.

23 **"tucked inside him":** Scott King, *Coretta*, 115.

24 **Coretta and Aminda Badeau Wilkins:** Scott King, *Coretta*, 116.

25 **"Yes, Mommy," Yolanda replied:** "Coretta Scott King interview," box 22, folder 9, tape 30, Alden and Allene G. Hatch Papers, George A. Smathers Libraries, University of Florida.

26 **"You who have":** "Progress Hailed by Peace Women," *New York Times*, November 2, 1963; "Strike for Peace at UN," *Daily News* (New York), November 2, 1963.

27 **Wilson presented her:** "Progress Hailed by Peace Women"; "Mrs. M.L. King in WSP Protest," *New York Amsterdam News*, November 16, 1963; "Strike for Peace at UN."

27 **"There cannot be peace":** Mabs Kemp, "'Women Strike for Peace' Hear Mrs. Martin L. King," *Baltimore Afro-American*, November 16, 1963.

28 **"hurried trip to Washington":** Sue Cronk, "She Feels Left Out—of Jail: Mrs. Martin Luther King Jr.," *Washington Post*, November 4, 1963.

28 **of "constant fear":** Cronk, "She Feels Left Out—of Jail."

28 **"I had no words":** Scott King, *Coretta*, 117.

29 **"the white youths":** Rowland Evans and Robert Novak, "Bomb-Banner Rides on Civil Rights Coattails," December 30, 1963.

29 **"I can never really be free":** P. Bernard Young Jr., "Cheers, Plaque for Leader's Wife," *Norfolk* (VA) *Journal and Guide*, May 2, 1964.

29 **youngest person ever:** Coretta Scott King, *My Life with Martin Luther King Jr.* (Holt, Rinehart and Winston, 1969), 1–3; Scott King, *Coretta*, 119.

30 **more active and public role:** Scott King, *My Life with Martin Luther King Jr.*, 1–3; "Interview with Coretta Scott King, Nobel Prize," Alden and Allene G. Hatch Papers, George A. Smathers Libraries, University of Florida.

30 **"threat of death":** Kathryn Johnson, "Years of Threats Told by Mrs. Martin Luther King," *Palo Alto Times*, October 21, 1964.

30 **"most notorious liar":** Mary Pakenham, "Hoover Calls Rev. King Liar," *Chicago Tribune*, November 19, 1964.

31 **"The FBI had become our enemy":** Scott King, *Coretta*, 121; Ralph David Abernathy, *And the Walls Came Tumbling Down: An Autobiography* (Harper & Row, 1989), 309; Eig, *King*, 404–5.

32 **"What the hell":** "Lyndon Johnson and McGeorge Bundy on 27 May

1964," Tape WH6405.10, Citation #3522, Presidential Recordings Digital Edition, prde.upress.virginia.edu/conversations/9060284.

32 **"If women would"**: "Mrs. King Asks Women to Help in Rights Fight," *Los Angeles Times*, March 7, 1965.

33 **"penned in invisible ink"**: Scott King, *Coretta*, 133.

34 **"by the timidity"**: Muriel Dobbin, "Dr. King Asks Settlement in Vietnam," *Baltimore Sun*, March 3, 1965; Jack Nelson, "King Eulogizes Slain Negro as Rights Martyr," *Los Angeles Times*, March 4, 1965.

34 **"I don't see"**: Roy Reed, "Alabama Police Use Gas and Clubs to Rout Negroes," *New York Times*, March 8, 1965.

34 **FBI agents filed**: "King's Wife Says Cause Would Go On Without Him," *Baltimore Afro-American*, March 20, 1965.

34 **path of nonviolence**: "King's Wife Says Cause Would Go On Without Him."

35 **that "[laid] bare"**: Lyndon B. Johnson, Special Message to the Congress, March 15, 1965, The American Presidency Project, presidency.ucsb.edu /node/242211.

35 **"The real hero"**: Johnson, Special Message to the Congress, March 15, 1965.

35 **"It is in South Africa"**: Luix Overbea, "Negro Role in Society Is Defined," *Winston-Salem Journal*, March 22, 1965.

36 **full citizenship, equal treatment**: Overbea, "Negro Role in Society Is Defined."

36 **"Mother to Son"**: Overbea, "Negro Role in Society Is Defined"; Scott King, *Coretta*, 139.

36 **President Johnson federalized**: Ben A. Franklin, "Field Commanders in Alabama Linked by 'Hot Line' to Pentagon," March 22, 1965.

37 **"Finally our lives"**: Scott King, *Coretta*, 139.

37 **At the Pentagon**: Franklin, "Field Commanders in Alabama Linked by 'Hot Line' to Pentagon."

37 **"The President desires"**: Memorandum # 328, Presidential Decisions with Respect to Vietnam, 4/6/1965, "NSAM 328 Presidential Decisions w/Respect to Vietnam," National Security Action Memorandums, NSF, Box 6, LBJ Presidential Library, accessed January 31, 2025, discoverlbj.org/item /nsf-nsam328.

38 **no clear explanation**: Irving Berstein, *Guns or Butter: The Presidency of Lyndon Johnson* (Oxford University Press, 1996), 534–35.

38 **"Both the President"**: William Westmoreland, "Vietnam in Perspective," *Military Review*, January 1979, 37.

38 **"felt the urge"**: Lydia Saad, "Gallup Vault: The Urge to Demonstrate," Gallup Vault, April 20, 2016, news.gallup.com/vault/190886/gallup-vault -urge-demonstrate.aspx; Jason Long, "Organized Labor and the Vietnam

Antiwar Movement: Early Union Mobilization," *Crimson Historical Review* 5, no. 1 (Fall 2022): 18.

39   **"American mothers will not"**: "He Graduates in June '65, Will He Die in Vietnam in June '66?," *New York Times*, June 26, 1965.

39   **nearly seventy-five thousand US troops**: Richard Eders, "Johnson Starts Sweeping Survey of Vietnam Role," *New York Times*, July 22, 1965.

39   **Polls showed 26 percent**: George Gallup, "U.S. Public Sharply Divided on Vietnam," *Los Angeles Times*, July 2, 1965.

39   **"Each of us"**: Ruth McCoy, "Your Chicago," *Chicago Defender*, April 27, 1965; Lillian Calhoun, "Confetti," *Chicago Defender*, April 27, 1965; "4 Rights Leaders at Presbyterian Confab," *Chicago Defender*, May 20, 1965; "Long Way to Go in Rights Push Says Mrs. King," *Chicago Defender*, June 12, 1965.

CHAPTER 2: SKIP

41   **"These five soldiers"**: President Lyndon Johnson, "Medal of Honor Ceremony," C-SPAN, November 19, 1968, https://www.c-span.org/program /the-presidency/medal-of-honor-ceremony-for-vietnam-veterans/443386.

42   **"jumped like frogs"**: Tom Ricke, "Medal of Honor Winner Dies in Holdup Attempt," *Detroit Free Press*, May 1, 1971.

42   **"It came as a shock"**: "Ex-GI Recalls How He Won His Medal of Honor," *Battle Creek Enquirer*, November 20, 1968.

42   **"The ceremony was"**: "Won Medal of Honor 1968—Slain in Detroit 1971," *Boston Globe*, May 1, 1971.

43   **"That's my big brother"**: Saul Friedman, "Dave's Big Brother's a Hero," *Detroit Free Press*, November 20, 1968.

44   **Joyce gave him**: Ricke, "Medal of Honor Winner Dies in Holdup Attempt."

44   **"We did not want"**: Eric D. Lawrence, "Alumni of Northwestern High Honor Classmate's Acts of Bravery in War," *Detroit Free Press*, September 18, 2012.

45   **"He's not related"**: "Citizens Protest Police Manhandling of Boy Suspect," *Michigan Chronicle*, June 30, 1956.

45   **"Most of these kids"**: Jim Treloar, "'They're Just Dumb,' Slum Teacher Says," *Detroit Free Press*, September 27, 1966; Jim Treloar, "What the Schools and Students Need," *Detroit Free Press*, September 28, 1966.

46   **"It is not merely"**: Ernest Smith, "A Northwestern Teacher Supports Boycott: A Million Merediths," *Illustrated News* (Detroit), October 29, 1962.

46   **"Segregated Northwestern's chief defect"**: Smith, "A Northwestern Teacher Supports Boycott."

47 **"See what has been done"**: Betty de Ramus, "Meet Jessie Kennedy, Dynamic Woman with Realistic Plans," *Michigan Chronicle*, June 13, 1964.

47 **Current Topics Study Club**: *The Norwester* yearbook, Northwestern High School, 1966.

48 **"This social revolution"**: Jeanne Theoharis, *King of the North: Martin Luther King Jr.'s Life of Struggle Outside the South* (The New Press, 2025), 107; Martin Luther King Cobo Hall Speech, 1963, BlackPast.org, blackpast .org/african-american-history/martin-luther-king-cobo-hall-speech -june-23-1963.

48 **Reading *The Iliad***: *The Norwester* yearbook; Hilary Hayden, "Classics in the Inner City School," *The Classical World* 60, no. 3 (November 1966): 93–98.

49 **"I've seen her around for years"**: Hayes B. Jones, "The Martyrdom of Alice Herz," *Fact* (July–August 1965): 11–17; Jon Coburn, "Making a Difference: The History and Memory of 'Women Strike for Peace,' 1961–1990" (PhD diss., Northumbria University, 2015), 117–21; David Jones, "Woman, 82, Sets Herself Afire in Street as Protest on Vietnam," *New York Times*, March 18, 1965.

49 **"to appropriate endless billions"**: Jones, "The Martyrdom of Alice Herz."

49 **Rosa Parks and Congressman John Conyers**: Jon Coburn, "'I Have Chosen the Flaming Death': The Forgotten Self-Immolation of Alice Herz," *Peace & Change* 43, no. 1 (January 2018): 41.

50 **"Negroes have caught hell"**: "The War in Viet Nam," 1965, GI Press Collection, Wisconsin History Society Archives, https://content.wisconsinhis tory.org/digital/collection/p15932coll8/id/80749/; "Mississippi Negroes Being Urged to Dodge Draft," *New York Times*, July 31, 1965; "Viet Nam War Victim Buried," *Enterprise-Journal* (McComb, MS), July 28, 1965.

51 **"unsuitable for military service"**: "Army Releases Fasting Soldier," *Gazette and Daily* (York, PA), July 17, 1965.

51 **"Mississippi Negroes Being Urged"**: "Mississippi Negroes Being Urged to Dodge Draft."

51 **"close to treason"**: Simon Hall, *Peace and Freedom: The Civil Rights and Antiwar Movements in the 1960s* (University of Pennsylvania Press, 2005), 28.

51 **"It is very easy to understand"**: "MFDP and Viet Nam," Mississippi Freedom Democratic Party, July 31, 1965, crmvet.org/docs/pr/650731_mfdp _pr_vietnam.pdf.

52 **"In Mississippi and Washington"**: Hall, *Peace and Freedom*, 31–32; Cabell Phillips, "350 Vietnam Protesters Are Arrested in Capital," *New York Times*, August 10, 1965.

52 **"Negroes better than anyone else"**: Daniel S. Lucks, *Selma to Saigon: The*

Civil Rights Movement and the Vietnam War (The University Press of Kentucky, 2014), 75.

52 **Dozens had been splattered:** Hall, *Peace and Freedom*, 31–32; Phillips, "350 Vietnam Protesters Are Arrested in Capital."

53 **"For many young Americans":** "Doubling the Draft," *Life*, August 20, 1965, 30.

53 **shared those memories:** "White Lutheran Pastor Wants Black Co-Pastor," *Detroit Free Press*, October 18, 1969.

54 **"I later peed in my pants":** B. J. Shorak, Robert Thornton, National Court Reporters Association, and Keegan C. Stitt, "Robert Thornton Collection, Personal Narrative," loc.gov/item/afc2001001.98021.

54 **"They wanted it the hard way":** Mary Penick Motley, ed., *The Invisible Soldier: The Experience of the Black Soldier, World War II* (Wayne State University Press, 1975), 171.

55 **"We don't serve":** Motley, ed., *The Invisible Soldier*, 171–72.

55 **handed out anti-draft leaflets:** Charles Ferrell, "A Tribute to General Baker," *The Black Scholar*, October 11, 2014, theblackscholar.org/a-tribute-to-william-bill-watkins-by-w-f-santiago-valles.

55 **His politics were shaped:** Robyn Spencer, Emilye Crosby, Nishani Frazier, Wesley Hogan, and Hasan Kwame Jeffries, "Rethinking and Un-teaching Entrenched Movement Narratives: A Virtual Roundtable," *Fire!!!* 2, no. 2 (2013): 102–6; David Goldberg, "Detroit's Radical," *The Jacobin*, May 2014, jacobin.com/2014/05/detroit-s-radical-general-baker.

56 **"With all of this blood":** General G. Baker, "Letter to Draft Board 100 Wayne County, Detroit, Michigan," *Soulbook*, Spring 1965, 133–34.

56 **"My fight is for Freedom":** Baker, "Letter to Draft Board 100 Wayne County, Detroit, Michigan."

57 **"I was not interested":** Katrina May interview, January 19, 2024.

58 **"You couldn't turn on the news":** Katrina May interview, January 19, 2024.

58 **"This is not a new war":** Katrina May interview, January 19, 2024.

59 **"tall, dark, and handsome":** "Party Date," *Michigan Chronicle*, August 28, 1965; Katrina May interview, January 19, 2024.

61 **first Black American awarded:** Bethanne Kelly Patrick, "Selfless Act Transforms Young Veteran into a Battlefield Legend," Military.com, March 1, 2017, military.com/history/pfc-milton-lee-olive-iii-profile.html; Brian Scott MacKenzie, "Pfc. Olive, Civil Rights Activist & War Hero," *Medium*, October 23, 2015, brianscottmackenzie.medium.com/pfc-olive-civil-rights-activist-war-hero-41ecf1495eda.

61 **"I thought of taking sleeping pills":** "A Hero's Father Reflects on Fate,"

Michigan Chronicle, May 28, 1966; MacKenzie, "Pfc. Olive, Civil Rights Activist & War Hero"; Dianna Carter-Williams, "Milton 'Skipper' Lee Olive III," Mississippi Public Broadcasting, February 3, 2020, mpbonline .org/blogs/mississippi-public-broadcasting/milton-skipper-lee-olive-iii.

62 **"but some of us are still"**: "A Hero's Father Reflects on Fate"; MacKenzie, "Pfc. Olive, Civil Rights Activist & War Hero"; Carter-Williams, "Milton 'Skipper' Lee Olive III."

62 **"My first wife died"**: "A Hero's Father Reflects on Fate."

CHAPTER 3: "SHE EDUCATED ME"

63 **"My friends are concerned"**: Jonathan Eig, *King: A Life* (Farrar, Straus and Giroux, 2023), 474.

65 **"the war has to go on"**: "25,000 Viet Protesters Throng U.S. Capital," *Atlanta Constitution*, November 28, 1965.

65 **"we got very little satisfaction"**: Max Frankel, "Demonstrators Decorous," *New York Times*, November 28, 1965.

65 more than twenty-five thousand marchers: "For Many Would-Be Marchers, the Wait for Buses Was in Vain," *New York Times*, November 28, 1965.

65 **"Our members are veterans"**: Homer Bigart, "More Bus Drivers Refusing to Carry Pacifists," *New York Times*, November 27, 1965.

65 We do not want you: "A Message to Our Sons in Vietnam," *Washington Post*, November 26, 1965.

66 **"Freedom and destiny in America"**: John Herbers, "Typical Marcher: Middle-Class Adult," *New York Times*, November 28, 1965.

66 **"in spite of the bombings"**: Taylor Branch, *At Canaan's Edge: America in the King Years, 1965–68* (Simon & Schuster, 2007), 385.

66 **"Unless America learns"**: "25,000 Viet Protesters Throng U.S. Capital."

66 **"would not have been"**: Frankel, "Demonstrators Decorous."

66 **"I expected to see"**: "Throng of 20,000 Marchers in Protest of Vietnam War," *Washington Post*, November 28, 1965.

66 lollipop-shaped placard: Frankel, "Demonstrators Decorous."

67 **"Free Gasoline and Matches"**: "Throng of 20,000 Marchers in Protest of Vietnam War."

67 a skywriting plane: "Anti-Viet Policy Marches in D.C. to Face Opposition," *Baltimore Sun*, November 26, 1965.

67 **"I wouldn't call myself a pacifist"**: Walt Harrington, "Not Rich, Not Famous," *Washington Post*, February 26, 1994.

68 largest US protest: "Organizer Says Vietnam March Is Proof Many Oppose War," *Washington Post*, November 29, 1965.

68 "absolutely no competence": "Dodd Rips King U.N. Remarks," *Chicago Tribune*, September 12, 1965; Branch, *At Canaan's Edge*, 329.

69 "If a Negro minister": David Lawrence, "Dr. King's Correspondence with Hostile Governments," *Hartford Courant*, September 16, 1965; Thomas Jackson, *From Civil Rights to Human Rights: Martin Luther King, Jr., and the Struggle for Economic Justice* (University of Pennsylvania, 2007), 313.

69 "I really don't have the strength": Eig, *King*, 471.

69 "The sparsity of civil rights leaders": Herbers, "Typical Marcher: Middle-Class Adult."

69 "There's too many white folks here": Herbers, "Typical Marcher: Middle-Class Adult."

70 "the great majority": Robert B. Semple Jr., "President Backs Right to Dissent on Vietnam War," *New York Times*, November 27, 1965.

70 "raising our voices": Robert B. Semple Jr., "Johnson Grieves over Toll in War," *New York Times*, November 27, 1965.

70 more than thirteen hundred: "Vietnam Conflict—U.S. Military Forces in Vietnam and Casualties Incurred: 1961 to 1972," table 590, Statistical Abstract of the United States, 1977 (US Department of Commerce, Bureau of the Census, 1980), 369.

70 passage from Aeschylus: Philip Potter, "GI Casualty List Stirs President," *Baltimore Sun*, November 25, 1965.

70 "Our aim is not only": Lyndon B. Johnson, "Annual Message to the Congress on the State of the Union," January 8, 1964, The American Presidency Project, presidency.ucsb.edu/node/242292.

71 "to mount a decisive war": Daniel S. Lucks, *Selma to Saigon: The Civil Rights Movement and the Vietnam War* (The University Press of Kentucky, 2014), 92.

71 "Vietnam has distorted": "Vietnam Strains U.S. Budget Seams," *Christian Science Monitor*, December 1, 1965.

71 "The cup of peril": Lyndon B. Johnson, "Annual Message to the Congress on the State of the Union," January 12, 1966, The American Presidency Project, presidency.ucsb.edu/node/238437.

71 "My foreign policy": Lyndon B. Johnson, "The President's Prologue and Epilogue to 'This America,'" October 3, 1966, The American Presidency Project, presidency.ucsb.edu/node/238391; Sheyda Jahanbani, "'Through a Narrow Glass,' Compassion, Power, and Lyndon Johnson's Struggle to Make Sense of the Third World," in Mark Atwood Lawrence and Mark Updegrove, eds., *LBJ's America: The Life and Legacies of Lyndon Baines Johnson* (Cambridge University Press, 2024), 284.

71 "The 'War on Poverty' may": Arnold Sawislak, "Viet Nam Expected to Cut Poverty Funds," *Chicago Defender*, January 6, 1966; Arnold Sawislak,

"'War on Poverty' May Learn How It Feels to Be Poor," *Los Angeles Sentinel*, January 20, 1966.

72 **"If our country can spend"**: "Words of the Week," *Jet*, December 22, 1966; Lawrence Allen Eldridge, *Chronicles of a Two-Front War: Civil Rights and Vietnam in the African American Press* (University of Missouri Press, 2012), 34–35.

72 **"shot down on the battlefield"**: "Dr. King to Weigh Civil Disobedience If War Intensifies," *New York Times*, April 2, 1965.

72 **"The Great Society is now"**: Arthur Schlesinger Jr., *The Bitter Heritage: Vietnam and American Democracy, 1941–1966* (Houghton Mifflin, 1967), 50.

72 **"only thing that could"**: James Forman, *Sammy Younge, Jr.: The First Black College Student to Die in the Black Liberation Movement* (Grove Press, 1968), 138.

73 **"You haven't heard of"**: Forman, *Sammy Younge, Jr.*, 193

73 **all-white jury**: US Department of Justice, Civil Rights Division, "Marvin L. Segrest, Samuel L. Younge, Jr.—Notice to Close File," March 28, 2011.

73 **"I wanted some action"**: Forman, *Sammy Younge, Jr.*, 246.

73 **"People were just filling the streets"**: Forman, *Sammy Younge, Jr.*, 252.

74 **"Every time the paintbrush hit"**: Forman, *Sammy Younge, Jr.*, 253–54.

74 **"Here was a man"**: John Lewis, *Walking with the Wind: A Memoir of the Movement* (Simon & Schuster), 374.

74 **"We didn't need to look"**: Lucks, *Selma to Saigon*, 113.

74 **"We believe the United States government"**: "Rights Unit Says U.S. Is Aggressor," *New York Times*, January 7, 1966.

75 **"A vote for Bond"**: Dan Berger, *Stayed on Freedom: The Long History of Black Power Through One Family's Journey* (Basic Books, 2023), 118.

76 **"You didn't want us"**: John Neary, *Julian Bond: Black Rebel* (William Morrow & Company, 1971), 95.

76 **"Each draft notice begins"**: Eldridge, *Chronicles of a Two-Front War*, 51.

76 **"Sammy getting killed"**: Julian Bond, *Julian Bond's Time to Teach: A History of the Southern Civil Rights Movement* (Beacon Press, 2021), 295.

76 **"the courage of draft-card burners"**: Lucks, *Selma to Saigon*, 116.

76 **"glaring, sad and tragic example"**: Lucks, *Selma to Saigon*, 116.

76 **NAACP head Roy Wilkins**: Lucks, *Selma to Saigon*, 115.

77 **violated his First Amendment rights**: Lucks, *Selma to Saigon*, 118.

78 **"War will never cease"**: Lucks, *Selma to Saigon*, 172.

78 **"We aren't doing enough"**: Lucks, *Selma to Saigon*, 173.

78 **"Bond's Right to Dissent"**: "Citizens Committee for Julian Bond" advertisement, *New York Times*, January 20, 1966.

78 **"absolute support for our brother"**: John Parry, "15 African Envoys Fete Bond in N.Y.," *Atlanta Constitution*, January 22, 1966.

78 "I support Bond": King, "My Dream: Bond and the Constitution," *Chicago Defender*, January 29, 1966.

79 said everything: "Africa, 1619": Berger, *Stayed on Freedom*, 136.

80 "I'm not giving them": Berger, *Stayed on Freedom*, 139–42.

80 WE MOURN THE DRAFTING: Berger, *Stayed on Freedom*, 143.

81 Carmichael's rise symbolized: Berger, *Stayed on Freedom*, 125–48.

81 "I felt uncomfortable with it": Oral history interview with Julian Bond, interviewed by Elizabeth Gritter, November 1 and 22, 1999. Interview R-0345. Southern Oral History Program Collection in the Southern Oral History Program Collection (#4007), Southern Historical Collection, Wilson Library, University of North Carolina at Chapel Hill. Published by Documenting the American South, docsouth.unc.edu/sohp/R-0345/menu.html.

81 walked out of the chamber: Horowitz and Theoharis, eds., *Julian Bond's Time to Teach*, 296.

82 "The level of poverty": Jeanne Theoharis, *King of the North: Martin Luther King Jr.'s Life of Struggle Outside the South* (The New Press, 2025), 190.

82 "I've never seen anything like it": Gene Roberts, "Rock Hits Dr. King as Whites Attack March in Chicago," *New York Times*, August 6, 1966.

82 "big and bold" programs: Eig, *King*, 500, 507.

83 "This is not an easy time": D. J. R. Bruckner, "Dr. King Sees 'Desolate Days' for Rights Drive," *Los Angeles Times*, October 1, 1966.

83 Kings' personal phone calls: James Reston, "Washington: The Kennedy-Hoover Controversy," *New York Times*, December 14, 1966.

83 "We've assumed all along": "Report the FBI Bugs Dr. M. King's Phone," *Philadelphia Tribune*, December 17, 1966.

83 "If the FBI wants": "King Widow Speaks," *Baltimore Sun*, May 29, 1972.

84 "not even a battle": "Statement of the Reverend Martin Luther King, Jr.," *Federal Role in Urban Affairs: Hearings Before the United States Senate Committee on Government Operations, Subcommittee on Executive Reorganization*, December 15, 1966, 2966–70.

84 most forceful public condemnation: Robert Semple, Jr., "Dr. King Scores Poverty Budget," *New York Times*, December 16, 1966; Jean White, "King Calls for Action on Guaranteed Income," *Washington Post*, December 16, 1966; "King Warns Anew," *Chicago Defender*, December 17, 1966; Martin Nolan, "Dr. King Hits 'Ill-Considered' Vietnam War," *Boston Globe*, December 16, 1966.

84 "Martin had been content": Scott King, *Coretta*, 149; Coretta Scott King, *My Life with Martin Luther King Jr.* (Holt, Rinehart and Winston, 1969), 272–73.

84 **determined to preserve that legacy:** Edythe Scott Bagley, *Desert Rose: The Life and Legacy of Coretta Scott King* (University of Alabama Press, 2012), x.

85 **deployed 385,000 military personnel:** "Vietnam Conflict—U.S. Military Forces in Vietnam and Causalities Incurred: 1961 to 1972," 369.

CHAPTER 4: BASIC TRAINING

87 **"When I graduated":** "New Way of Living Begins for 3,639 January Grads!," *Michigan Chronicle*, February 5, 1966; *The Norwester* yearbook, Northwestern High School, 1966.

87 **joined the Michigan National Guard:** Branden Hunter, "Rest in Power Congressman Conyers," *Michigan Chronicle*, October 30–November 5, 2019.

88 **"I like to think":** John Wisely, "John Conyers: Korean War Service Broadened Views," *USA Today*, July 1, 2013.

88 **"I was drawn to":** "'The Dean' Congressman John Conyers Jr.," *Michigan Chronicle*, October 30–November 5, 2019.

88 **"mother of the civil rights movement":** Jeanne Theoharis, *The Rebellious Life of Mrs. Rosa Parks* (Beacon Press, 2013); "Mrs. M.L. King Here to Fete Rosa Parks," *Michigan Chronicle*, April 3, 1965.

88 **"I do not support":** "Viet Nam Supplemental," *CQ Almanac*, 1965 (21st ed.), 180–81.

88 **"just a skirmish":** "Conyers Calls War on Poverty Just a Skirmish," *Michigan Chronicle*, October 23, 1965.

89 **it meant everything:** "March in Protest," *Michigan Chronicle*, March 27, 1965; "Tour High School," *Michigan Chronicle*, November 20, 1965.

89 **"He made people in this town":** Simeon Booker, "A New Face in Congress," *Ebony*, January 1965, 76.

89 **proud to have steady work:** Thomas Sugrue, *The Origins of the Urban Crisis: Race and Inequality in Postwar Detroit* (Princeton University Press, 1996).

90 **not ready to go steady:** Katrina May interview, February 12, 2024.

91 **18.3 percent of the US military:** Jack Raymond, "Negro Death Ratio in Vietnam Exceeds Whites," *New York Times*, March 10, 1967.

91 **"Negroes Dying Faster Than Whites":** "Negroes Dying Faster Than Whites in Vietnam," *New York Amsterdam News*, March 19, 1966.

91 **"It is not likely":** "Two Wars," *New York Amsterdam News*, January 8, 1966.

91 **fewer than 2 percent:** *In Pursuit of Equity: Who Serves When Not All Serve? Report of the National Advisory Commission on Selective Service* (US Government Printing Office, 1967), 75, 80–81.

91 Grand Dragon of the Ku Klux Klan: James Westheider, *The African American Experience in Vietnam: Brothers in Arms* (Rowman & Littlefield, 2007), 29.

91 "We sure let him slip": Julian Bond, "How the Draft Dodged Me," *New York Times,* February 15, 1992.

92 "The draft deferment test": Jean Carper, *Bitter Greetings: The Scandal of the Military Draft* (Grossman, 1967), 89.

92 "If you can't learn anything": "Teachers, Cleage Battle over Crisis in Schools," *Michigan Chronicle,* May 28, 1966.

92 "Black Men! Whitey's plan": Herman Graham III, *The Brothers' Vietnam War: Black Power, Manhood, and the Military Experience* (University of Florida Press, 2003), 28.

92 "I think we're being killed off": Graham, *The Brothers' Vietnam War,* 21.

92 "I feel good about it": Sol Stern, "When the Black GI Comes Back from Vietnam," *New York Times Magazine,* March 24, 1968.

93 that "race is irrelevant": Whitney Young Jr., "To Be Equal: Integration Seen Faster in War," *Baltimore Afro-American,* February 19, 1966.

93 66 percent of Black soldiers: Thomas Johnson, "The U.S. Negro in Vietnam," *New York Times,* April 29, 1968.

93 two thirds of Black respondents: "Hostility Is Found to Draft Lottery," *New York Times,* November 13, 1966.

93 "unjust, immoral, and illegal": Fort Hood Three Defense Committee, "The Fort Hood Three: The Case of the Three G.I.'s Who Said 'No' to the War in Vietnam," GI Press Collection, Wisconsin History Society, 1966, https://content.wisconsinhistory.org/digital/collection/p15932coll8/id /54495/.

95 "We are going to give you": Frederick Wiseman, director, *Basic Training* (1971).

96 "What is the spirit": James Gillam, *Life and Death in the Central Highlands: An American Sergeant in the Vietnam War, 1968–1970* (University of North Texas Press, 2010), 16.

97 "We want no wider war": "Vietnam: A Television History; Why Vietnam?," 1965, WGBH, American Archive of Public Broadcasting (GBH and the Library of Congress), Boston, MA, and Washington, DC, accessed July 23, 2024, americanarchive.org/catalog/cpb-aacip-15-1g0ht2gc5k.

97 others laughed uncomfortably: David Cortright, *Soldiers in Revolt: GI Resistance During the Vietnam War* (1975; repr., Haymarket, 2005), 246.

97 "The man is out to kill": Wiseman, *Basic Training.*

98 "proud of being a Marine": "Diamond Jim Can't Believe Son Is Dead," *Michigan Chronicle,* October 29, 1966.

98   After seeing the head wound: B. J. Shorak, Robert Thornton, National
      Court Reporters Association, and Keegan C. Stitt, "Robert Thornton Collec-
      tion, Personal Narrative," loc.gov/item/afc2001001.98021; "Marine Dies in
      Action in Vietnam," *Southwest Topics-Wave* (Los Angeles), November 3, 1966.

99   "You don't leave that kind": Shorak et al., "Robert Thornton Collection,
      Personal Narrative."

99   "like someone poking hard": Frank Murray "Thousands of U.S. Soldiers
      Suffer Loss in Hearing," *Des Moines Tribune*, August 21, 1969.

100   staging comedy skits: Barry Davis interview, February 29, 2024.

100   "Everybody would say": Barry Davis interview, February 29, 2024.

101   "The poor of America": Homer Bigart, "M'Namara Plans to 'Salvage'
      40,000 Rejected in Draft," *New York Times*, August 24, 1966; Ted Sell,
      "New Draft Plan," *Los Angeles Times*, August 24, 1966.

101   "a world run by strong men": Daniel Patrick Moynihan, memo to Harry
      McPherson, July 16, 1965, LBJ Library, Office Files of Harry McPherson,
      Box 21, McPherson: Civil Rights-1965 (2); Geoffrey Jensen, "A Parable of
      Persisting Failure: Project 100,000," in Geoffrey Jensen and Matthew
      Stith, eds., *Beyond the Quagmire: New Interpretations of the Vietnam War*
      (University of North Texas Press, 2019), 152.

102   "Very possibly our best hope": Lawrence Baskir and William Strauss,
      Chance and Circumstance: The Draft, the War and the Vietnam Generation
      (Random House, 1978), 125–26.

102   "If 100,000 nonwhite men": Jensen, "A Parable of Persisting Failure: Proj-
      ect 100,000," 152.

102   Nearly 40 percent: Lisa Hsiao, "Project 100,000: The Great Society's An-
      swer to Military Manpower Needs in Vietnam," *Vietnam Generation* 1, no.
      2 (1989).

102   without politically risky steps: Robert McNamara, "Social Inequities: Ur-
      ban's Racial Ills," *Vital Speeches of the Day*, December 1, 1967, 102.

103   businesses in Canada: Christian Appy, *Patriots: The Vietnam War Remem-
      bered from All Sides* (Penguin, 2004), 166.

103   "a kind of class warfare": James Fallows, *The National Defense* (Random
      House, 1981), 133.

103   "discriminatory and undemocratic": William Westmoreland, "Vietnam in
      Perspective," *Military Review*, January 1979, 37.

103   "at least my mother": Peter Gelzinis, "Skin Color Can't Break Bonds Made
      in Vietnam," *Boston Herald*, November 17, 2018, bostonherald.com/2017
      /09/28/gelzinis-skin-color-cant-break-bonds-made-in-vietnam.

103   men from working-class neighborhoods: Christian Appy, *Working-Class War:
      American Soldiers and Vietnam* (University of North Carolina Press, 1993), 12.

103 **More people from South Boston:** Matthew Medsger, "Vietnam Memorial Dedicated for 41st Time to 25 South Boston Lives Lost," *Boston Herald*, September 18, 2022; Brian Wright O'Connor, "Vietnam Falls, Harvard Shrugs," *The Harvard Crimson*, September 26, 2017.

103 **Latino neighborhoods in Los Angeles:** Steven Cuevas, "The Invisible Force: Latinos at War in Vietnam," *KQED*, May 25, 2015, https://www .kqed.org/news/10534280/the-invisible-force-latinos-at-war-in-vietnam.

103 **"They got our boys":** Carolyn Woods Eisenberg, *Fire and Rain: Nixon, Kissinger, and the Wars in Southeast Asia* (Oxford University Press, 2023), 49.

104 **highest known death toll:** O. J. Spivey, "New Documentary Honors Edison High School's Fallen Vietnam War Troops," *Philadelphia Tribune*, November 9, 2021.

104 **At Northwestern High:** "Earns Purple Heart," *Michigan Chronicle*, March 12, 1966; "Purple Heart Is Awarded Posthumously," *Michigan Chronicle*, August 6, 1966; "Tragedy Marks Reunion," *Michigan Chronicle*, March 4, 1967.

104 **"baby, that is nothing":** Clyde Taylor, ed., *Vietnam and Black America: An Anthology of Protest and Resistance* (Doubleday, 1973), 271.

104 **one of 382,000 men:** "Induction Statistics," Selective Service System, sss .gov/history-and-records/induction-statistics.

CHAPTER 5: BREAKING SILENCE

105 **a thunderous explosion:** Coretta Scott King, *Coretta: My Life, My Love, My Legacy* (Henry Holt and Co., 2017), 47–48; Coretta Scott King, *My Life with Martin Luther King Jr.* (Holt, Rinehart and Winston, 1969), 117; Jonathan Eig, *King: A Life* (Farrar, Straus and Giroux, 2023), 159.

105 **wake-up call:** Scott King, *Coretta*, 49.

106 **"when I made the commitment":** Scott King, *Coretta*, 51.

107 **"For countless thousands of children":** William F. Pepper and Benjamin Spock, "The Children of Vietnam," *Ramparts* 5, no. 7 (January 1967): 44–68.

107 **"dramatize and propagandize":** "Supplemental Correlation Summary, Subject: Coretta Scott King," June 7, 1971, FBI file.

107 **"Nothing will ever taste":** David Garrow, *Bearing the Cross: Martin Luther King, Jr., and the Southern Christian Leadership Conference* (William Morrow, 1986), 543.

108 **"There is an existential moment":** Daniel S. Lucks, *Selma to Saigon: The Civil Rights Movement and the Vietnam War* (The University Press of Kentucky, 2014), 189.

108 **Martin told his advisers:** Eig, *King*, 514.

108 **"Unless we have a peaceful world":** Doris Giller, "Her Involvement Not Planned, Says Mrs. Martin Luther King," *Montreal Star*, February 24, 1967.

109 **"we are engaged in a war":** Martin Luther King Jr., "The Casualties of the War in Vietnam," February 25, 1967, https://investigatinghistory.ashp.cuny .edu/module11D.php.

109 **"It challenges the imagination":** King, "The Casualties of the War in Vietnam."

109 **"Let me say finally":** King, "The Casualties of the War in Vietnam."

109 **"We entered this war":** Alex Coffin, "Many Have a Strong Feeling Against War," *Atlanta Constitution*, March 13, 1967.

110 **"scores of arguments":** Coffin, "Many Have a Strong Feeling Against War."

110 **"the evils which breed war":** Coffin, "Many Have a Strong Feeling Against War."

110 **"combine the fervor":** "Dr. King Leads 5,000 Peace Marchers in Chicago Stroll," *Baltimore Afro-American*, April 1, 1967.

110 **"Hate America" movement:** Eig, *King*, 516.

112 **"broken and eviscerated":** Martin Luther King Jr., "Beyond Vietnam: A Time to Break Silence," April 4, 1967, https://www.americanrhetoric.com /speeches/mlkatimetobreaksilence.htm.

112 **more like a professor:** King, "Beyond Vietnam"; Eig, *King*, 517–18.

113 **"I could never again":** King, "Beyond Vietnam."

113 **nation's most influential magazines:** "Dr. King's Disservice to His Cause," *Life*, April 21, 1967; Kenneth Crawford, "King and the Soldiers," *Newsweek*, April 17, 1967; "A Tragedy," *Washington Post*, April 6, 1967; "Dr. King's Error," *New York Times*, April 7, 1967; Lucks, *Selma to Saigon*, 198.

113 **"Dr. King has done a disservice":** "Dr. King's Error."

114 **"the wrong track":** Jackie Robinson, "An Open Letter to Dr. Martin L. King," *Chicago Defender*, May 13, 1967.

114 **"serious tactical mistake":** John Sibley, "Bunche Disputes Dr. King on Peace," *New York Times*, April 13, 1967.

114 **advocated for continued bombing:** "Senator Has Changed His Mind," *Norfolk* (VA) *Journal and Guide*, April 1, 1967.

114 **done "irreparable harm":** Lucks, *Selma to Saigon*, 197.

114 **"Is it wrong":** "Wilkins in Bitter Attack on Dr. King's Peace Stand," *Chicago Defender*, April 20, 1967.

114 **"much of the draft card burnings":** "Dr. King's Tragic Doctrine," *New Pittsburgh Courier*, April 15, 1967.

114 **"equally as determined":** Lawrence Allen Eldridge, *Chronicles of a Two-*

Front War: Civil Rights and Vietnam in the African American Press (University of Missouri Press, 2012), 107–9.

115 **"dismayed, and so am I"**: Peter Kihss, "Westmoreland Decries Protests," *New York Times*, April 25, 1967.

115 **"unrelenting military, political and psychological pressure"**: Tom Wicker, "Westmoreland Tells Congress U.S. Will Prevail," *New York Times*, April 29, 1967.

115 **never spoke again**: Lucks, *Selma to Saigon*, 199; Eig, *King*, 523.

115 **initially disapproved of his son's stand**: Scott King, *My Life with Martin Luther King Jr.*, 273.

115 **vital role for both of them**: Scott King, *My Life with Martin Luther King Jr.*, 273.

116 **"You cannot believe in peace"**: Scott King, *My Life with Martin Luther King Jr.*, 273.

116 **"When the Pope spoke"**: Scott King, *My Life with Martin Luther King Jr.*, 273–74.

116 **"a lot of the congregation"**: "CSK Interview," box 22, folder 8, tape 24, Alden and Allene G. Hatch Papers, George A. Smathers Libraries, University of Florida.

117 **Union members marched**: William O'Brien, "Visitors by Bus, Air, in March," *San Francisco Examiner*, April 16, 1967.

117 **"the hippie character"**: Mike Culbert, "War Protest Marchers Filled Kezar Stadium," *Berkeley Daily Gazette*, April 17, 1967.

117 **Marchers plucked lilies**: "San Francisco March Attracts Thousands," *Redlands Daily Facts*, April 15, 1967.

117 **Residents opened their apartment windows**: Rix Blair, "March Was Quite a Show for San Francisco," *Berkeley Daily Gazette*, April 17, 1967.

117 **"I believe in their right"**: Lynn Ludlow, "Youth Dominates March," *San Francisco Examiner*, April 16, 1967.

118 **"U.S. Serviceman Appreciation Week"**: "'Support GIs' Week Is Rolling," *San Francisco Examiner*, April 16, 1967.

118 **"You can't undo the work"**: "'Support GIs' Week Is Rolling."

118 **called American militarism a "cancer"**: "60,000 Rally Against War," *Press Democrat* (Santa Rosa, CA), April 16, 1967.

118 **"Fellow peacemakers," she began**: "Huge Crowds March to Protest War," *Modesto Bee*, April 16, 1967.

118 **"I know what bombing does"**: Lynn Ludlow, "Youth Dominates March," *San Francisco Examiner*, April 16, 1967.

119 **"For God's sake"**: Paul Hofman, "50,000 at San Francisco Peace Rally," *New York Times*, April 16, 1967.

119 **more than 125,000 protesters:** Darius Jhabvala, "King, at UN, Implores U.S. 'Stop the Bombing,'" *Boston Globe*, April 16, 1967.

119 **"We are willing to make":** Jhabvala, "King, at UN, Implores U.S. 'Stop the Bombing.'"

119 **"Hey, hey, L.B.J.":** Douglas Robinson, "100,000 Rally at U.N. Against Vietnam War," *New York Times*, April 16, 1967.

119 **"I had learned how to maim":** Gary Rader, "Draft Resistance," *New York Review of Books*, September 14, 1967.

120 **"white persons of good will":** Douglas Robinson, "Throngs to Parade to the U.N. Today for Antiwar Rally," *New York Times*, April 15, 1967.

120 **antiwar protests erupted:** "Protesters on March in Many Cities," *Oakland Tribune*, April 16, 1967.

120 **updates from FBI Director Hoover:** "LBJ Gets Reports on Protests," *San Francisco Examiner*, April 16, 1967.

120 **"The worldwide Communist apparatus":** "Demonstrations Will Prolong War," *Berkeley Gazette*, April 17, 1967.

120 **"bullets and mortar shells":** Roy Reed, "Johnson, in Medal Ceremony, Warns That Dissent Has Price," *New York Times*, May 3, 1967.

120 **"Stop the bombing":** Ken Burns, director, *The Vietnam War*, episode 5, 2017.

121 **"We aim at more":** "King Plans Anti-War Campaign," *Washington Post*, April 24, 1967; "King Seeks Volunteers for 'Vietnam Summer,'" *Los Angeles Times*, April 24, 1967.

121 **"Only the terrible constancy":** David Halberstam, "The Second Coming of Martin Luther King," *Harper's Magazine*, August 1, 1967, 48, 51.

121 **"Can we see the President?":** David Holmberg, "Viet Protesters Waited in Rain for a Message," *Washington Daily News*, May 18, 1967; "Dr. Spock, Mrs. King Lead 200 Peace Marchers to White House," *Atlanta Constitution*, May 18, 1967.

122 **"Dirty lousy traitors":** "Egg Hits Spock at White House War Protest," *Courier-Journal* (Louisville, KY), May 18, 1967.

122 **"They don't realize":** "Egg Hits Spock at White House War Protest."

122 **"I Ain't Got Time to Die":** Willa Mae Rice, "From This Pew," *Pittsburgh Courier*, May 27, 1967.

122 **"God called him":** Willa Mae Rice, "An Interview with 'The King's Lady,'" *Pittsburgh Courier*, June 3, 1967.

123 **Thirty people were arrested:** "Sit-in Escalates into Riot," *Boston Globe*, June 3, 1967.

123 **"Slavery could not have lasted":** "Mrs. King Sings in Beverly," *Boston Globe*, August 21, 1967.

123 **"We women gave you our sons"**: "You Can't Shut Out the Millions of Americans Who Oppose Your War in Vietnam," *New York Times*, September 18, 1967.

123 **"Not My Sons"**: "Women's March Erupts into Washington Melee," *Los Angeles Times*, September 21, 1967.

124 **"My war is being fought"**: "Mom of 'No Go' G.I. Picket[s] White House," *Philadelphia Tribune*, September 23, 1967.

124 **"It's time for the women"**: "CSK Interview," box 22, folder 8, tape 24, Alden and Allene G. Hatch Papers, George A. Smathers Libraries, University of Florida.

124 **appeared in *The New York Times***: "Mrs. Martin Luther King Jr. Says Join Me in Washington January 15," *New York Times*, January 11, 1968.

124 **"History shows us"**: Coretta Scott King et al., "Women Cry Out Against War," *Atlanta Constitution*, January 10, 1968.

125 **"We've had 10,000 women"**: James McGarry, "Women Planning Capital March, *Boston Globe*, January 14, 1968.

125 **"I don't think in terms"**: John Portlock, "Before Riverside: Black Antiwar Activism, 1917–1967" (PhD dissertation, University of Rochester, 2019), 325.

125 **"After my son returned"**: "Cleveland Mother Is Proud of Son Who Denounces U.S.," *Tampa Tribune*, November 25, 1967.

126 **"I'm with them one hundred percent"**: "Tuck Brothers Speak Out Against the Vietnam War," *Cleveland Call and Post*, December 2, 1967; "Women Plan Peace March," *Cleveland Call and Post*, January 13, 1968.

126 **"Mrs. King and Mrs. Wilson"**: Dorothy McCardle, "It Was Too Tame for the Radicals," *Washington Post*, January 16, 1968.

126 **"The Burial of Traditional Womanhood"**: Say Burgin, "Understanding Antiwar Activism as a Gendering Activity: A Look at the U.S.'s Anti–Vietnam War Movement," *Journal of International Women's Studies* 13, no. 6 (December 2012): 23.

127 **"He got . . . in a state of depression"**: Eig, *King*, 530

127 **"He talked about death"**: Eig, *King*, 538.

127 **"plague Congress and the President"**: Ben A. Franklin, "Dr. King Plans Mass Protest in Capital June 15," *New York Times*, March 20, 1968.

127 **"We believe the highest patriotism"**: Ben A. Franklin, "Dr. King to Start March on the Capital April 22," *New York Times*, March 5, 1968.

128 **"I must say I'm very disappointed"**: Carl Greenberg, "Dr. King Asks Johnson Defeat," *Los Angeles Times*, March 17, 1968.

128 **"rise of a 'messiah'"**: Eig, *King*, 532.

128 **recruiting "ghetto informants"**: Eig, *King*, 535, 541

128 underwent major surgery: Scott King, *Coretta*, 154.

128 "Martin was home": Edythe Scott Bagley, *Desert Rose: The Life and Legacy of Coretta Scott King* (University of Alabama Press, 2012), 233.

128 "What good will freedom be": "Lady Pacifist Visits Hanoi Women," *Boston Globe*, April 13, 1968.

129 "I wanted to give you": Scott King, *Coretta*, 155.

129 "Before we met each other": Carolyn Lewis Washington, "Mrs. King Upholds Non-Violent Action," *Washington Post*, March 29, 1968.

CHAPTER 6: AMBUSH

131 millions of Americans: Joel Achenbach, "Did the News Media, Led by Walter Cronkite, Lose the War in Vietnam?," *Washington Post*, May 25, 2018.

131 "It seems now": CBS News, "Report from Vietnam: Who, What, When, Where, Why?," February 27, 1968.

133 "Our job was running road convoys": Thomas Lamar Owens interview, March 13, 2024.

133 hundreds of thousands of gallons: Department of the Army, "4th Infantry Division Operational Report: Lessons Learned," January 31, 1968, 87.

133 "No task was more disliked": Donn Starry, *Mounted Combat in Vietnam* (Department of the Army, 2022), 106.

133 "Tanks were big-ass targets": Dwight W. Birdwell and Keith William Nolan, *A Hundred Miles of Bad Road* (Presidio, 2000), 162.

133 built for combat in Europe: Starry, *Mounted Combat in Vietnam*, 7.

133 "You'd learn more": Barry Davis interview, February 29, 2024.

134 In Skip's first three months: Starry, *Mounted Combat in Vietnam*, 79.

134 More than eight thousand American vehicles: Starry, *Mounted Combat in Vietnam*, 107.

135 "always on my mind": Starry, *Mounted Combat in Vietnam*, 5.

135 "One chapter talks": Ken Neeld interview, February 23, 2024.

135 "The tank was home": Thomas Lamar Owen interview, March 13, 2024.

135 "If you have been together": Jack Mountcastle interview, February 28, 2024.

136 "I was in combat": Jack Mountcastle interview, February 28, 2024.

138 "You don't have to treat them": Bill McGraw, "He Helped Start 1967 Detroit Riot, Now His Son Struggles with the Legacy," *Detroit Free Press*, December 29, 2016, freep.com/story/news/local/michigan/detroit/2016/12/29/detroit-riot-william-scott-race/95675688.

138 nearly ten thousand people: Matthew D. Lassiter and the Policing and Social Justice History Lab, "Days of the Uprising: 12th Street Blind Pig," *Detroit Under Fire: Police Violence, Crime Politics, and the Struggle for Racial*

Justice in the Civil Rights Era (University of Michigan Carceral State Project, 2021), policing.umhistorylabs.lsa.umich.edu/s/detroitunderfire/page /blind-pig1.

138 **"You could hear the tanks"**: Katrina May interview, January 17, 2024.

139 **turned "ghostly empty"**: Katrina May interview, January 17, 2024.

139 **"The majority of them"**: Katrina May interview, January 17, 2024.

139 **"theater of combat"**: "Afro Americans!," Series 1, Box 5, Folder 1, Wallace Terry Papers, Schomburg Center for Research in Black Culture, New York Public Library.

140 **"They say we're fighting"**: Herman Graham III, *The Brothers' Vietnam War: Black Power, Manhood, and the Military Experience* (University of Florida Press, 2003), 113.

140 **request a "captain's mast"**: Committee for GI Rights, *Kangaroo Court-Martial: George Daniels and William Harvey, Two Black Marines Who Got 6 and 10 Years for Opposing the Vietnam War* (Committee for GI Rights, 1969); David Cortright, *Soldiers in Revolt: GI Resistance During the Vietnam War* (1975; repr., Haymarket, 2005), 52; Christian Appy, *American Reckoning: The Vietnam War and Our National Identity* (Viking, 2015), 140–41.

140 **"Frankly I'm mixed up"**: David Parks, *GI Diary* (Harper & Row, 1968), 115–16.

140 **"a little too casual about death"**: Parks, *GI Diary*, 93.

140 **"I can't wait"**: Parks, *GI Diary*, 91.

141 **Battle of Dak To**: Department of the Army, "The Battle for Dak To: 4th Infantry Division, 25 Oct–1 Dec 67 (After Action Report)," January 3, 1968; John Schlight, *The War in South Vietnam: The Years of the Offensive, 1965–1968* (Air Force History and Museums Program, 1999).

141 **"The Communists seemed bent**: Peter Arnett, "Dak To: Fiercest of Viet," *Boston Globe*, November 26, 1967.

142 **"In a conventional war"**: Arnett, "Dak To: Fiercest of Viet."

142 **"Victory and defeat"**: Lee Lescaze, "Dakto: The Enemy's Choice," *Washington Post*, November 25, 1967.

142 **"beginning of a great defeat"**: "Westmoreland Says End of War Beginning to Come into View," *Globe and Mail* (Toronto), November 23, 1967.

142 **"We military people"**: Orr Kelley, "Military Says 'War Nearly Won,'" *Boston Globe*, November 26, 1967.

142 **majority of Americans**: "Harris Poll Finds Most Support War," *New York Times*, December 31, 1967; "A Gallup Poll Finds 59% of Americans Would Continue War," *New York Times*, November 11, 1967.

142 **"acts of disloyalty"**: "Poll Finds Johnson Reverses His Popularity Loss," *New York Times*, December 5, 1967.

143 **"Always ready to accentuate"**: John Mountcastle interview, February 28, 2024.

143 **"Failure to rapidly replace tanks"**: Department of the Army, "4th Infantry Division Operational Report: Lessons Learned," January 31, 1968.

144 **waves of enemy soldiers**: Department of the Army, "4th Infantry Division Operational Report: Lessons Learned," January 31, 1968; Congressional Medal of Honor Citation, "Dwight Hal Johnson," November 19, 1968.

145 **with his .45-caliber pistol**: Congressional Medal of Honor Citation, "Dwight Hal Johnson."

145 **"The difference between what Dwight did"**: John Mountcastle interview, February 28, 2024.

145 **"He was really close"**: Jon Nordheimer, "From Dakto to Detroit," *New York Times*, May 26, 1971.

146 **"When the tank blew up"**: Nordheimer, "From Dakto to Detroit."

146 **holding off the attackers**: Congressional Medal of Honor Citation, "Dwight Hal Johnson"; "U.S. Units Escape Traps in Vietnam," *New York Times*, January 16, 1968.

146 **"He saved the lives"**: Tom Stanton, "A Hero in Vietnam, Detroit Died a Tragic Death 3 Years Later," *Detroit Free Press*, December 4, 2022.

146 **"When it was all over"**: Nordheimer, "From Dakto to Detroit."

146 **"I don't know how many"**: "Won Medal of Honor 1968—Slain in Detroit 1971," *Boston Globe*, May 1, 1971.

146 **"The berserk state is ruinous"**: Jonathan Shay, *Achilles in Vietnam: Combat Trauma and the Undoing of Character* (Atheneum, 1994), 98.

146 **One memory from the frenzy**: Nordheimer, "From Dakto to Detroit."

PART 2

CHAPTER 7: AMERICA BELONGS TO US

152 **"I have the sad responsibility"**: Coretta Scott King, *Coretta: My Life, My Love, My Legacy* (Henry Holt and Co., 2017), 162.

152 **"I have never seen such courage"**: Robert Anglin, "A Widow Marches," *Boston Globe*, April 9, 1968.

152 **"the tears would roll"**: Scott King, *Coretta*, 172.

153 **who remained at Camp David**: Robert Barkdoll, "Humphrey to Represent Government at Funeral," *Los Angeles Times*, April 9, 1968.

153 **more than fifty members of Congress**: "Who's Who Attending Funeral," *Atlanta Constitution*, April 10, 1968.

153 **"He gave his life"**: "Mrs. King's Statement," *Boston Globe*, April 7, 1968.

153 **"To lose great men"**: Scott King, *Coretta*, 176–77.

153 **more than eighty thousand demonstrators**: Michael Stern, "87,000 March in War Protests Here," *New York Times*, April 28, 1968.

154 **"Ten Commandments on Vietnam"**: Coretta Scott King, "10 Commandments on Vietnam," American Rhetoric, April 27, 1968, https://www.ameri canrhetoric.com/speeches/corettascottkingvietnamcommandments.htm.

155 **"Veterans for Peace in Vietnam"**: David Holmstrom, "New York Parades Air War Dispute," *Christian Science Monitor*, April 30, 1968.

155 **"until the last gun is silent"**: Coretta Scott King, "10 Commandments on Vietnam."

156 **largest of dozens**: "Both Sides Have Their Day," *Boston Globe*, April 28, 1968.

156 **"We are not being saved"**: Stern, "87,000 March in War Protests Here."

156 **Tens of thousands more**: "Protesters Active Around World," *Globe and Mail* (Toronto), April 29, 1968.

156 **calling for "poor power"**: Joseph Sterne, "Rally Hears Mrs. King's March Plea," *Baltimore Sun*, May 2, 1968.

157 **"I must remind you"**: Joseph Sterne, "King Widow Leads Trek by Mothers," *Baltimore Sun*, May 13, 1968; Judith Martin and Carolyn Lewis, "Coretta King: From His Footsteps to Her Own," *Washington Post*, June 16, 1968.

158 **"Long live the King"**: "Mrs. King Lifts Spirits of Poor March," *Washington Post*, May 31, 1968.

158 **"With all due respect"**: Coretta Scott King, "We May Yet Not Only Survive, We May Triumph," *Harvard Alumni Bulletin*, July 1, 1968; Bertram Waters, "Somber Class Day for Harvard," *Boston Globe*, June 13, 1968.

159 **"Has not power heard"**: Coretta Scott King, "We May Yet Not Only Survive, We May Triumph," *Harvard Alumni Bulletin*, July 1, 1968.

159 **"unlawfully, willfully, and knowingly"**: Michael Steward Foley, "When the Government Went After Dr. Spock," *New York Times*, June 14, 2018.

159 **"What is the use of physicians"**: Daniel Lang, *Patriotism Without Flags* (Norton, 1974), 40.

160 **"Her speeches show it"**: Martin and Lewis, "Coretta King: From His Footsteps to Her Own."

161 **"campaign of conscience"**: Mary Wiegers, "Coretta King Stresses Women Power," *Washington Post*, June 20, 1968.

162 **"physical lesson" on when to not**: Wallace Terry, *Bloods: Black Veterans of the Vietnam War: An Oral History* (Presidio Press, 1984), 167.

163 **"another war being fought in Vietnam"**: Wallace Terry, "Black Power in Viet Nam," *Time*, September 19, 1969.

163 "not to make a big thing": Gerald F. Goodwin, *Race in the Crucible of War: African American Servicemen and the War in Vietnam* (University of Massachusetts Press, 2023), 89.

163 "We are supposed to be American": Goodwin, *Race in the Crucible of War*, 89.

163 Black troops began organizing groups: Herman Graham III, *The Brothers' Vietnam War: Black Power, Manhood, and the Military Experience* (University of Florida Press, 2003), 100.

163 "protect ourselves from the force": "Black Panther Party Platform and Program," October 1966, https://archive.org/details/Blackpntrs10Pnt.66.

164 largest domestic airlift: John Kifner, "Thousands of U.S. Troops Mobilized for Guard Duty at Democratic Convention," *New York Times*, August 25, 1968.

164 "We feel that we've done enough": "Armed Forces: The Defiant 43," *Time*, September 13, 1968.

164 Each was later court-martialed: "3 More Convicted in Protest at Fort," *New York Times*, September 29, 1968.

165 "How could I fire": Aretha Watkins, "Is Army Punishing GI, One of 'Fort Hood 43'?," *Michigan Chronicle*, January 11, 1969.

165 "shoot to kill any arsonist": "Nation: Should Looters Be Shot?," *Time*, April 26, 1968.

165 a "police riot": Daniel Walker, *Rights in Conflict: The Violent Confrontation of Demonstrators and Police in the Parks and Streets of Chicago During the Week of the Democratic National Convention of 1968* (Bantam Books, 1968).

166 "Julian Bond has the axe handle": Jim Rankin, "Lester and Julian?," *Atlanta Constitution*, August 28, 1968.

166 "national judgment on the war": Michael Long, ed., *Race Man: Julian Bond Selected Works, 1960–2015* (City Lights Books, 2020), 44.

166 "poverty, racism, and war": Long, ed., *Race Man*, 44.

167 "If this dream is deferred": Long, ed., *Race Man*, 50.

167 "Both parties would give": Ethel Payne, "So This Is Washington," *Chicago Defender*, July 6, 1968.

167 who fed ice cream: Sara Davidson, "Rockefeller Debates Hecklers in Atlanta," *Boston Globe*, May 24, 1968; Ethel Payne, "Humphrey's Big Dilemma," *Chicago Defender*, July 13, 1968.

167 he would appoint Coretta: "McCarthy Model Cabinet Lists Rockefeller," *Globe and Mail* (Toronto), August 16, 1968.

167 vicious red-baiting: Scott King, *Coretta*, 216.

167 Nixon attended the funeral: Dwight Chapin, *The President's Man: The Memoirs of Nixon's Trusted Aide* (William Morrow, 2022), 68–90.

169 **"lesser of the evils"**: Alex Coffin, "Mrs. King Backs Humphrey-Muskie," *Atlanta Constitution*, October 30, 1968; Juan Williams, "How Would America Be Different If King Had Lived?," *Washington Post*, April 3, 1988.

169 **"I think his opponents"**: Coffin, "Mrs. King Backs Humphrey-Muskie."

169 **"Millions of black people"**: "Conyers Mostly Anti-Nixon," *Baltimore Sun*, October 25, 1968.

169 **"help President Nixon"**: "Mrs. King to Aid Nixon 'If He Is Right,'" *Norfolk* (VA) *Journal and Guide*, November 9, 1968.

169 **"a sense of somebodiness"**: Carolyn Lewis, "A Negro Mother's Big Job," *Washington Post*, September 6, 1968.

170 **"America belongs to us"**: Lewis, "A Negro Mother's Big Job."

CHAPTER 8: HONOR

171 **"If I ask you to marry"**: Katrina May interview, July 11, 2024.

173 **"The adjustment period"**: James T. Gillam, *War in the Central Highlands of Vietnam, 1968–1970* (Edwin Mellon Press, 2006), vi; Gerald F. Goodwin, *Race in the Crucible of War: African American Servicemen and the War in Vietnam* (University of Massachusetts Press, 2023), 208.

174 **offered little to help veterans**: Richard Kulka, ed., *Trauma and the Vietnam War Generation* (Brunner/Mazel, 1990), xxviii.

174 **"gross stress reactions"**: Ghislaine Boulanger, "Diagnosis and Its Discontents: Chaim Shatan and the Definition of Military Trauma," *Studies in Gender and Sexuality* 21, no. 3 (2020): 219.

174 **"I been livin' with Vietnam"**: Wallace Terry, *Bloods: Black Veterans of the Vietnam War: An Oral History* (Presidio Press, 1984), 14.

174 **"Once you've fought in Vietnam"**: Goodwin, *Race in the Crucible of War*, 210.

174 **"When Skip came home"**: Jon Nordheimer, "From Dakto to Detroit: Death of a Troubled Hero," *New York Times*, May 26, 1971.

175 **"He had a stack of pictures"**: Nordheimer, "From Dakto to Detroit."

175 **"We went around to place"**: Tom Ricke, "Medal of Honor Winner Dies in Holdup Attempt," *Detroit Free Press*, May 1, 1971.

175 **"The big question is still"**: Thomas A. Johnson, "Negro in Vietnam Uneasy About U.S.," *New York Times*, May 1, 1968.

175 **"The Army was supposed to teach"**: Geoffrey Jensen, *The Racial Integration of the American Armed Forces: Cold War Necessity, Presidential Leadership, and Southern Resistance* (University Press of Kansas, 2023), 270.

175 **"It gave you a feeling"**: Goodwin, *Race in the Crucible of War*, 214.

176 **"even black senior officers"**: Eduardo Lachica, "After Retiring from

Highest Ranks of Military, Black Officers Find Dearth of Job Opportunities," September 28, 1987; Harry Summers Jr., "Red Badge of Courage: Earned and Ignored," *Los Angeles Times*, November 5, 1987.

176 **unemployment rate for Black veterans:** B. Drummond Ayres Jr., "Job Outlook Is Bleak for Vietnam Veterans," *New York Times*, June 5, 1971; Kopp Michelotti and Kathryn Gover, "The Employment Situation of Vietnam Era Veterans," *Monthly Labor Review* 95, no. 12 (December 1972): 13.

176 **"If the average Vietnam veteran":** Goodwin, *Race in the Crucible of War*, 207.

176 **just days before King's service:** "Military Rites for Marine Ronald Dobbs," *Michigan Chronicle*, April 13, 1968.

176 **"It was crushing to all":** Katrina May interview, January 17, 2024.

176 **"This is a bitter time":** Robbie McCoy, "'Why War?' Plagues Bereaved Parents of Felled Marine," *Michigan Chronicle*, March 2, 1968.

177 **"That was a trying time":** Katrina May interview, January 17, 2024.

177 **He read about the turmoil:** "Why Conyers Came Out for HHH," *Michigan Chronicle*, October 26, 1968.

177 **"I didn't do nothing, Ma":** Nordheimer, "From Dakto to Detroit."

178 **alongside four other recipients:** Robert Maynard, "Johnson Gives Medal of Honor to Five Heroes," *Washington Post*, November 20, 1968.

179 **"Other brave men will be called":** Michael Posner, "Black Soldier Among Five to Get Medal of Honor," *Chicago Defender*, November 20, 1968.

179 **"I want to remind you":** Maynard, "Johnson Gives Medal of Honor to Five Heroes."

180 **"Specialist Johnson's conspicuous gallantry":** "Medal of Honor Ceremony," November 19, 1968, c-span.org/video/?409914-1/medal-honor-ceremony-vietnam-veterans.

180 **"Honey, what are you crying about?":** Nordheimer, "From Dakto to Detroit."

180 **"I'm thrilled and proud":** Agnes Stewart, "Congressional Medal of Honor Won by Detroiter," *Michigan Chronicle*, November 23, 1968.

181 **"Face It Girl, It's Over":** Andy Badale and Francis Hayward Stanton, "Face It Girl, It's Over," performed by Nancy Wilson, *The Ed Sullivan Show*, November 24, 1968, YouTube, youtube.com/watch?v=vxMRaYt9Yhs.

182 **photo of the reunited family:** "U.S. to Allow Hero's Deported Father to Return," *Hartford Courant*, November 22, 1968; "U.S. Deported Stepfather of Medal of Honor Winner," *New York Times*, November 24, 1968.

182 **"His return was my Christmas present":** John Oppendahl, "Hero's Present to Mom," *Detroit Free Press*, December 24, 1968; "Honored GI's Parents Will Be Reunited," *Sacramento Bee*, November 21, 1968.

182 **"My father couldn't wait"**: "Katrina Lyn May Marries Medal of Honor Hero," *Michigan Chronicle*, February 1, 1969.

183 **"My mom and I went dress shopping"**: Katrina May interview, July 11, 2024.

183 **"We did sightseeing"**: Katrina May interview, January 19, 2024.

183 **"It's really ironic"**: Tom Stanton, "A Hero in Vietnam, Detroit Died Tragic Death 3 Years Later," *Detroit Free Press*, December 4, 2022.

184 **"a living recruiting poster"**: "Father Back in States, Viet Hero Re-enlists," *Michigan Chronicle*, December 28, 1968; "Medal Winner Gets New Duty Around Detroit," *Columbus Ledger* (Columbus, GA), December 19, 1968; Peter Davis, "Vietnam: 30 Years On," *Bangor Daily News* (Bangor, ME), April 30, 2005.

184 **"People were really listening"**: Fred Halstead, *GIs Speak Out Against the War: The Case of the Ft. Jackson 8* (Pathfinder Press, 1970), 81.

185 **"I'm not a Republican"**: Malcolm X, "The Ballot or the Bullet," April 3, 1964, https://teachingamericanhistory.org/document/the-ballot-or-the-bullet/.

185 **"Malcolm X laid his rap"**: Halstead, *GIs Speak Out Against the War*, 32.

185 **"I figured it must be"**: Halstead, *GIs Speak Out Against the War*, 74.

185 **"We, as GIs, are forced"**: "GIs United Against the War in Vietnam Statement of Aims," in Halstead, *GIs Speak Out Against the War*, 98.

186 **"It is our right to think"**: "GIs United Against the War in Vietnam Statement of Aims," in Halstead, *GIs Speak Out Against the War*, 98.

186 **"Fort Jackson Eight"**: The army admitted one of those arrested was an informant, lowering the number of defendants from nine to eight.

186 **growing network of antiwar coffeehouses**: "Coffeehouse Is Center of GI Dissent in S.C. Army Town," *Washington Post*, April 3, 1969; David Cortright, *Soldiers in Revolt: GI Resistance During the Vietnam War* (1975; repr., Haymarket, 2005), 53.

186 **"the most important victory to date"**: Ben A. Franklin, "Army Bars Trial of 3 Antiwar GI's," *New York Times*, May 21, 1969.

187 **"right to express opinions"**: "Antiwar Group Says Army Cautions Generals on Dissent," *Washington Post*, June 16, 1969; "Pentagon to Allow Protest in Services," *New York Times*, September 16, 1969.

187 **"the military reservation is fast becoming"**: Leroy Aarons, "Protesters in Army Are Increasing," *Washington Post*, April 17, 1969.

187 **be known as Malcolm X High**: CC Douglas, "Malcolm X Day Observed Widely," *Michigan Chronicle*, March 1, 1969.

187 **Skip worried that the students**: Jim Ingram, "Army Shared Blame in Hero's Death?," *Michigan Chronicle*, May 8, 1971.

187 **"We object to the Army"**: "Black Medal Winner 'Exploited' by Military," *Michigan Chronicle*, February 15, 1969.

188 **Not only was Detroit**: "City to Honor Viet War Hero," *Michigan Chronicle*, February 15, 1969.

189 **"We are aware that the American"**: "'Thank You, Detroit,'" *Michigan Chronicle*, March 1, 1969.

189 **"Acts of great bravery"**: "Westy: Made Reds Come to Talks," *Ironwood Daily Globe* (Ironwood, MI), February 20, 1969.

189 **latest Gallup poll**: George Gallup, "Public Views Swing Toward 'Get Out' or 'All-Out' in War," *Miami Herald*, March 23, 1969.

189 **"He's a marked man"**: "Eight Medal of Honor Winners Honor Ninth," *Detroit Free Press*, February 19, 1969.

190 **"Only God and myself"**: "Eight Medal of Honor Winners Honor Ninth."

CHAPTER 9: MORATORIUM

191 **"I see this war"**: "Mrs. King's Vigil," *Globe and Mail* (Toronto), October 16, 1969.

191 **"will not give his life"**: "Americans Show Distaste for War in Heavy Turnout," *Atlanta Constitution*, October 16, 1969.

191 **"the very fabric and fiber"**: "Mrs. King's Vigil," *Globe and Mail* (Toronto), October 16, 1969.

192 **"Are you prepared"**: William Raspberry, "His Own Quiet Way," *Washington Post*, November 3, 2003.

192 **marchers softly sang**: "Candles Burn Before White House," *Baltimore Sun*, October 16, 1969.

192 **was "obviously aware"**: "Right to White House," *Boston Globe*, October 16, 1969.

193 **"his worst day in office"**: Terrace Wills, "Wide Support Surprises Organizers of Nation-wide U.S. War Protests," *Globe and Mail* (Toronto), October 15, 1969.

193 **"If mankind wishes to survive"**: "Mrs. King Gets Love Prize," *Atlanta Constitution*, January 19, 1969; "Mrs. King in Audience with Pope Paul VI," *Afro-American*, February 1, 1969.

194 **"on the side of peace"**: Richard Nixon, "Inaugural Address," January 20, 1969, The American Presidency Project, https://www.presidency.ucsb.edu/node/239549.

194 **"I do not want guns"**: "Amnesty Asked for Deserters," *Baltimore Sun*, February 6, 1969.

195 **"very respectful hearing"**: William MacKaye, "Mrs. King, Clerics Talk Peace with Kissinger," *Washington Post*, February 6, 1969.

195 **his administration offered little clarity**: Carolyn Woods Eisenberg, *Fire and Rain: Nixon, Kissinger, and the Wars in Southeast Asia* (Oxford University Press, 2023), 48.

195 **"We fear the time is approaching"**: George Dugan, "Religious Leaders Bid Nixon Give Vietnam Policy," *New York Times*, February 22, 1969.

196 **"for what is happening in Vietnam"**: "How Patient Must We Be, Mr. Nixon?," *New York Times*, March 30, 1969.

196 **first woman to preach**: Tom McCarthy, "The World Today," *Star-Gazette* (Elmira, NY), March 15, 1969.

196 **"Ultimately the power of the spirit"**: Muriel Brown, "Mrs. King in London," *Washington Post*, March 17, 1969; Florence Mouckley, "'I See the Dawn of a New Day,'" *Christian Science Monitor*, March 21, 1969.

197 **Thousands of people gathered**: "A Nation Recalls Death of Dr. King," *New York Times*, April 5, 1969.

197 **dozens of other cities**: "Memorial Rallies Urge Rededication to King's 'Dream,'" *Washington Post*, April 5, 1969.

197 **paused for a photo**: Alex Coffin, "Widow, Mayor Start King Memorial Rites," *Atlanta Constitution*, April 5, 1969.

197 **"Make King's Dream a Reality"**: Coffin, "Widow, Mayor Start King Memorial Rites."

197 **"thousands of other ways"**: James Dickenson and Sidney Blumenthal, "Nixon Papers Harsh on Dr. King," *Washington Post*, December 2, 1986; Robert Jackson and Paul Houston, "Nixon Papers Show Concern for the Trivial," *Los Angeles Times*, December 2, 1986.

197 **Nixon sent Robert Finch**: "A Nation Recalls Death of Dr. King," *New York Times*, April 5, 1969.

198 **large GI-civilian antiwar demonstrations**: Ben A. Franklin, "Army Is Worried Over Increase in Aggressive Antiwar Militancy by Soldiers," *New York Times*, April 6, 1969.

198 **"Let us save America"**: "New Coalition Rallies Here," *Atlanta Constitution*, April 7, 1969.

198 **"dare to struggle to right wrongs"**: Robert Kilpatrick, "Response Urged by Mrs. King," *New Haven Register*, February 25, 1969.

198 **"paint on a crumbling house"**: "Dr. King's Widow Says Changes Are Needed," *Birmingham Post-Herald*, April 1, 1969; "King's Widow Demands Rescue of Black Children," *Arizona Republic*, April 1, 1969; "U.S. Must Save 'Lost Generation,' Says Mrs. King," *Chicago Defender*, April 1, 1969.

199 **The group's president, Katie E. Whickam:** Libby Neidenbach, "Beauty and the Ballot: New Orleans Civil Rights Activist Katie Whickam," Historic New Orleans Collection, September 14, 2023, hnoc.org/publications/first -draft/beauty-and-ballot-new-orleans-civil-rights-activist-katie-whickam.

199 **"What kind of country":** Len Lear, "Mrs. King Tells Beauticians to Enter Political Arena," *Philadelphia Tribune*, August 9, 1969.

199 **"America has confronted its conscience":** Robert Hey, "Viet Storm," *Christian Science Monitor*, October 17, 1969.

200 **"The war has destroyed the hopes":** "Right to White House," *Boston Globe*, October 16, 1969.

200 **"They surely see us":** "Americans Show Distaste for War in Heavy Turnout," *Atlanta Constitution*, October 16, 1969.

200 **"I felt like throwing up":** Nancy Zaroulis and Gerald Sullivan, *Who Spoke Up?: American Protest Against the War in Vietnam, 1963–1975* (Doubleday, 1984), 275.

200 **"Don't get rattled":** "The Night Nixon Moved America," November 3, 2010, nixonfoundation.org/2010/11/the-night-that-moved-america.

200 **"most prestigious leader":** Ethel Payne, "Mrs. King Lights Candle to Peace, Husband's Dream," *Chicago Defender*, October 18, 1969.

200 **hundreds of local newspapers:** Eisenberg, *Fire and Rain*, 86–87.

201 **"destined to go down in history":** "October 15: A Day to Remember," *Newsweek*, October 27, 1969; Eisenberg, *Fire and Rain*, 87; Stanley Karnow, *Vietnam: A History* (Penguin, 1983), 599; "Strike Against the War," *Time*, October 17, 1969.

201 **"Unless he can assert":** "Strike Against the War."

201 **"Our fight is here":** Paul Valentine, "Candlelight Walk Caps Day in City," *Washington Post*, October 16, 1969.

201 **"Our black brothers in Vietnam":** "Mrs. King to Speak," *Baltimore Afro-American*, October 18, 1969.

201 **"I die in Vietnam":** "War Protest on Wednesday Expected to Be Generally Peaceful," *New York Times*, October 12, 1969.

201 **students boarded commuter trains:** "M-Day," *Los Angeles Times*, October 19, 1969.

201 **Bankers in New York:** Eisenberg, *Fire and Rain*, 86.

201 **seventy-six crosses were arranged:** "War Protest on Wednesday Expected to Be Generally Peaceful."

202 **"He was killed last week":** Eisenberg, *Fire and Rain*, 86.

202 **etched a peace symbol:** "M-Day."

202 **"Bomb the birds":** "Flag's Use Symbolized U.S. Division Over Viet Moratorium Day," *The Register* (Santa Ana, CA), October 16, 1969.

202 **In Lexington, Massachusetts:** "War Protest on Wednesday Expected to Be Generally Peaceful."

202 **"costing America its soul":** John Herbers, "Vietnam Moratorium Observed Nationwide by Foes of the War," *New York Times*, October 16, 1969.

202 **tallied Moratorium march estimates:** "Americans Show Distaste for War in Heavy Turnout," *Atlanta Constitution*, October 16, 1969.

202 **"Dr. King was probably more right":** Daniel S. Lucks, *Selma to Saigon: The Civil Rights Movement and the Vietnam War* (The University Press of Kentucky, 2014), 234.

203 **"We have a right to suspect":** Wills, "Wide Support Surprises Organizers of Nation-wide U.S. War Protests."

203 **"travesty upon the sacrifices":** Valentine, "Candlelight Walk Caps Day in City."

203 **"We feel the moratorium":** Valentine, "Candlelight Walk Caps Day in City."

203 **defied Mayor John Lindsay's order:** "Flag's Use Symbolized U.S. Division Over Viet Moratorium Day."

203 **"On city flagpoles":** Homer Bigart, "Rallies Here Crowded, Orderly," *New York Times*, October 16, 1969.

204 **"to bring the war in Vietnam":** James Naughton, "Nixon Challenges Protest Leaders," *New York Times*, October 15, 1969.

204 **"Have you ever been inside":** "Troops Count Cost of Vietnam's Hamburger Hill," *The Guardian* (London), May 24, 1969.

204 **"writing it in a hurry":** "Vietnam One Week's Dead," *Life*, June 27, 1969.

205 **commitment to "Vietnamization":** Richard Nixon, "Address to the Nation on the War in Vietnam," November 3, 1969.

205 **"I would be untrue":** Nixon, "Address to the Nation on the War in Vietnam."

205 **"And so tonight":** Nixon, "Address to the Nation on the War in Vietnam."

205 **show of public approval:** "Nixon Declares 'Silent Majority' Backs His Speech," *New York Times*, November 5, 1969.

206 **"We've got those liberal bastards":** Karnow, *Vietnam*, 600.

206 **"It is hard to escape":** "Nixon Said Nothing New—Mrs. King," *Norfolk* (VA) *Journal and Guide*, November 8, 1969.

206 **"These predictions of violence":** "Dr. Spock, Mrs. King Accuse U.S. of Intimidating Anti-War Marchers," *Boston Globe*, November 9, 1969.

208 **"We are not here to break":** Richard Harwood, "Largest Rally in Washington History Demands Rapid End to Vietnam War," *Washington Post*, November 16, 1969.

208 **"What in the world":** Bryan Curtis, "Mr. Goodell Goes to Washington," *Grantland*, February 4, 2013, grantland.com/features/roger-goodell-father-senator-charles-goodell.

208 **"we cannot afford the humiliation"**: "Huge Crowd Continues March," *Fort Worth Star-Telegram*, November 16, 1969.

208 **watching college football**: "Massive Peace Rally Ends on Violent Note," *Hartford Courant*, November 16, 1969.

208 **Buckeyes' 42–14 victory**: "Nixon Telephones Woody Hayes," *Buffalo News*, November 17, 1969.

208 **"He was totally absorbed"**: Robert Levering, "How Anti-Vietnam War Protests Thwarted Nixon's Plans and Saved Lives," *Waging Nonviolence*, November 12, 2019, wagingnonviolence.org/2019/11/anti-vietnam-war -moratorium-mobilization-nixon.

209 **"measures of great consequence and force"**: William Burr and Jeffrey Kimball, *Nixon's Nuclear Specter: The Secret Alert of 1969, Madman Diplomacy, and the Vietnam War* (University of Kansas Press, 2015).

209 **"were becoming increasingly slim"**: Richard Nixon, *RN: The Memoirs of Richard Nixon* (Grosset & Dunlap, 1978), 54.

209 **58 percent of Americans**: Lydia Saad, "Gallup Vault: Hawks vs. Doves on Vietnam," May 21, 2016, news.gallup.com/vault/191828/gallup-vault-hawks -doves-vietnam.aspx.

CHAPTER 10: "NOBODY'S A HERO FOREVER"

212 **make sense of the atrocity**: "Viets Slain; U.S. Officer Held," *Newsday*, November 13, 1969.

212 **interviewed Paul Meadlo**: "'So I . . . Killed 10 or 15,'" *Washington Post*, November 25, 1969.

213 **"I raised my son"**: "'So I . . . Killed 10 or 15.'"

214 **"to the silence"**: Bill Black, "Vietnam Atrocities Merely American 'Business as Usual,'" *Michigan Chronicle*, December 13, 1969.

214 **joined seventy-five thousand demonstrators**: Robert Toth, "75,000 Hold Quiet Protest Against War Near White House," *Los Angeles Times*, May 10, 1970.

214 **"Our society is critically ill"**: "Coretta King Sees Nation Near Fascism," *Washington Post*, June 1, 1970.

214 **first soldier from Detroit**: James Cole, "Local GI Killed in Cambodia," *Michigan Chronicle*, May 30, 1970.

215 **"He was the best dad"**: Katrina May interview, July 11, 2024.

215 **"Nothing ever seemed to bother him"**: Rita Griffin, "Real-Life Story Was More 'Frightening Than Dramatic,'" *Michigan Chronicle*, April 3, 1982.

215 **His daily behavior became erratic**: Griffin, "Real-Life Story Was More 'Frightening Than Dramatic.'"

215 "We'd be watching television": Katrina May interview, February 12, 2024.

215 "Then he'd get angry": Griffin, "Real-Life Story Was More 'Frightening Than Dramatic.'"

215 "dog and pony show": Katrina May interview, February 12, 2024.

215 "Dwight was a hot property": Jon Nordheimer, "From Dakto to Detroit: Death of a Troubled Hero," *New York Times*, May 26, 1971.

216 "trying to suck him dry": Katrina May interview, February 12, 2024.

216 "I hadn't won the Medal": Tom Tiede, "They Are Capable of Error . . . and of Decency," *Daily Olympian* (Olympia, Washington), August 12, 1971.

216 "The military refused to believe": Griffin, "Real-Life Story Was More 'Frightening Than Dramatic.'"

216 "I had to handcuff myself": Nordheimer, "From Dakto to Detroit."

216 "know how to break away": Katrina May interview, January 17, 2024.

217 "had turned from a loving husband": Griffin, "Real-Life Story Was More 'Frightening Than Dramatic.'"

217 "The first day Dwight arrived here": Nordheimer, "From Dakto to Detroit."

217 he would go AWOL: Nordheimer, "From Dakto to Detroit."

218 "When they gave it to me": Aretha Watkins, "Dwight Johnson Sought Help . . . and Found None," *Michigan Chronicle*, May 8, 1971.

218 "put it down on paper": Watkins, "Dwight Johnson Sought Help . . . and Found None."

219 "eats away at your inner being": Wallace Terry, *Bloods: Black Veterans of the Vietnam War: An Oral History* (Presidio Press, 1984), 128.

219 70 percent of Black veterans: *Legacies of Vietnam: Comparative Adjustment of Veterans and Their Peers* (Committee on Veterans Affairs, U.S. House of Representatives), March 9, 1981, 47.

219 "Skip was something special": Nordheimer, "From Dakto to Detroit."

219 "Ma, I'm not taking a thing": Nordheimer, "From Dakto to Detroit."

220 Several neighbors turned hostile: Griffin, "Real-Life Story Was More 'Frightening Than Dramatic.'"

220 "Subject is bright": Nordheimer, "From Dakto to Detroit."

220 What hurt most: Nordheimer, "From Dakto to Detroit."

221 "He didn't confide in his mother": Nordheimer, "From Dakto to Detroit."

221 "What would happen": Nordheimer, "From Dakto to Detroit."

221 "in the psycho ward": Nordheimer, "From Dakto to Detroit."

222 When officials could not reach him: Nordheimer, "From Dakto to Detroit."

222 "like they were repossessing them": Katrina May interview, February 12, 2024.

222 **bought a 1967 Mercury for $850**: Nordheimer, "From Dakto to Detroit."

222 **called him a "traitor"**: Jim Ingram, "Army Shares Blame in Hero's Death?," *Michigan Chronicle*, May 8, 1971.

223 **"so troubled and tense"**: Ingram, "Army Shares Blame in Hero's Death?"

223 **"summer soldiers and sunshine patriots"**: Thomas Paine, "The American Crisis," American Battlefield Trust, December 23, 1776, https://www.bat tlefields.org/learn/primary-sources/american-crisis.

223 **delivered by William Crandell**: Judd Arnett, "Two Who'll Testify About 'War Crimes,'" *Detroit Free Press*, January 27, 1971.

223 **"all of Indochina aflame"**: Vietnam Veterans Against the War, *The Winter Soldier Investigation: An Inquiry into American War Crimes* (Beacon Press, 1972), 1.

224 **"I was ordered to shoot him"**: Gene Goltz, "Vets Tell Tales of Horror," *Detroit Free Press*, January 31, 1971.

224 **"Kill anything you want to kill"**: Vietnam Veterans Against the War, *The Winter Soldier Investigation*, 52; Todd Gitlin, "Ghost War," *Salon*, August 24, 2004.

224 **Calley was the only person convicted**: Homer Bigart, "Calley Guilty of Murder of 22 Civilians at Mylai," *New York Times*, March 30, 1971.

224 **"to prove that war crimes"**: John Peterson, "Mock Trial of US 'War Crimes' in Vietnam," *Boston Globe*, February 1, 1971.

224 **more than three hundred substantiated allegations**: Nick Turse, *Kill Anything That Moves: The Real American War in Vietnam* (Metropolitan Books, 2013), 14.

224 **"I consider these men patriots"**: "Congressman Conyers and Vets of Winter Soldier Investigation," February 18, 1971, Pacifica Radio Archives, North Hollywood, California.

225 **"It would seem that the massacre"**: John Conyers, "Congressman John Conyers Calls for War Testimony by Veterans," February 5, 1971, displaced films.com/sir-no-sir-archive/archives_and_resources/library/investiga tions/winter_soldier_investigation/conyers.html.

225 **"an outcry by young men"**: "Echoes of Atrocity," *Detroit Free Press*, February 2, 1971.

225 **"They said the shrinks could join"**: Wilbur Scott, *The Politics of Readjustment: Vietnam Veterans Since the War* (Routledge, 1993), 15.

225 **"The rap groups became known"**: Andrea Recarte, "Unveiling Chaim Shatan: An Analyst Unveiling War Wounds" (PhD diss., City University of New York, 2018), 55.

226 **Lifton and Shatan began pushing**: Murry Engle, "Behind the Capture of the Lincoln Memorial," *Honolulu Star-Bulletin*, December 31, 1971; Rob-

ert Jay Lifton, *Home from the War: Learning from Vietnam Veterans* (Simon & Schuster, 1974).

226 **"post-Vietnam syndrome"**: Gerald Nicosia, *Home to War: A History of the Vietnam Veterans' Movement* (Crown, 2001), 159.

226 **"When one comes back"**: Congressional Record, vol. 117, part 8, April 6, 1971, 9978.

226 **"a disservice to my country"**: James Naughton, "200,000 Rally in Capital to End War," *New York Times*, April 25, 1971; Daryl Lembke, "150,000 Ask Peace in 6-Hour Parade in San Francisco," *Los Angeles Times*, April 25, 1971.

226 **"serving my country"**: "Veterans Discard Medals in War Protest at Capitol," *New York Times*, April 24, 1971.

227 **"The country doesn't know it yet"**: "And the Anguish of a Veteran," *Washington Post*, April 25, 1971.

227 **"I have a story I'm writing"**: Nordheimer, "From Dakto to Detroit."

227 **Katrina kissed him goodbye**: Nordheimer, "From Dakto to Detroit."

228 **a Johnnie Walker and a Pabst**: Tom Ricke, "Medal of Honor Winner Dies in Holdup Attempt," *Detroit Free Press*, May 1, 1971.

228 **pulled a gun from beneath**: Ricke, "Medal of Honor Winner Dies in Holdup Attempt."

228 **"I kept pulling the trigger"**: Nordheimer, "From Dakto to Detroit."

228 **the early morning hours**: Katrina May interview, February 12, 2024.

229 **"he went into that store"**: Lawrence DeVine, "Did He Find Life Too Painful?," *Detroit Free Press*, April 6, 1982.

229 **"They say he shot somebody"**: "Medal of Honor Veteran's Holdup Slaying Puzzling," *Escanaba Daily Press* (Escanaba, MI), May 3, 1971.

229 **"Nobody's a hero forever"**: Dorothy Storck, "Medal of Honor Memory Jag," *Philadelphia Inquirer*, October 4, 1976.

CHAPTER 11: MAKING THE PEACE

231 **"Let us declare"**: John Hauragan and Irna Moore, "Peace Rally Temper Quickens," *Washington Post*, April 25, 1971.

231 **many in the crowd had marched**: Hauragan and Moore, "Peace Rally Temper Quickens."

231 **"war presents a very serious problem"**: "Conversation Between President Nixon and His Assistant for National Security Affairs (Kissinger)," April 21, 1971, National Archives, Nixon Presidential Materials, White House Tapes, Oval Office, Conversation 484–13; Carolyn Woods Eisenberg, *Fire and Rain: Nixon, Kissinger, and the Wars in Southeast Asia* (Oxford University Press, 2023), 291.

232 **267,000 US troops in Vietnam:** "Force in Vietnam Is Cut to 267,000," *New York Times*, May 11, 1971.

232 **"the public all they should know":** George Gallup, "The Gallup Poll: Nixon, Like Johnson, Faces Credibility Gap on Vietnam," *Baltimore Sun*, May 23, 1971.

232 **"We must force our government":** Hauragan and Moore, "Peace Rally Temper Quickens."

232 **"Fort McClellen GIs":** "250,000 Demonstrators March for 'Peace Now,'" *Miami Herald*, April 25, 1971.

233 **collecting draft cards and war medals:** Roland Powell, "Kerry, Mrs. King Denounce Viet in Capitol Protest," *Buffalo Evening News*, April 24, 1971.

233 **"There is no way to bring":** "250,000 Demonstrators March for 'Peace Now.'"

233 **"They forced us to return":** Hauragan and Moore, "Peace Rally Temper Quickens."

233 **"the struggle of one month":** "Mrs. King Hails Vets' D.C. Protest," *Boston Globe*, May 23, 1971.

233 **"a contribution we must make":** Hauragan and Moore, "Peace Rally Temper Quickens."

233 **"forget about the other war":** Hauragan and Moore, "Peace Rally Temper Quickens."

234 **"Our nation's preoccupation":** "King's Widow Calls for Peace, End to Racism," *Hartford Courant*, June 21, 1971.

234 **"While we have spent billions":** James Naughton, "200,000 Rally in Capital to End War," *New York Times*, April 25, 1971.

234 **"tie the anti-Vietnam war movement":** SAC, Los Angeles, letter to FBI Director, April 29, 1968, FBI files.

234 **urged the House Un-American Activities Committee:** "We Still Have a Choice, Mrs. King Tells Marchers," news clipping with notes [n.d., ca. October 1969], FBI files.

235 **"single most important thing":** Coretta Scott King, letter to Ruth Gage-Colby, March 26, 1971, FBI files.

235 **"uppity," "Queen," and "Black Jackie":** Henry Leifermann, "'Profession: Concert Singer, Freedom Movement Lecturer,'" *New York Times*, November 26, 1972; Roy Reed, "Widow of Dr. King Hopes Center Will Keep His Philosophy Alive," *New York Times*, January 10, 1972.

235 **"When I experienced the attacks":** Coretta Scott King, *Coretta: My Life, My Love, My Legacy* (Henry Holt and Co., 2017), 187–89.

235 **"Medal of Honor GI Killed":** "Medal of Honor GI Killed," *Atlanta Constitution*, May 1, 1971.

235 **featured an AP article:** "Too Much Too Soon Blamed for Hero's Death in Holdup," *Atlanta Journal*, May 3, 1971.

235 **Nordheimer's deeply reported:** Nordheimer, "From Dakto to Detroit," *New York Times*, May 26, 1971.

236 **"In many ways American students":** Andrew Malcolm, "C.C.N.Y. Graduates Hear Mrs. King," *New York Times*, June 2, 1971.

237 **described the government's arrogance:** "Vietnam: The Public's Need to Know," *Washington Post*, June 17, 1971.

237 **"America's public enemy number one":** Richard Nixon, "Remarks About an Intensified Program for Drug Abuse Prevention and Control," June 17, 1971.

237 **no evidence of widespread addiction:** Jeremy Kuzmarov, *The Myth of the Addicted Army: Vietnam and the Modern War on Drugs* (University of Massachusetts Press, 2009).

238 **"Addicts instead of the war itself":** Robert Jay Lifton, *Home from the War: Vietnam Veterans, Neither Victims nor Executioners* (Simon & Schuster, 1973), 125–26.

238 **blame the My Lai massacre:** Kuzmarov, *The Myth of the Addicted Army*, 8.

238 **a "Heroin Plague":** "Marijuana—The Other Enemy in Vietnam," *U.S. News & World Report*, January 26, 1970; "The Heroin Plague," *Newsweek*, July 5, 1971; Kuzmarov, *The Myth of the Addicted Army*, 44.

238 **"The specter of highly weapons-trained":** "The New Public Enemy No. 1," *Time*, June 28, 1971.

238 **one in four people:** Mimi Cantwell, "Veterans in Prison," U.S. Dept. of Justice, Bureau of Justice Statistics, 1981; Jason Higgins, *Prisoners After War: Veterans in the Age of Mass Incarceration* (University of Massachusetts Press, 2024), xii.

239 **Coretta's transformed countenance:** Alice Walker, "The Growing Strength of Coretta King," *Redbook*, September 1971.

239 **"fragility and formality":** Walker, "The Growing Strength of Coretta King."

239 **"Periodically Martin and I":** Walker, "The Growing Strength of Coretta King."

240 **"When he was assassinated":** Walker, "The Growing Strength of Coretta King."

241 **"It will be 50 years":** Reed, "Widow of Dr. King Hopes Center Will Keep His Philosophy Alive."

241 **"widow of Dr. King":** Reed, "Widow of Dr. King Hopes Center Will Keep His Philosophy Alive."

241 **"How well I understood":** Scott King, *Coretta*, 184.

241 **"My main focus":** Scott King, *Coretta*, 216.

241 **"We shall shun like the plague"**: Leonard Moore, *The Defeat of Black Power: Civil Rights and the National Black Political Convention of 1972* (Louisiana State University Press, 2018), 56–57.

242 **"This is a historic event"**: Ethel Payne, "Set Permanent Political Unit," *Chicago Defender,* March 13, 1972.

242 *National Black Political Agenda*: *The National Black Political Agenda* (National Black Political Convention, 1972), 28–29, 34; David Stein, "'This Nation Has Never Honestly Dealt with the Question of a Peacetime Economy': Coretta Scott King and the Struggle for a Nonviolent Economy in the 1970s," *Souls* 18, no. 1 (January–March 2016): 86.

242 **"topsy-turvy morality"**: Stein, "'This Nation Has Never Honestly Dealt with the Question of a Peacetime Economy,'" 86–87.

243 **"Nixon's dogs eat better"**: "Thousands March in Capital to Protest Nixon Welfare Plan," *Chicago Tribune,* March 26, 1972; "30,000, Many of Them Children, Protest Nixon Welfare Policies," *New York Times,* March 26, 1972.

243 **work to eliminate "systemic violence"**: Henry Woodhead and Gregory Jaynes, "Mrs. King Has Ideal Candidate," *Atlanta Constitution,* April 20, 1972.

244 **"alternative to it must be found"**: Sharon Taylor, "Mrs. Coretta King Addresses L.A. Clubs," *Los Angeles Sentinel,* May 25, 1972.

244 **"Martin wrote five books"**: "Mrs. Martin Luther King Inaugurates Black History Month at Cheyney State," *Philadelphia Tribune,* February 13, 1972.

244 **"militancy without purpose is unproductive"**: Doc Young, "The Subject Is . . . ," *Los Angeles Sentinel,* April 13, 1972.

244 **"the most militant of militants"**: Sharon Taylor, "Mrs. Coretta King Addresses L.A. Clubs," *Los Angeles Sentinel,* May 25, 1972.

244 **"Our study of the secret files"**: Jack Anderson, "Black Activists Are FBI Targets," *Washington Post,* May 16, 1972.

245 **plotted to assassinate him**: Mark Feldstein, *Poisoning the Press: Richard Nixon, Jack Anderson, and the Rise of Washington's Scandal Culture* (Farrar, Straus and Giroux, 2010), 340.

245 **ordered the mining of Haiphong Harbor**: John Darnton, "Antiwar Protests Erupt Across U.S.," *New York Times,* May 10, 1972.

245 **"Resolution to Impeach Richard M. Nixon"**: "A Resolution to Impeach Richard M. Nixon as President of the United States," *New York Times,* May 31, 1972.

245 **"gangrene of Vietnam"**: Carmen Fields, "Political Policies Create Radicals,

Mrs. King Says," *Boston Globe*, May 22, 1972; "King Widow Speaks," *Baltimore Sun*, May 29, 1972.

246 **"Mr. Nixon will have reduced"**: "President Plans a 12,000-Man Cut in Vietnam Force," *New York Times*, August 30, 1972.

246 **"people know the war is wrong"**: Charles DeBenedetti, *An American Ordeal: The Antiwar Movement of the Vietnam Era* (Syracuse University Press, 1990), 323.

246 **"Peace is at hand"**: "Kissinger Asserts That 'Peace Is at Hand,'" *New York Times*, October 27, 1972.

247 **national observance of King's birthday**: "U.S. Marks Birthday of Slain Dr. King," *Philadelphia Daily News*, January 16, 1973.

247 **"He believed in America"**: "LBJ Buried Near His Texas Birthplace," *Boston Globe*, January 26, 1973.

247 **"it would be hypocritical"**: "Nixon Leads U.S. in Mourning 'a Man of Unshakable Courage,'" *Los Angeles Times*, January 23, 1973.

247 **signed a ceasefire agreement**: Flora Lewis, "Vietnam Peace Pacts Signed," *New York Times*, January 28, 1973.

248 **"Vietnam Peace Hope Dim"**: Sylvan Fox, "Vietnam Peace Hope Dim," *New York Times*, March 29, 1973.

248 **"we could solve the unemployment problem"**: Stein, "'This Nation Has Never Honestly Dealt with the Question of a Peacetime Economy,'" 89.

248 **ensure jobs for all Americans**: David Stein, "Why Coretta Scott King Fought for a Job Guarantee," *Boston Review*, May 17, 2017.

248 **"This nation has never honestly dealt"**: Stein, "'This Nation Has Never Honestly Dealt with the Question of a Peacetime Economy,'" 81.

249 **more than 30 percent**: Michael Getler Washington, "Rising Black GI Ratio Worries Army," *Washington Post*, August 14, 1973.

249 **one in every three army GIs**: Martin Blinkin and Mark Eitelberg, *Blacks and the Military* (Brookings Institution Press, 1982).

249 **"The rising number of blacks"**: Washington, "Rising Black GI Ratio Worries Army."

249 **recruiters found that economic necessity**: Drew Middleton, "Armed Forces Recruitment Increases with the Help of a Sagging Economy," *New York Times*, January 26, 1975.

249 **"a commentary on our nation"**: Charles Moskos Jr., *The American Enlisted Man: The Rank and File in Today's Military* (Russell Sage Foundation, 1970), 153.

250 **"Most Americans with decent economic prospects"**: Earl Graves, "The Military and Our Fair Share," *Black Enterprise*, July 1980.

250 **"you have to ask why"**: David Binder, "Army Head Favors Volunteers," *New York Times*, February 11, 1977.

CHAPTER 12: RESTORED TO HONOR

251 **"We can never judge another person"**: Michael Graham, "Errant Hero Is Forgiven in Death," *Detroit Free Press*, May 6, 1971.

251 **Outside the church**: Graham, "Errant Hero Is Forgiven in Death."

252 **neighborhood residents paid their respects**: Barry Davis interview, February 29, 2024.

253 **northeast section of the cemetery**: "War Hero Slain in Holdup Is Buried in Arlington," *Philadelphia Inquirer*, May 7, 1971.

253 **"hanging up on people"**: Katrina May interview, January 19, 2024.

253 **"They kept pushing him"**: Dorothy Storck, "Medal of Honor Memory Jag," *Philadelphia Inquirer*, October 4, 1976.

253 **"I'd wake up in the middle"**: Katrina May interview, February 12, 2024.

254 **"Baby, I know you're angry"**: Katrina May interview, January 19, 2024.

254 **"I just let it go"**: Katrina May interview, January 19, 2024.

254 **"There are thousands of war veterans"**: "Speaker Says Honor Veterans," *Hartford Courant*, June 1, 1971.

255 **"impact of a modern tragedy"**: Henry Rosset, "The Post-Vietnam Syndrome," *New York Times*, June 12, 1971.

255 **"When soldiers are hailed as heroes"**: Samuel Brooks, "Psychiatrist Underscores Need for Reorientation of Vietnam Veterans," *Michigan Chronicle*, March 10, 1973.

256 **if his symptoms had been properly**: Wilbur Scott, *The Politics of Readjustment: Vietnam Veterans Since the War* (Routledge, 1993), 43–44.

256 **"the first public acknowledgment"**: Chaim Shatan, "The Grief of Soldiers: Vietnam Combat Veterans' Self-Help Movement," *American Journal of Orthopsychiatry* 43 (July 1973); Samuel Brooks, "Psychiatrist Underscores Need for Reorientation of Vietnam Veterans," *Michigan Chronicle*, March 10, 1973.

256 **"No soldier ever really survives"**: Robert Jay Lifton, *Home from the War: Vietnam Veterans, Neither Victims nor Executioners* (Simon & Schuster, 1973), 38–39.

256 **National Veterans Resource Project**: Andrea Recarte, "Unveiling Chaim Shatan: An Analyst Unveiling War Wounds" (PhD diss., City University of New York, 2018), 50.

257 **"saved the government hundreds of millions"**: Chaim Shatan, "Afterword— Who Can Take Away the Grief of a Wound?," in Ghislaine Boulanger and

Charles Kadushin, eds., *The Vietnam Veteran Defined* (Taylor & Francis Group, 1986), 176.

257 **"There was no escaping it"**: Richard Wesley interview, September 29, 2023.

258 **"my generation's Ira Hayes"**: Richard Wesley interview, September 29, 2023.

258 **Wesley's play brought pivotal moments**: Richard Wesley, *Strike Heaven on the Face* (1972; Alexander Street Press, 2003).

259 *Medal of Honor Rag*: Kevin Kelly, "Lead Players Save a Perfunctory Revival of 'Cat on a Hot Tin Roof,'" *Boston Globe*, May 24, 1974; Kevin Kelly, "'Medal of Honor' a Must-See," *Boston Globe*, April 17, 1975; Richard Coe, "Poignant Polished 'Medal,'" *Washington Post*, January 27, 1976; Clive Barnes, "'Medal of Honor Rag' Relives Trauma of Vietnam," *New York Times*, March 29, 1976; Elaine Welles, "Clifton Davis Returns to the Stage in 'Medal of Honor Rag,'" *Philadelphia Tribune*, September 25, 1976.

259 **"there were no parades or ceremonies"**: John O'Connor, "Medal of Honor Rag,' a Veteran's Problems," *New York Times*, April 6, 1982.

259 **Reviewers often took as much space**: Edwin Wilson, "The Personal Anguish of Vietnam," *Wall Street Journal*, March 31, 1976.

259 **"a succinct and moving dramatization"**: R. H. Gardner, "A Drama About a Real Tragedy," *Baltimore Sun*, February 6, 1976; Ernie Santosuosso, "Critics Recommend: 'Medal of Honor,'" *Boston Globe*, April 25, 1975.

259 **"The facts remain the facts"**: Clive Barnes, "Death of a Hero," *New York Times*, February 29, 1976.

260 **"It was more frightening"**: Rita Griffin, "Real-Life Story Was More 'Frightening Than Dramatic,'" *Michigan Chronicle*, April 3, 1982.

260 **"We would better serve returning prisoners"**: Robert Jay Lifton, "Heroes and Victims," *New York Times*, March 28, 1973.

260 **"Peace came Saturday"**: "Whose 'Honorable Peace'?," *Michigan Chronicle*, February 3, 1973.

261 **"The President and his aides"**: John Conyers Jr., "Why Nixon Should Have Been Impeached," *The Black Scholar* 6, no. 2 (October 1974): 3–5.

261 **Congress ultimately voted down**: Carolyn Woods Eisenberg, *Fire and Rain: Nixon, Kissinger, and the Wars in Southeast Asia* (Oxford University Press, 2023), 7.

261 **"This action closes a chapter"**: John Finney, "Ford Unity Plea," *New York Times*, April 30, 1975.

261 **"Now that the curtain of surrender"**: "The Agony of Defeat," *Chicago Defender*, May 3, 1975.

262 **"There were people thinking"**: Katrina May interview, January 19, 2024.

262 **"How do you tell a kid"**: Thomas Fox, "Terrors of Viet War Led Hero to Holdup and Death, VA Rules," *Detroit Free Press*, March 20, 1977.

263 **"Johnson's criminal behavior"**: Fox, "Terrors of Viet War Led Hero to Holdup and Death, VA Rules."

264 **"completely confused, bitter, distrustful and depressed"**: Fox, "Terrors of Viet War Led Hero to Holdup and Death, VA Rules."

264 **retroactive benefits to 1974**: "War Hero's Widow Wins Battle for G.I. Benefits," *New York Times*, March 23, 1977; "Hero's War Stress Wins Wife Pension," *Montreal Star*, March 24, 1977; "The Robber Hero's Award," *Evening Post* (UK), March 24, 1977.

264 **"It took me six years"**: Katrina May interview, January 19, 2024.

265 **"those who felt"**: Fox, "Terrors of Viet War Led Hero to Holdup and Death, VA Rules."

265 **"Restored to Honor"**: "Restored to Honor," *Michigan Chronicle*, April 23, 1971.

265 **"It's been hard"**: "Did Hero Find Life Too Painful?," *Detroit Free Press*, April 6, 1982.

EPILOGUE

267 **"Fellow citizens, we cannot"**: Collins George, "'Lincoln Portrait' with Mrs. King Opens Detroit's Negro History Week," *Detroit Free Press*, February 6, 1972.

269 **discovery of strontium 90**: Cora Weiss, "Cascading Movement for Peace: From Women Strike for Peace to UNSCR 1325," *Social Justice* 46, no. 1 (2019): 14.

269 **"It is very nice to drink"**: Daniel S. Lucks, *Selma to Saigon: The Civil Rights Movement and the Vietnam War* (The University Press of Kentucky, 2014), 152.

269 **at least two dozen countries**: Richard Grimmett, "Instances of Use of United States Armed Forces Abroad, 1798–2009," Congressional Research Service, January 27, 2010.

270 **"We must demand justice"**: Karlyn Barker and Peter Perl Washington, "250,000 Assemble to Mark '63 March," *Washington Post*, August 28, 1983.

270 **"with the same fervor"**: Scott Harris, "War Protesters Press Message to Lawmakers," *Los Angeles Times*, January 12, 1991.

270 **"wars are poor chisels"**: Louis Chu, "Coretta Scott King Urges Peace," *Atlanta Daily World*, January 23, 2003.

270 **"I don't want us to forget"**: Shaila Dewan and Elisabeth Brumiller, "At

Mrs. King's Funeral, a Mix of Elegy and Politics," *New York Times*, February 8, 2006.

270 **Bush's secret authorization:** Dewan and Brumiller, "At Mrs. King's Funeral, a Mix of Elegy and Politics."

271 **"but no more for the poor":** Ron Walters, "Rev. Joseph Lowery," *Chicago Defender*, February 23, 2006.

271 **"President Bush will pay tribute":** Jesse Jackson, "President Bush and Mrs. King," *Los Angeles Sentinel*, February 6, 2003.

271 **Her coffin was placed:** Dewan and Brumiller, "At Mrs. King's Funeral, a Mix of Elegy and Politics."

272 **opposed war but supported warriors:** "Guns vs. Butter: Many Blacks Oppose American Role in War," *Wall Street Journal*, January 25, 1991.

272 **"The unemployed are not pawns":** David Stein, "'This Nation Has Never Honestly Dealt with the Question of a Peacetime Economy': Coretta Scott King and the Struggle for a Nonviolent Economy in the 1970s," *Souls* 18, no. 1 (January–March 2016): 92, 95.

274 **"How could you little wimps":** Wilbur Scott, *The Politics of Readjustment: Vietnam Veterans Since the War* (Routledge, 1993), 68.

274 **more than a hundred vet centers:** Scott, *The Politics of Readjustment*, 70–71.

274 **"I took so much flak":** Chaim Shatan, "'A True Child of Trauma'—Sarah Haley: 1939–1989," *Journal of Traumatic Stress* 3, no. 3 (1990): 479.

275 **"the things the veterans appreciate":** Joseph Shapiro, "Psychiatrist Who Counsels Vets Wins Genius Grant," National Public Radio, September 25, 2007, npr.org/2007/09/25/14682035/psychiatrist-who-counsels-vets-wins -genius-grant.

275 **"Until we end wars":** Jonathan Shay, *Achilles in Vietnam: Combat Trauma and the Undoing of Character*, 209.

276 **"I was just driving":** Christopher Johnson interview, February 12, 2024.

CREDITS

p. 154: Hulton Archive/Getty Images

p. 158: Bob Fitch Photography Archive, Department of Special Collections, Stanford University Library

p. 161: Bettmann Archive/Getty Images

p. 168: Bob Fitch Photography Archive, Department of Special Collections, Stanford University Library

p. 173: Katrina May personal collection

p. 178: White House Photographic Office

p. 179: Walter P. Reuther Library, Archives of Labor and Urban Affairs, Wayne State University

p. 182: Photograph by Jimmy Tafoya. Copyright © Detroit Free Press—USA TODAY NETWORK via Imagn Images

p. 188: Walter P. Reuther Library, Archives of Labor and Urban Affairs, Wayne State University

p. 192: *U.S. News & World Report* magazine photograph collection (Library of Congress)

p. 207: Bettmann Archive/Getty Images

p. 240: Bettmann Archive/Getty Images

p. 252: Photograph by Steve Thompson. Copyright © Detroit Free Press—USA TODAY NETWORK via Imagn Images

p. 264: Copyright © Detroit Free Press—USA TODAY NETWORK via Imagn Images

INDEX

Note: Italicized page numbers indicate material in photographs or illustrations.